THE PURITAN REVOLUTION
AND
EDUCATIONAL THOUGHT

THE PURITAN REVOLUTION

AND

EDUCATIONAL THOUGHT

Background for Reform

RICHARD L. GREAVES

RUTGERS UNIVERSITY PRESS
New Brunswick, New Jersey

Copyright © 1969 by Rutgers University, the State University of
New Jersey
Manufactured in the United States of America
Library of Congress Catalogue Card Number: 78-96029
SBN: 8135-0616-6

Acknowledgments

Happily, an author's task is a stimulating one. Incisive criticism, invaluable advice, and welcome encouragement come from many sources. To the following, as well as to the many friends silently acknowledged, I express my gratitude:

To the William Andrews Clark Memorial Library, University of California at Los Angeles, for a postdoctoral research fellowship which enabled me to begin this study.

To the National Endowment for the Humanities for a postdoctoral research fellowship which enabled me to complete the work.

To Provost Richard Schlatter of Rutgers University for scholarly inspiration and for writing the Foreword.

To Dr. Geoffrey Nuttall of the University of London and Dr. E. P. Y. Simpson of Massey University, New Zealand, for thorough training in the discipline of intellectual and ecclesiastical history.

To Dr. John New of the John Carter Brown Library, Brown University, and Dr. Richard Harvey of Ohio University, for helpful criticism in the early stages of the study.

To President Mark Curtis of Scripps College and Dr. Ted Underwood of the University of Minnesota for making special studies of their own available to me.

To my former colleagues Dr. Donald Barnes and Professor David Brawner for helpful advice.

To the staffs of the William Andrews Clark Memorial Library, the Huntington Library, the Library of Congress, and the libraries of the University of California at Los Angeles, Harvard University, Yale University and the University of Illinois for their efficient service.

And most of all to the one person without whose faithful encouragement and help this study could not have been completed, and to whom this book is dedicated: Judith Rae Greaves.

R. L. G.

June, 1969

Foreword

The history of education and of educational philosophy is still in a primitive state of development. Trained historians have, until recently, shied from a subject which seemed to be a banality in the hands of pious memorialists of schools and universities celebrating their centennials and tricentennials, and so on *ad infinitum*. But recently there has been a change.

We now know something of the changes in higher education brought about by the needs of the new ruling elites of the Renaissance—the age of *The Prince, The Book of the Courtier, The Utopia,* and *The Christian Knight*. We are beginning to learn about the changes which the new science brought about, or failed to bring about, in the universities of Europe in the early modern period. Finally, we are beginning to understand a little more about the educational revolution which accompanied the Protestant Reformation.

In Protestant lands—England, Scotland, Switzerland, New England, Holland, and parts of Germany and France—education was regarded as a principal weapon in the fight to extirpate popery. But the Protestant educational reforms were in fact more than religious in origin and effect and were connected with radical changes taking place in the structure of European society. (An interesting recent discussion of new concepts and new methods in English educational history is Lawrence Stone, "Literacy and Education in England 1640–1900," *Past and Present*, number 42, February, 1969, which appeared too late to be included in Professor Greaves's bibliography.)

The age of the Puritan Revolution in England is of the greatest interest to the historian of education. Here for the first time in history emerged grandiose schemes for a system of universal education for all social classes—and a beginning in the direction of putting the schemes into effect was at least attempted.

More important, the educational theorists of the day went beyond the humanistic idea of education as a training for "the complete gentleman" and beyond the Protestant notion of the training of a Bible-reading citizenry capable of understanding the thorny mysteries of Reformed theology: They, or at least the theorists connected with the radical sectarians, saw and described the connection between the educational system and the economic, social and political institutions of the day. They advocated educational revolution as a part of the general revolution which they wanted. In reaction, defenders of the *status quo* came to see the traditional system of education, or lack of it, as an important bastion of law and order.

If the reader wishes historical studies to have a bearing upon contemporary problems, then Professor Greaves's book will surely please him. For the men of seventeenth-century England of whom he writes raised most of the modern questions: Who should control the educational system? How should it be financed? What should be taught? Who should be educated (or who is educable)? How is excellence to be measured and maintained? Finally, since they saw education as an important cog in the whole social structure, they thought of educational revolution as impossible unless accompanied by general revolution, by the creation of the good society. But in the short run they had to try to wrest the educational system from the grip of the present Establishment as part of a general attempt to overthrow that Establishment and to replace it by a new and better Establishment (not, of course, to be called by that name!).

Most of the persons whom Professor Greaves discusses are lesser men than Milton and Locke whose educational treatises are major documents in intellectual history, although they may be less instructive to the modern reader concerned with education today. Moreover, Professor Greaves does discuss more than the educational theorists of the Cromwellian period. Nevertheless, the main strength of his book seems to me to lie in his careful and full account of the educational theories of the Puritan Revolution in England—a much fuller account than we have had before. He has contributed significantly both to our knowledge of the English Revolution and our knowledge of the history of education.

                                                        Richard Schlatter

Rutgers University
June, 1969

Contents

THE PURITAN REVOLUTION
AND
EDUCATIONAL THOUGHT

CHAPTER ONE

The Intellectual and Social Milieu of Puritan England

The revolutionary ferment which gripped England in the decades between 1640 and 1660 brought forth demands for reforms that were not solely political. The social structure of England was subjected to withering criticism from a host of zealous critics who demanded a new educational system, a complete overhaul of England's legal structure, a reordering of religious affairs, care for the poor, and a more equitable economic basis for society. Most of the criticisms and proposed remedies had some merit; others were simply the unrealistic visions of utopian dreamers, divorced from the harsh realities of mid-seventeenth century life. The sectaries, who echoed the social concerns of the Old Testament prophet Amos as they cried out for the reformation of society, were among the most outspoken critics. Liberal Puritans also played a major role, with both groups reflecting Baconian ideals.

In the seventeenth century ecclesiasticism and religious dogma still held the minds and souls of men in a rigid bondage. Cromwellian England witnessed the final attempt of religious fervor to dominate the political structure of society. That attempt ended in the politico-religious settlement of 1689 and the abdication by the church of its theocratic political claims. Yet the divorce of religion from the mundane affairs of human society and government was hardly apparent to the Englishman of the mid-seventeenth century. It was difficult for even such a proponent of secularism as Thomas Hobbes adequately to grasp. The kind of thinking that most influenced the vast majority of Englishmen of this era was thinking clothed in religious garb. To a people not yet accustomed to think in secular, rational terms, the religious arguments provided the hearers and readers an intellectual vocabulary adapted to their understanding. Such an intellectual approach had the *sine qua non* for any acceptable action or thought—the conviction that it was sanctioned by the Divine. Hence, Thomas Hobbes, one of the truly great minds at work in the Cromwellian era, enjoyed less influence than John Owen, William Dell, John Bunyan, John Saltmarsh, John Webster, William Walwyn, George Fox, and John Lilburne.

The preaching and writing of the sectaries, those to the left of the vast Puritan host, were of particular significance. Yet any attempt to define the terms sectary, Puritan, and Anglican precisely is exceptionally difficult. Ecclesiastical, theological, political, psychological, and socioeconomic factors have all been used by historians to reach an acceptable definition. The problem is compounded by the fact that the groups to which the terms refer were undergoing a process of evolutionary change throughout the sixteenth and seventeenth centuries, and doubly compounded by the fact that, so far as ideology is concerned, the same term often applies in the same period to more than one group. In the 1640s, for example, some men gave their political allegiance to the Puritans while maintaining Anglican religious views. For the purpose of this study, which embraces the mid-seventeenth century, these groups are described without an attempt to arrive at definitions applicable to the sixteenth and seventeenth centuries as a whole. Nor will it be necessary to develop definitions extensive enough to embrace all the idiosyncrasies of a given group: The ways these groups differed significantly from one another in terms of basic ideologies will suffice.

The *sectaries* were predominantly separatists in their ecclesiology and were opposed to any form of *jure divino* ecclesiastical polity. They were antiliturgical in their approach to worship, preferring simplicity in their church services. Theologically they were not uniform, but embraced Calvinism, Antinomianism, mysticism, and even tinges of Arminianism, often in combination (e.g., Antinomianism and mysticism). Epistemologically the sectaries differed from both Anglicans and Puritans in their religious antirationalism and anti-intellectualism. Sectaries manifested strong tendencies toward primitivism in religion, politics, economics, and society, and were essentially antiprofessional in their attitude toward the clergy, lawyers, medical doctors, and professors of divinity. Generally, but not exclusively, they represented the interests of the lower classes.

Puritans preferred the possibility of reforming the existing ecclesiastical establishment to the alternative of separatism, though between 1660 and 1662 many were forced by their consciences to follow the separatist path of nonconformity. Puritans embraced episcopacy, presbyterianism, and congregationalism as a church polity. Although they adamantly rejected *jure divino* episcopacy, some Puritans applied that concept to presbyterian or congregational polity. In worship the Puritans preferred a purified and simple liturgy, dignified but not excessively formal. Theologically the Puritans were Calvinists, either moderate or strict, depending upon whether they were a part of the Zwingli-Bullinger-Tyndale tradition or the Calvin-Perkins-Ames tradition.[1] Epistemologically they differed sharply from the sectaries by retaining rationalism in religion, though that rationalism was subordinated to faith and empiricism. The Puritans were moderately primitivistic in their religious and socioeconomic views, but not nearly so much as the sectaries. Puritans were not antiprofessional, though they were not averse to criticizing the legal class in England. It is impossible to identify the Puritans with any class, though the middle class tended to prefer Puritanism.

Anglicans believed in a state church with an episcopal polity. Liturgical in their worship, they preferred a formal service dignified by the use of clerical dress and symbolic gestures. Theologically, few if any Anglicans in the mid-seventeenth century were willing to embrace Calvinism fully. Instead Anglican theology retained its "belief in the innate rationality of fallen man, in a hierarchical relationship between grace and nature, [and] in a sacramental way to Heaven. . . ."[2] Furthermore Anglicans demonstrated no interest in either the Sabbatarianism or the forensic emphasis common in Puritanism. Nor was Anglican theology concerned with covenant thought in the way that Puritanism was. Anglican epistemology gave a greater role to human reason than did that of the Puritans, though no Protestant thought has ever been thoroughly rationalistic. The primitivism characteristic of the sectaries and moderately embraced by the Puritans did not interest the Anglicans, nor were they inclined toward antiprofessionalism. Anglicans cannot be identified with any socioeconomic class.

Prior to the two decades 1640–1660, a dialogue on political and religious issues occurred between the Puritans and the Anglicans, but with the accession of Puritans to political power in the 1640s that dialogue shifted to debates between the Puritans and the sectaries. The dialogue continued to include ecclesiastical questions (primarily involving polity), theological questions (which began to reveal disenchantment with Calvinism), and political questions (concerned with power and suffrage). Moreover, these controversies revealed an increased awareness of the need for broad social reforms. In these dialogues the sectaries and more liberal Puritans demanded revolutionary reforms, often forcing the more conservative Puritans to defend a social structure they themselves realized needed changing.

Such a defense was inevitable on the part of the conservatives, for not only did the sectaries demand legal and economic reforms,[3] but they also launched vigorous attacks on the ecclesiastical and educational establishments—the twin pillars of the state. No Puritan of any kind could envisage a Holy Commonwealth without a reformed church and piously oriented schools. The sectaries' criticism of these establishments from the pulpit and in the press meant a war of ideas and words. Whether or not the radicals were intent on destroying ecclesiasticism, as some were, mattered not. Nor did it matter that the basic sectarian concern was not to destroy but to reform the universities. What did matter to the Puritans was that the educational and ecclesiastical systems were under attack.

SOCIAL UNREST AND EDUCATIONAL REFORM

The sectaries did not criticize the educational system simply because they believed they possessed better concepts of the nature of the curriculum and pedagogical methods, as did the liberal Puritans. This they did believe, but their critiques of education were also an integral part of their discontent with the entire social structure. As the universities were constituted in the 1640s and 1650s they principally served the privileged classes, as they had since their founding, though scholarships were making it possible for those of lesser means to attend. The Puritans, like their predecessors, had attained prestigious positions in the universities and, through them, often in church and state. Having once attained those positions, their reforming ardor tended to mellow into a complacent conservatism, though the Independents were able to maintain something of their reformist zeal. The Puritans felt their earlier attack on England's *status quo* was justified, for they were the elect fulfilling a divine mission, but now that they in turn were being attacked, their task was to defend the divine way against the forces of anarchy in England. It was, to quote a Puritan defender, "the Devills plot, to root out Learning." [4]

Even under the relatively liberal rule of Oliver Cromwell the universities tended to remain a bastion for the support of the ruling powers. The government could hardly allow the universities to become hotbeds of political discontent, sending forth revolutionaries determined to overthrow it. Properly supervised and staffed, the universities might instead provide the government with sympathetic recruits to perform its tasks and intellects to defend its policies. The point was not lost on Cromwell, who had more than a cursive interest in education. It was not by accident that his "recommendations for degrees to be conferred by Oxford seldom failed to note the religio-political as well as the professional qualifications for such honors." [5]

There were other reasons for the suspicion with which the Puritans viewed the attacks of the sectaries on education. Epistemologically the sectaries stressed the role of the Spirit, who could reveal knowledge equally to poor as well as rich, to peasant as well as gentry. If so, then the masses as well as the divines were equally able to discern the will of God, provided the Spirit was willing. This attack on the expert in religion was also an attack against the state, for the ecclesiastical structure was in reality a department of the state. It was a Puritan axiom that "the Minister and Magistrate [are] to go hand in hand together," or, in the words of a conservative writer, "as the ruine of Learning will bring ruine on the Church, so on the State; no Minister, no Statesman. . . ." [6] If the common man, using Scripture and enlightened by the Spirit, might discover all necessary religious truth, might not the common man also, using Magna Charta or the dictates of natural law discoverable by reason, arrive at the conclusion that he had a right to speak for himself in political matters? What originated as an epistemological question in religion had important political ramifications that caused the Puritans concern. It was no idle thought that prompted one Puritan preacher to warn his Cambridge audience that the sectaries "preach that all must be carried on by the power and might of the Spirit, but I am sure they fly to visible power, and invocate the secular arme." [7]

Perry Miller suggested that "as long as common folk were kept abject before a mystery which they could not themselves understand or criticize, they would meekly and fearfully pay their tithes and never dream of laying rude hands upon university endowments." [8] As far as the Puritan defenders of the educational system in the 1640s and 1650s were concerned, there is reason to accept this observation, but with qualification. The published sermons of the university-trained Puritans often included Latin, Greek, or Hebrew phrases, which the man in the pew was unable to understand. Nor was the man in the pew apt to follow the tedious details of the preacher's arguments, put there more for the benefit of his fellow clergymen than his own congregation. Some of this pedantism was utilized simply to awe the congregation and remind them of their inexpertness in religion. The eminent Puritan divine Richard Baxter (1615–1691) wrote:

> It is most desirable that the Minister should be of parts above the people so far as to be able to teach them and awe them and manifest their weaknesses to themselves. . . . See that you preach . . . some higher points that stall their understandings. . . . Take up some profound questions (such as the Schools voluminously agitate) and . . . make it as plain as you can, that they may see that it is not your obscure manner of handling, but the matter itself that is too hard for them, and so may see that they are yet but children that have need of milk.[9]

The Essex Puritan Giles Firmin (1614–1697) admitted the generality of this practice when he complained that "there hath been a too great Idolizing of Learning, and abusing it in Sermons, by reciting of the Fathers, or School-men, some men fondly making, it may be, a quarter of their Sermons to be Latine, or Greek sentences out of them, and then turning them into English, to make people admire them, and conclude them to be great Schollars. . . ." [10] Yet there was also a genuine concern on the part of the Puritans to instill in their congregations a sound knowledge of religious principles. Meetings in private homes for biblical study and prayer, even though directed by laymen, were ordinarily encouraged. Nevertheless the Puritan regarded university-trained clergy as a *sine qua non* to develop an educated congregation: Sectarian criticism of the teaching of divinity in the universities was a threat to this ideal.

The enigma posed by the relationship of religion and knowledge, which was a basic cause of the disagreement between Puritans and sectaries, was inherent in Protestant thought. "From the time of the Anabaptists at Münster," Perry Miller observed, "Protestant theologians strove with might and main to keep justification by faith from becoming a justification of illiteracy." [11] The Puritan problem was to prevent such an occurrence, and in doing so to avoid the pitfalls of an educated but equal congregation of saints and an uneducated congregation subservient to the whims of the clergy. The threat posed by the sectaries involved both a tendency toward the political and spiritual equalization (or "levelling") of the saints, and the thorough spiritualization of religious knowledge, rendering it unnecessary to study divinity in the universities. Such an outlook resulted from a reaction to Puritan legalism and the sterile debates on ecclesiastical polity in the 1640s. It was also a reaction to the fact that traditional clerical education at Oxford and Cambridge had tended to bolster a tyrannical government and social system. *Cadit quaestio:* The educational structure had to be reformed.

CHANGING EMPHASES IN HIGHER EDUCATION

One of the conservative Puritan apologists for education, the Presbyterian Thomas Hall (1610–1665), summarized the Puritan view of the primary role of schools: "If there be a Ministery, then there must be Schools of learning, and Universityes. If the end be allowed, the means conducing to that end must not be denied," and there must exist adequate "Schools, those Nurseries for the Church. . . ." [12] An anonymous writer in 1648 made the same point, adding that more schools were to be erected to train youths in education and godliness for both the church and the state. [13] The culmination of that education came at Oxford or Cambridge, where studies remained much as they had been in the preceding half century. Officially Cambridge was governed by her Elizabethan statutes of 1570, while Oxford in the 1640s and 1650s continued to operate according to the Laudian statutes of 1636. It has been demonstrated, though, that these statutes were not fully operative in the late sixteenth and early seventeenth centuries. [14] Hence they do not present a completely accurate picture of what the educational program was like, though they are the indispensable starting place for a study of that program.

The Elizabethan statutes operative at Cambridge required an undergraduate in arts to reside at the university for a minimum of sixteen terms, during which he was to attend university lectures in rhetoric, logic, and philosophy. It was common, however, for a student to be

able to take his degree in less than the required number of terms.[15]
At Oxford the Laudian statutes specified that students in the faculty
of arts attend sixteen terms or four years, during which they were
required to attend the public lectures of the university. Sons of peers
and the eldest sons of baronets and knights were permitted to take
the B.A. degree at Oxford in three years. Students working toward
the M.A. at Oxford were required to spend an additional three years
or twelve terms at the university, though exceptions were frequently
made. At Cambridge too the M.A. examinations followed an additional three years of study beyond the B.A. Having attained the
M.A. degree, a student could proceed at Cambridge, for example,
to take the B.D. after an additional seven years. This was also true
at Oxford, which required a final four years of study for the D.D.,
whereas Cambridge demanded five for the same degree. Medical
studies were likewise lengthy, with Oxford, for example, requiring
three years beyond the M.A. for the B.M. degree, and an additional
four years beyond that for the doctorate in medicine. It was usual,
however, for candidates for higher degrees to receive dispensations
permitting them to study for the degree as nonresidents, thus cutting
down the expenses for professional degrees considerably.

For the university undergraduate the main stress was slowly changing in the sixteenth and seventeenth centuries from the scholastic-
centered curriculum to one more inclusive of the natural sciences
and less concerned with logic. Emphasis on the latter had long been
traditional as a prerequisite for the study of scholastic theology.
Puritans flatly rejected scholastic theology as part of Popery, but
retained certain Nominalist premises, such as a distrust of reason and
an emphasis on authority to solve problems incapable of a rational
solution. Nor did the Puritans find it necessary to reject *in toto* the
traditional scholastic curriculum, now hallowed by centuries of usage.
At Oxford the undergraduate continued to study grammar, rhetoric,
moral philosophy, geometry, and Greek, as well as logic. Rhetoric,
which now included a survey of classical literature, was given an
expanded role in the curriculum at both universities. Classical studies
were furthered at Oxford and Cambridge by the founding of the
Craven scholarships in 1649. As one modern scholar observed, the
universities "were pervaded by a classical atmosphere." [16]

The Elizabethan statutes that governed academic life at Cambridge
specified the workings of the university in virtually every aspect
except for the curriculum. Rhetoric was required as a subject of

study for first-year undergraduates, with logic following in the second and third years and philosophy in the fourth. The lecturer in rhetoric was required to discuss Quintilian, Hermogenes, or Cicero; the lecturer in logic, Aristotle's dialectical works and Cicero's *Topics;* the lecturer in philosophy, Aristotle, Pliny, and Plato. In addition to attending lectures, undergraduates were also required to take part in academic exercises, especially scholastic disputations. William Haller has observed, however, that the Puritan instructors at Cambridge were really interested less in making their students scholastic disputants than preachers. Sermons were the subject of emphasis, with the primary authority being the Bible rather than Aristotle and his fellow ancients. Presumably the entire range of subjects in the curriculum was examined with a view to the application of that knowledge to ministerial duties.[17]

One rather atypical program of studies for Cambridge undergraduates is the curriculum usually attributed to the Puritan Richard Holdsworth, Fellow of St. John's in 1613, Master of Emmanuel beginning in 1637, and a Royalist supporter in the civil war. Holdsworth, a professor at Gresham College from 1629 to 1637, presumably laid greater stress on science than did his fellow tutors. His first-year pupils delved into logic, ethics, physics, history, grammar, classical literature, geography, the writings of Erasmus, and the New Testament. Prior to commencing their second year of studies, students were asked to review Latin and Greek grammar. Then they were ready to begin a new year of studies concentrating on ethics, physics, metaphysics, classics, and oratory. In the third year they faced more classics, oratory, ethics, and physics, as well as history. Fourth-year students would, in addition to participating in disputations, read more Aristotle, a compendium of divinity, the *Institutes* of Justinian, other classics, and perhaps a compendium of medicine.[18]

A set of rules drawn up by the Anglican James Duport, Fellow of Trinity College, Cambridge, was more conservative in its approach to education, stressing conduct and manners as well as speculative, disputative learning.[19] Duport's approach was probably more common at Cambridge than Holdsworth's.

Linguistic studies remained part of the curriculum at the universities, with both Latin and Greek expected of undergraduate students. At Oxford the undergraduates, commencing in their third year of studies, and the Bachelors were required to attend Greek lectures. Emphasis on the classical languages must not have been popular with the students, however, for as early as 1600 at Cambridge the tutors and pupils were communicating in English rather than in Latin. The college statutes, which customarily specified that Latin was to be spoken at mealtimes in the college halls, were ignored in this respect. Yet the traditional practice was still valued to the extent that the parliamentary committee responsible for supervising the Visitors at Oxford ordered, in July, 1649:

> That the Visitors of the Universitie of Oxon be required to see either the Latin or Greeke be stricktly and constantly exercised and spoken, in their familier discourse within the said severall Colledges and Halls respectively, and that noe other language be spoken by any Fellow, Scholar, or Student whatsoever.[20]

The regulations had little effect, but language study nevertheless continued as a required subject for all undergraduates.

The weakest area of the curriculum was the natural sciences. In the early seventeenth century famous scientists and mathematicians did not hold university posts. At Oxford the situation had become worse than at Cambridge, for the Laudian statutes caused the sciences to stagnate by not allowing for change. At Cambridge, where university control of the curriculum was less strict, tutors had the option to have their pupils read recent scientific works, but "most tutors were not interested in the new experimental sciences, and some even overlooked the work of ancient scientists." [21] In Holdsworth's curriculum, for example, the science a student learned was Aristotelian. Generally the textbooks used were medieval rather than modern. Lecturers on medicine were required to proceed by commenting on Hippocrates and Galen. The Tomlins lecturer on anatomy, whose position was endowed in 1622, did not practice dissection. The cosmography and geography lecturers were required to comment on Pliny, Strabo, and Plato. Cambridge did not have a chair of mathematics until 1663. The Puritan John Wallis (1616–1703), who took his B.A. (1637) and M.A. (1640) at Emmanuel College, where he had come under the influence of Holdsworth, retrospectively wrote in 1697: "Mathematics . . . were scarce looked upon as academical studies, but rather mechanical; as the business of traders, merchants, seamen, carpenters, surveyors of lands, or the like; and perhaps some almanac-makers in London. . . . For the study of mathematics was at that time more cultivated in London than in the universities." [22]

The Elizabethan statutes that governed Cambridge required that a professor of astronomy teach and interpret Ptolemy just when the Copernican theory began to gain increasing acceptance among scientists. Of significance for the future of the teaching of the natural sciences at Oxford was the establishment in 1619 of the chairs of geometry and astronomy by Sir Henry Savile (1549–1622), Warden of Merton College. The statute specifying the duties of the Savilian Professor of Astronomy is particularly interesting. It was

> his duty to explain the whole of the mathematical economy of Ptolemy, . . . applying in their proper place the discoveries of Copernicus, Gexber, and other modern writers . . . provided, however, that he may lay before his auditors, by way of introduction to the arcana of the science, the sphere of Proclus, or Ptolemy's hypotheses of the planets. . . . It will also be the business of the professor of Astronomy to explain and teach . . . the whole science of optics, gnomonics, geography, and the rules of navigation in so far as they are dependent on mathematics. He must understand, however, that he is utterly debarred from professing the doctrine of nativities and all judicial astrology without exception.[23]

Although this statute clearly opened the door to the teaching of the Copernican theory, the first two Savilian Professors of Astronomy, John Bainbridge and John Greaves, probably upheld the Ptolemaic theory.[24] In 1648 and 1649, due to the shift in the balance of political power in England, a number of Royalists at Oxford were compelled to leave. One of the replacement professors was Seth Ward (1617–1689). As Savilian Professor of Astronomy, Ward propounded the Copernican theory. The Sedleian Professor of Natural Philosophy at Oxford, whose chair had been endowed in 1622, had no such freedom, but was bound by the Laudian statutes, since William Sedley had left it up to the university to select the subject matter for the Sedleian Professor. Inasmuch as the Laudian statutes specified that the subject matter must be Aristotelian thought and theory, there was little hope for significant scientific advancement from the Sedleian Professor. Most students seem to have been unconcerned about the whole situation: "At the time the Savilian lectures were inaugurated, and for many years afterwards, there was little interest in either geometry or astronomy on the part of the average student, and had not fines been imposed for absence at lectures they would not have attended them at all." [25]

The programs at the universities leading to master's degrees generally featured a wider range of subjects than those offered the undergraduate. The Oxford M.A. student studied moral philosophy, astronomy, geometry, natural philosophy, metaphysics, history, Greek, and Hebrew. At Cambridge, according to the Elizabethan statutes, the M.A. student was expected to attend lectures in such subjects as philosophy, astronomy, drawing, and Greek. Hebrew, theology, and history were commonly studied as well. At either university one might also study Arabic, since a chair for that subject had been established at Cambridge in 1632 and at Oxford by Laud in 1636.

The level of attainment achieved by the two universities in the 1640s and 1650s has been praised by seventeenth century and modern historians. The Earl of Clarendon, a Royalist sympathizer, observed of Oxford:

> It might reasonably be concluded that this wild and barbarous de-population would even extirpate all that learning, religion, and loy-alty, which had so eminently flourished there; and that the succeed-ing ill husbandry, and unskilful cultivation, would have made it fruitful only in ignorance, profanation, atheism, and rebellion; but . . . the goodness and richness of that soil could not be made barren by all that stupidity and negligence.

Clarendon noted that when Charles II ascended the throne in 1660 he found Oxford (and presumably Cambridge also) "abounding in excellent learning, and devoted to duty and obedience, little inferior to what it was before its desolation. . . ."[26] There was also admira-tion in the words of Thomas Sprat (1635–1713), the historian of the Royal Society, when he said of Oxford in the Cromwellian period: "The University had, at that time, many members of its own, who had begun a free way of reasoning; and was also fre-quented by some Gentlemen, of Philosophical Minds, whom the misfortunes of the Kingdom, and the security and ease of a retirement among Gown-men, had drawn thither."[27] Sprat was thinking espe-cially of men such as Seth Ward, John Wilkins, the Warden of Wadham College (1648), John Wallis, Savilian Professor of Geom-etry (1649), and Jonathan Goddard, the Warden of Merton College (1651), who had come to Oxford after the collapse of the Royalist cause. The criticism of one writer who longed, in 1656, for the days "when Oxford and Camebridge were Universities, and a Colledge more learned then a Town-Hall; when the Buttery and Kitchin could

speak Latine, though not Preach . . . ," [28] was obviously founded
on political bias.

Cromwell and his Puritan associates were responsible for much of
the improvement that was made in the universities. Cromwell himself
became Chancellor of Oxford, while maintaining a strong interest in
the affairs of Cambridge and the three Scottish universities. Under
Cromwell the Scottish universities had their revenues increased and
the city of Edinburgh received a College of Physicians.[29] In the face
of demands for the expansion of the English universities, he approved
the founding of a new school at Durham. He founded or re-founded
scores of elementary schools, and also directed that commissioners
be sent throughout the country to ascertain educational needs. It is
unduly harsh to say of the period, as the English author Albert
Mansbridge did, that "the Protectorate, in spite of its conscientious
reforming zeal, exhausted the Universities by the atmosphere of
suspicion and inquisition which it involved." [30] Such a harsh judgment
was probably based on the politically-motivated criticisms of the
Royalist Anthony Wood. The observation of Maurice Ashley that
"the Puritan influx tended to encourage discipline and application in
the universities and to awaken them from lethargy and a traditional
curriculum" would be more accurate. It was Ashley's judgment that
"it was a golden age for education." [31]

The Debate on Religion and Learning

The sectaries were adamant that it was not a golden age for
education, and they set about to prove their point in the 1640s and
1650s. The resulting debate raged in the press and in the pulpit,
outside the universities as well as within their walls. The debate was
inevitable in light of the evangelical piety common to Puritans and
sectaries,[32] for it gave rise to dichotomous interpretations. The first
aspect of this piety was its strong biblicism, which fostered in the
conservative element of Puritanism distinct tendencies toward either
legalism (as in Richard Baxter) or a strong concern with polity (as
with most Presbyterians). In reaction to this, the same biblicism led
to an emphasis on spiritualism and the development of a lay piety
which favored the Spirit to the educated clergy and the state church.
Evangelical piety stressed, in the second place, personal experience,
which led in some circles to a spiritualistic faith bordering on or em-

bracing mysticism. This was particularly true when biblicism produced a reaction against formalism and legalism. Those Puritans who
were formalistic and legalistic emphasized personal experience, but
controlled and codified it in accordance with scriptural precedents
interpreted by educated clergy. Finally, evangelical piety regarded
as important the idea that knowledge of God was revealed in the
world. Already accustomed to an inductive method in the analysis
of religious experience, it was a comparatively easy step for the Puritan or the sectary to transfer that method to the study of the natural
world. When that occurred, he was on the threshold of embracing
the new science.[33] The intense combination of the first two of these
elements of evangelical piety in the sectaries, coupled with the third
among the more intelligent of their number, made it inevitable that a
debate on the existing educational system should occur. For that
system taught an academic rather than a spiritualistic divinity; it
stressed classical and linguistic studies rather than Scripture and Spirit
alone; it maintained the interests of professional classes as opposed
to the laity, and it was too slow (according to both progressive Puritans and sectaries) in accepting recent developments in science.

There were other factors involved in the debate, one of which per-
tained to ecclesiological considerations. Because ministers not properly ordained were long barred from the pulpit by state law, a fierce
controversy over the nature and validity of ordination broke out in
England.[34] Each side claimed divine sanction for its particular view
of ordination. The question of a university education as a necessary
prerequisite did not enter into the debates between the Anglicans and
the Presbyterians, but with the spread of the Independents and the
sectaries, not all of whom had university training, the question was
raised. Once the question had been injected into the debate, it was not
long before the sectaries began to assail the whole system of higher
and lower education as nonutilitarian and out of touch with modern
needs and advances in knowledge. The sectaries did not wish to
destroy the universities, but they were insistent upon a thorough-
going reform of the curriculum and related academic matters.

Another factor involved in the debate was a basic resentment
against the clergy and the professors as upholders of a social order
which the sectaries found intolerable. The Leveller William
Walwyn, grandson of a bishop but a member of no particular sect
himself, voiced the feeling of all sectaries when he wrote of the Puritan clergy: "When they commend Learning, it is not for Learnings

sake, but their owne; her esteeme gets them their Livings and pre-
ferments; and therefore she is to be kept up, or their Trade will goe
downe." [35] In this context it was not learning itself that was being
condemned, but the Puritan attempt to use learning to maintain, in
the eyes of the sectaries, their politico-social position. University
degrees continued to be, in Puritan England as well as in Stuart England, the requisite keys to civil and ecclesiastical appointments, preserving political and religious power for the educated.

The literature of the debate is fairly extensive, and the parties involved numerous. In the 1640s the central issue in these debates was
whether or not unordained men could preach, regardless of their
educational status. Yet the issue of the necessity of higher education
for preachers was present, for as early as 1641 the Puritan leader
Robert Greville (1608–1643), Lord Brooke, described the views of
those who opposed the necessity of education for the ministry.[36] Lord
Brooke himself did not agree with these views, but, manifesting a
liberal spirit, he pleaded that they should be given a fair hearing. In
the same year an anonymous author published an account of a Holborn cobbler identified only as Mr. Vincent, who reputedly
preached at St. George's, Southwark, "that all those who would not
preach as Coblers, and Tinkers, were damned." Opposed to both
episcopacy and monarchy, Vincent purportedly contended that any
who preached or prayed other than by the moving of the Spirit were
offenders of God destined to damnation; no human learning was
necessary to be a minister.[37]

In 1646, Giles Workman criticized the more liberal views of the
Independent lay preacher John Knowles. Workman emphasized the
importance of a thorough knowledge of Hebrew, Greek, and Latin
(the latter because of the theological literature in that language) for
a minister as well as authority from the church to preach. Workman
was quite aware of the broader political implications of the right of
laymen to preach: "If ability to preach be sufficient to authorize one
to preach without any more adoo, then also ability to baptize, and to
take on them to rule, govern, and judge. . . ." [38] Knowles, a defender of lay preaching and a suspected Antitrinitarian, was quick to
assert that the Spirit could not be "cloyster'd up amongst the
Cleargy," and that "Tongues and Arts" were not necessary qualifications for preachers. Knowles also made the point that many laymen
were better educated than the clergy, and therefore, on that basis,
more qualified to preach than those who had been formally or-

dained.[39] Knowles himself, though not ordained, knew Greek and Latin.

In 1647 the Puritan Lazarus Seaman (d.1675), a staunch opponent of lay preaching and an advocate of *jure divino* Presbyterianism, came to the defense of the scurrilous Presbyterian diatribist, Thomas Edwards (1599–1647), whose biased and vindictive attack against the sectaries had brought a predictable reaction. Seaman's brief defense of Edwards, published anonymously, opposed the growing tendency of the sectaries [40] to denounce human learning in religion. The title of his work speaks for itself: *Tub-Preachers Overturn'd or Independency to be Abandon'd and Abhor'd . . . in a Satisfactory Answer to a Lybellous Pamphlet, Intituled a Letter to Mr Thomas Edwards . . . Shewing the Vanity, Folly, Madness of the Deboyst Buff-Coate, Mechanick Frize-Coat, Lay Illiterate Men and Women, to Usurpe the Ministery.*[41] The title page listed twenty of the sectarian "tub-preachers" by name, including the Particular Baptists William Kiffin, Paul Hobson, and Thomas Patient, the General Baptists Thomas Lamb and Jeremiah Ives, and Praisegod Barbon, who was to give his name to Cromwell's Parliament of saints.

In August, 1650, a dispute occurred which resulted in a series of controversial tracts. The initial work was by the conservative Puritan Thomas Hall.[42] According to the title page, it was "occasioned by a dispute at Henly in Arden in Warwick-shire, Aug. 20. 1650. Against Laurence Williams, a Nailor-Publike-Preacher. Henry Oakes, a Weaver-Preacher. Hum. Rogers, (lately) a Bakers boy-Publike-Preacher." The title page tells its own story. Preaching by such an uneducated lay group provoked the indignation of Presbyterian Hall, one of the Commonwealth's staunchest defenders of an educated clergy and the existing system of education. Hall, however, did not go unchallenged. In the same year (1651) that his attack against lay preaching appeared, it was answered in sectarian tracts by William Hartley and Thomas Collier. Hartley, a radical sectary, opposed any attempt to make a distinction between clergy and laity "in the Common-wealth of Saints." Instead, preaching was a task assigned to all. Qualifications for that task were spiritual in nature and divinely bestowed. Christians were to preach "by vertue of Gospel abilities, [rather] then humane Letters Pattents." The value of education was not rejected, except as a qualification for the ministry. Hartley, in fact, called for a reformation of the universities, largely aimed at abolishing the study of theology.[43] Collier (*fl.* 1651–1691), an uneducated Baptist, argued against Hall that God used the intellectually weak as his ministers in order to prevent his servants from glorying in their academic attainments, and that there were "none but Asses in the things of God, who study Arts and Sciences, to help them to preach and prophesie. . . ." [44]

Collier's defense of uneducated lay preachers called forth replies the following year by John Ferriby and the astrologer Richard Saunders (1613–1687?), both of whom defended the conservative position. They affirmed the value of higher education for the ministry and rejected Collier's argument that men must rely on divine illumination alone to understand Scripture. The effect of Collier's position, Saunders believed, would be to "make the Scripture a Nose of Wax (as the Papists speake) pliable to any sense that the darknesse and vanity of mens minds will put upon it." [45]

While the controversy initiated by Thomas Hall raged, another Presbyterian, John Collinges (1623–1690), took up the gauntlet thrown by the sectaries. Firmly opposed to lay preaching, Puritan Collinges believed a university education was an excellent qualification—though not an absolutely necessary one—for a minister. Learning enabled a man "to interpret Scripture and understand the tongues, and to . . . Preach methodically and persuasively, &c." [46] Collinges was answered by the lawyer William Sheppard (d.1675?), shortly to become prominent in London legal circles. Sheppard did not regard university education as a prerequisite for the ministry, but insisted that he did not wish to be "thought to smell of the Levellers opinion, and to be an enemy to publike Preachers and preaching. . . ." Nevertheless, Sheppard's sectarian sympathies were clearly revealed when he insisted that all spiritually-gifted men had the right to preach publicly. They needed neither a university education nor ordination, though Sheppard did not automatically condemn those who possessed these qualifications. Uneducated lay preachers manifesting spiritual gifts needed only the "advice and approbation" of their fellow Christians. [47] Collinges, in reply, would allow such preaching only in cases of absolute necessity, and returned to his earlier remarks about the value of higher education (especially the study of the biblical languages) for the ministry. [48]

In the meantime the debate in general had altered; the nature of higher education was called into question by the sectaries. Puritan and general conservative concern about such criticism was real, though often masked by ridicule and crudity. Some did not scruple to misrepresent the sectaries' position, accusing them of wishing to destroy universities altogether. A piece of crude verse published in 1662, but very likely current the preceding decade, attempted to inculcate this erroneous view in the minds of the masses:

> Wee'l down with all the Versities,
>   Where Learning is profest,
> Because they practice and maintain
>   The language of the Beast;
> Wee'l drive the Doctors out of doors,
>   And parts what ere they be;
> Wee'l cry all Arts and Learning down
>   And hey then up go we.[49]

There were others who, like the Anglican Robert Boreman (d.1675), believed or, for propagandistic purposes, professed to believe, that the attack on the universities and the clergy was part of a sinister Jesuit plot—and hence, by implication, quite un-English.[50] Or the sectaries might be accused of ignorance and pride, wanting, in spite of their illiteracy, to "be equall with others, and not be despised for their ignorance." [51] The Puritan Joseph Sedgwick found the reason for the sectaries' attack in their "interest onely and domestick want . . . ," believing that if they were educated and of a better socioeconomic position they would extol higher education as essential for magistrates and ministers.[52] Looking back on the controversy in 1660, Thomas Hall wrote: "This whole brood of vipers have come forth . . . doting upon opinions, and under the pretext of piety . . . [have gone] about to overthrow Scriptures, Sacraments, universityes, all order and ordinances. . . ." [53] Implicit in Hall's accusation is the fact that the criticism of the sectaries was an indictment not only of the clergy and universities but also of the whole social framework. For this reason the Puritans could not afford to regard with levity the persistent criticism of the sectaries.

Sidrach Simpson (1600?–1655), the liberal Puritan author of a work in support of lay preaching, had become Master of Pembroke Hall, Cambridge, and, in March, 1654, one of the Commissioners for the Approbation of Preachers (i.e., a Trier). A leading member of the Independents, Simpson was finally imprisoned because he had dared to preach against Cromwell in 1655. Two years earlier he had delivered a commencement address at Cambridge [54] in which he stressed the importance of higher learning in religion. Strong objection was taken to his views by the sectary William Dell (d.1669), a former army chaplain who had been Master of Caius College, Cambridge, since 1649. Dell was notorious as far as the Puritans were concerned; Baxter described him as a man "who took Reason, Sound Doctrine, Order and Concord to be the intollerable Maladies of Church and State, because they were the greatest Strangers to his Mind." [55] In his reply to Simpson, Dell not only denied the necessity of university training for the ministry, but he also attacked Plato and Aristotle, philosophy in general, and divinity degrees. Dell's reply, *A Plain and Necessary Confvtation of Divers Gross and Antichristian Errors*, was published with his *Tryal of Spirits* in 1654. Roger Williams, in a letter dated February 15, 1655, observed that the latter book had been burned at Massachusetts Bay,[56] and it would therefore appear that Dell's reply to Simpson was also burned by the New England Puritans. In any case, Dell's reply to Simpson was attacked in 1655 by Charles Chauncy, the President of Harvard. Chauncy, a Puritan, observed that Dell's writings were "in few hands, & they that have them build much upon his judgment." Chauncy defended the study of arts and sciences in general, especially logic, rhetoric, and the biblical languages, as a suitable preparation for those preparing to preach. He recognized, furthermore, that the attack against the conservative clergy and the existing university program had become an Anglo-American problem of concern to Puritans on both sides of the Atlantic.[57]

Dell was also answered by Seth Ward, the Savilian Professor of Astronomy at Oxford, in an appendix to his book *Vindiciae Academiarum* (Oxford, 1654). Part of that appendix was directed against the criticisms of education made by Thomas Hobbes in his *Leviathan* (1651). Dell was harshly dealt with by Ward, but the Savilian professor treated Hobbes with more respect, choosing to think that Hobbes was merely out of touch with current developments in the universities: "The truth is . . . , about that time when Mr. Hobbs was conversant in Magdalen-Hall, the constitution and way of the University might (likely) be enclining to his Character of it, but now his Discourse seemes like that of the seaven sleepers, who after many yeares awaking, in vaine addressed themselves to act according to the state of things when they lay downe." [58]

Ward's primary concern was with neither Hobbes nor Dell, but with a probing criticism of higher education by the sectary John Webster, entitled *Academiarum Examen, or the Examination of*

as Master of Caius College, Cambridge.[64] Sedgwick could not resist making the caustic observation (aimed at Dell) that "Yelden Tithes, if exacted to the rigour, make a very fat Benefice." [65]

In the 1650s the Puritans and most of the sectaries found themselves debating with the Quakers as well as debating the subject of education. The Quakers, who played a major role in the sectarian movement, also criticized contemporary education. Richard Hubberthorn (1628–1662), a Lancashire Quaker and a friend of George Fox and George Whitehead, published a list of twenty-seven questions directed to the clergy in which he demanded to know why it was necessary to go to Oxford or Cambridge rather than to the Holy Spirit to receive training for the ministry. His reply came in 1654 from the Anglican Richard Sherlock (1612–1689), who had been ejected as chaplain of New College, Oxford, c.1648. The heart of Sherlock's rebuttal was the assertion that the Holy Spirit revealed the truths of the Gospel through the knowledge of the languages, arts, and sciences that were studied at such places as Oxford and Cambridge. Only with that knowledge could one successfully avoid being deceived in religious matters by human misconceptions and imagination.[66] Sherlock was in turn attacked by the Quaker founder, George Fox (1624–1691), who reasserted the Quaker belief that the teaching of the Spirit came without the use of any human means, including education.[67]

The debate gradually began to subside in the later 1650s, though the pamphlet wars continued. In 1658 a certain N.E., a religious conservative, asserted the necessity of ordination to preach, and was refuted the same year by the sectary Jeremiah Ives (*fl.* 1653–1674), a self-taught General Baptist. Ives contended that any man had the lawful right to preach, if he had a divine gift enabling him to do so. Higher education was not mentioned as a necessary prerequisite.[68] The following year (1659) the Puritan Immanuel Bourne (1590–1679), a Presbyterian rector in Leicestershire, came to the defense of the existing social structure in England in response to the attacks of the sectaries John Darker, Tobias Watson, and other Baptists. Bourne defended the necessity of an educated clergy, tithes, and infant baptism. The attack on the universities, he argued, was a subtle Popish plot "carried on by Quakers, some Anabaptists, and Familists . . . that they might more easily bring us back to the bondage of Popery, blind Superstition, and antichristian Tyranny." [69]

The defense of preaching by gifted but unordained ministers was also made by three East Anglian Independent ministers, Samuel Petto (1624?–1711), John Martin, and Frederick Woodall. The conservative case opposing their position was made by the Puritans John Collinges and Matthew Poole. Poole (1624–1679), a *jure divino* Presbyterian, was concerned about upholding the role of the universities as educators of the clergy. His concern was manifested in a plan to provide financial assistance to university students, especially those studying for the ministry.[70]

Thus the debate on higher learning and religion began and ended on the question of ordination. At its peak, however, the debate broadened to include the more significant problem of the nature and role of higher education in English society. It was at that stage of the debate that the participants delved into the issues raised by the great seventeenth century contributors to educational thought— Francis Bacon, Jan Comenius, Samuel Hartlib, and John Dury. Involved in the debate were questions relating to developments in the natural sciences, the validity of classical studies, pedagogical issues (especially in the teaching of foreign languages), and the broader problem of the nature, extent, and purpose of the educational program. It was no longer simply a religious issue that was at stake, but a question which affected the whole of society.

CHAPTER TWO

Utilitarian and Experimental Criteria in Educational Reform

The educational philosophy of Puritan and sectarian reformers was part of an intellectual tradition that originated in Elizabethan England and which was popularized by Francis Bacon in the Jacobean period. The diffusion of that tradition in the Caroline period and particularly in Puritan England gave rise to demands for educational reforms based on the criteria of utility and experience. Various Puritans and sectaries championed such criteria, arraying themselves as the Moderns in an intellectual debate with the Ancients. For the Moderns what mattered most was the practical and utilitarian—that which could provide effective relief for man's estate. Their position embraced or was compatible with a materialistic ideology which sought the physical prosperity of society. For the Ancients what mattered most was the welfare of the mind, which was to be attained by examining the writings of the classical world. Theirs was a non-materialistic philosophy which shunned the enthusiastic claims of the Moderns for the utilitarian value of experimental science. For the Ancients there was a strong urge to find all essential knowledge in classical literature and the Bible. For the Moderns, on the other hand, contemplation of the ancient wisdom of the classics paled in the light of new scientific knowledge, much of which had utilitarian implications.

THE BACONIAN-COMENIAN TRADITION

FRANCIS BACON

As the herald of modernity Francis Bacon rejected dependence on classical authorities, criticizing them for their attention to semantic arguments and neglect of reality. He condemned the reverence for antiquity manifested by contemporary scholars and their servility to classical authority, calling for the submission of knowledge to the practical test of experience. Like Descartes he sought to liberate the mind of man from the entrapments of prior notions, but unlike Descartes he rejected total reliance on the mind as the source of knowledge. Experience, not rationalization, was the key to the advancement of knowledge.

Bacon synthesized, systematized, and popularized the scientific thought of the sixteenth century. More important, he had a literary gift that enabled him to express the experimental, utilitarian approach to the discovery of knowledge in a way that won it acceptance with later generations of scientists and reformers. "Bacon's great service to 'science' was that he gave it an incomparable advertisement, by associating with it his personal prestige, his 'Elizabethan' glamour, and his great literary power." [1] He found a utilitarian element in scientific knowledge which he wished to direct to beneficial social ends—to the formation of a new Atlantis. The achievement of that utopian society was to result from the study of nature in accordance with his new *organum* and the application of the results to social reform. By emphasizing the social applications of scientific knowledge Bacon inspired later generations to seek a more just and prosperous society.

An important instrument in bringing about a better society was education. On this subject Bacon had a number of specific ideas for reform. Learning, he affirmed, must have a view to utility and action. He found it strange that the colleges of Europe devoted themselves solely to professional preparation (law, theology, and medicine) rather than to the study of arts and sciences in general. Both, he felt, were essential. The practice of universities largely limiting themselves to the training of lawyers, theologians, and medical doctors was inimical to the advancement of the sciences and harmful to states and governments. The latter were adversely affected because there was no specific program of education designed to train men for careers as statesmen; what future statesmen learned of value in the universities they had to glean from their training in the arts. How much better prepared they would be, Bacon claimed, if they concentrated more on history, modern languages, and "books of policy and civil discourse." [2] Men trained in these utilitarian subjects would be in a better position to guide their governments and further progress.

Bacon called for the establishment of a closer relation between the universities of Europe and the founding of a brotherhood of scholars to exchange ideas and data. He criticized the universities where he found that "everything is . . . adverse to the progress of science." Lectures and academic exercises were so ordered that any unusual thought was, he felt, impossible. "The studies of men in these places are confined and as it were imprisoned in the writings of certain authors, from whom if any man dissent he is straightway arraigned as a turbulent person and an innovator." The universities must learn to accept change, he contended, for the natural state of the arts (and he undoubtedly included the sciences) was one of perpetual growth. He also warned that there would be little progress in discovering the secrets of nature unless full allowance were made for expenses entailed in conducting experiments. He called for the appointment of suitable men to undertake an inquiry concerning areas of knowledge insufficiently explored. In his opinion it was essential to review the sciences to ascertain their state of development. He set out to accomplish this task in his treatise, *The Advancement of Learning.*[3]

During his lifetime Bacon's philosophy was not embraced by the Puritans, largely because of what H. R. Trevor-Roper has called "its courtly Jacobean clothes, its patrician elegance, its metropolitan urbanity and scepticism, its traces of the galleries and aviaries of York House, the gardens and fishponds of Gorhambury. . . ."[4] Undoubtedly Bacon's attachment to the court did create suspicion in the minds of Puritans, but that suspicion cannot have been furthered by what they actually read in his works. What probably retarded the acceptance of the Baconian philosophy more than anything else was the stifling intellectual climate of the latter years of James I and the entire reign of his son. With the collapse of the Laudian censorship and the old regime in the early 1640s came a freer intellectual climate. With it also came the need of Puritan leaders for a philosophy that would voice their desires for reforming the state and society. In the intellectual and revolutionary ferment of these years Bacon's philosophy became an inspiring force. Already his writings had influenced such men as William Ames, Sir Walter Ralegh, Lord Brooke, and John Robinson; others were to fall under his sway—Hugh Peter, James Harrington, George Wither, William Dell, Richard Baxter, William Walwyn, Thomas Goodwin, John Milton, Richard Overton, John Saltmarsh, Gerrard Winstanley, William Petty, and Anthony Burgess.[5] Baconian ideas were spread among the lower classes, especially after 1640, by the almanacs, which, selling for 1*d*. apiece, served to disseminate information widely and inexpensively. Bacon's thought apparently appeared in the weeklies also, though weekly readers seemed to have a "chronic thirst for pseudo-science" more than for genuine scientific developments.[6]

There was much in the thought of Bacon that influenced the Puritans and sectaries. Bacon's experimental approach in science was fairly compatible with the emphasis on personal experience in religion. His reluctance to rely on sources and his insistence on first-hand experience as the means to gain scientific knowledge was much the same methodology as Puritans and sectaries used to seek religious truth. Bacon's elevation of religion over scientific knowledge, though done not for religious but scientific reasons,[7] was compatible with the belief of both Puritans and sectaries in the superiority of religious over natural truth. The Puritans, however, could not have accepted the strongly irrational element which Bacon found in religion. This would have been acceptable to most sectaries. The Baconian emphasis on the usefulness of knowledge blended with the fervent spirit of religious and social activism that motivated many Puritans and sectaries, making Bacon a "source of the humanitarianism and social-mindedness which are so conspicuous in the period of Puritan domination."[8] The application of that social-mindedness to educational reform reflected Baconian ideas. His emphasis on the utilitarian aspects of education, his call for adequate training in history, modern languages, and politics, his pleas for closer cooperation among scholars and between universities, his criticism of the rigidity of the curriculum and the reliance on traditional authors, his dislike of Aristotelianism, his belief that logic and rhetoric should not be studied by students so early in their training, his demand for liberty of thought, his interest in trades, his concern for the advancement of scholarly research: all these points were enunciated by educational reformers in Puritan England. Whether they derived these concepts directly from the writings of Bacon or whether they came *via* his intellectual disciples of the Comenian group makes little difference to the fact that the fountain of inspiration for educational reform in Puritan England was ultimately Francis Bacon.

THE TRANSMISSION OF THE BACONIAN HERITAGE

Among those who propagated Baconian principles in Puritan England was a small group dedicated to educational and social reform which took its inspiration from the Bohemian Jan Amos Komensky (Comenius; 1592–1670). Comenius, a schoolmaster and Bohemian Brethren minister, was deeply influenced by Bacon in his formative years. During the Thirty Years' War he was driven from Bohemia by the Catholics. Finding refuge with a group of fellow Bohemians on a Polish estate at Leszno, he took the opportunity to study Bacon and write on education. Then, Samuel Hartlib in England offered him money, copies of Bacon's works, and an amanuensis. Comenius sent his writings to England for Hartlib to publish. Through the efforts of Hartlib, Comenius entered into correspondence with John Dury (1596–1680), then living in Sweden, where he too distributed Comenius' works.

In the Baconian tradition, Comenius insisted that learning be utilitarian as well as attractive, thereby preparing students to face the tasks of life. Furthermore, education must include more than memorization; students must examine the natural world. As for Bacon, so for Comenius, the observation of nature was a *sine qua non* for the attainment of knowledge, though Comenius placed less value on scientific experiment and the inductive method than did Bacon. The natural sciences were to be taught as a useful subject. Comenius himself wrote a treatise on physics entitled *Physicae ad Lumen Divinum Reformatae Synopsis Philodidactorum et Theodidactorum Censurae Exposita* (Leipzig, 1633).

For those capable and desirous of pursuing studies beyond their university education Comenius proposed the establishment of a universal "Didactic College" where the foremost scholars of the world were to reside to advance the arts and sciences *ad gloriam Dei.* This conception of a universal college was derived by Comenius from Bacon's *New Atlantis,* in which the latter described his House of Solomon where great scholars sought to advance the frontiers of human knowledge. Comenius viewed his "Didactic College" as having "the same relation to other schools that the belly bears to the other members of the body; since it will be a kind of workshop, supplying blood, life, and strength to all." [9]

Comenius had a direct interest in the advancement of academic scholarship. From Bacon he had received inspiration about the progress to be made through the use of the inductive method. His plan to enlist a body of men to gather the sum total of human knowledge in a magnum opus to be entitled *Pansophia* was much like Bacon's call for a body of eminent scholars to survey scientific knowledge. Again, as in the case of Bacon the dream was never fulfilled, but the aspirations of both men bore testimony to their conviction that, in general, knowledge could not be compartmentalized. Unlike Bacon, however, Comenius did not believe in the necessity of separating religious and human knowledge. Puritans, therefore, would have found Baconian principles more agreeable in the modified form in which Comenius interpreted them to England than in the way in which Bacon himself stated them.

Comenius' friend, Samuel Hartlib (c.1600–1670), was a Pole. As a young man Hartlib had journeyed to England where he studied at Cambridge and came into contact with Baconian ideas. Beginning in 1638 "he threw himself into works of charity, collected money for Protestant refugees from Poland, Bohemia, and the Palatinate, set up a short-lived school, on Baconian principles, at Chichester, and finally, in 1630, moved to London and lived permanently in Duke's Place, Holborn." [10] Throughout the 1630s, he championed the views of Comenius and Dury, who, with himself, were the philosophers of the English opposition party and the articulators of Baconian reform. With parliamentary approval Hartlib invited Comenius and Dury to England in mid-1641, with the promise of patronage by James Ussher, Archbishop of Armagh, Lord Brooke, John Williams, Archbishop of York, John Selden, and John Pym, leader of the House of Commons. Dury arrived in London in June and was given an honorary post as chaplain to the Earl of Leicester, Strafford's successor. Comenius followed in September. When political conditions in England prohibited Pym and other Puritan leaders from supporting Comenius' plans for educational reform, he left for Sweden in June, 1642. [11]

In the Baconian tradition Hartlib maintained a distinct interest in science and education, counting among his friends John Milton, Robert Boyle, Seth Ward, and John Wallis. Another friend was the Comenian Hezekiah Woodward (1590–1675), who stressed the importance of science and of emphasizing things rather than words in education. Hartlib knew Samuel Foster, Professor of Astronomy at Gresham College, and admired the work of the astronomer Jeremiah Horrocks, a pioneer in the theory of universal gravitation, a contributor to a more accurate estimate of the solar parallax, and an intermediate link between Johannes Kepler and Isaac Newton.[12]

Hartlib's writings on education embodied the ideas of Bacon and Comenius, stressing the utilitarian ideal. He proposed that the educational system include four kinds of schools, the first of which was to train the "Vulgar" students whose occupations would be mechanical. The second type of school was to train the young gentry and nobility, whose responsibilities would ultimately be fulfilling offices in the state. The third kind of school (essentially a college of education) was to prepare scholars in the arts and sciences. The fourth type of school (a theological seminary) was for instruction in divinity. "The right Ordering of these Schooles," he wrote, "is to bee lookt upon as the Maine Foundation of a Reformed-Commonwealth, without which no other work of Reformation will ever bee effectuall." [13]

Hartlib argued that statesmen would be better able to govern if they availed themselves of the utilitarian information (statistical, economic, etc.) which could be supplied by an invisible college of cooperating scholars, of which he volunteered to be the secretary. Such men, having placed themselves in the service of the state, would be able to "improve husbandry, teach languages, forward inventions, compile statistics, educate the Red Indians, the Irish, the poor, recommend domestic servants, welcome—perhaps convert—the Jews, interpret the Apocalypse." [14] The proposal for such a project was put forth in 1647 as an office of addresses comprising several branches. The office was to be open to all men to aid in fulfilling their needs. Of particular interest was the office of communication, whose task was to promote practical inventions, serve as a clearing house for ideas, promote piety and ecumenicity in religion, correspond with librarians concerning books and manuscripts, and publish the results of its work annually to professors at Oxford and Cambridge and the heads and masters of all colleges and halls.[15]

Dury did not leave England with Comenius, but remained to continue the work of reformation. He moved in impressive circles: Robert Boyle was his uncle by marriage; the younger children of Charles I were his pupils by virtue of parliamentary appointment;

Henry Oldenburg, a German Protestant and later Secretary of the Royal Society, was his son-in-law; he corresponded with Henry Robinson and probably knew Milton.[16] Dury served as a member of the Westminster Assembly of Divines and as Keeper of the King's Library.

Dury's ideas on education were governed by his concept of education's function, which he defined as the preparation of "every one for the industrie and employment in the society of men, whereunto by reason of his birth, he may have a right, or by reason of his naturall parts he may by others be called, or of his own accord lawfully apply himself." Education was also, in the Puritan manner, to provide students with suitable religious instruction. Nothing was to be taught except that which was useful to society. Recognizing the need for pedagogical and curriculum changes in the schools in order to make this philosophy of education fully operative, Dury called—essentially on religious grounds—for the "reforming and facilitating all the meanes of humane learning for the schooles as well of old as young Schollers." Aware of the need for reforms in higher as well as lower education, he criticized (as the sectaries would later do) the monopolizing of higher learning by the two universities and called for the strengthening of the English system of education. Aware of the problems that confronted the Comenians in establishing their program of reform, he cautioned that those who "are habituated to a custome of their owne, and thinke themselves to be Doctors and Masters of Sciences, are not easily brought by the sight of any booke, though never so well penned, to alter their course of teaching." [17]

Dury criticized pedagogy which made students "learn by heart the General Rules, sentences, and Precepts of Arts, before they are furnished with any matter whereunto to apply those Rules and Precepts." Students were consequently led "into a Maze of subtile and unprofitable Notions; whereby their mindes are puft up with a windy conceit of knowledge . . . ; for their heads are filled with certain termes and empty shewes of learning. . . ." The remedy entailed teaching the essence of things with terms; teaching arts and sciences capable of sensual perception alone by sense entirely rather than by tradition or reason; relying on sensual perception in other arts and sciences as much as possible; avoiding all superfluities in instruction; building on prior knowledge wherever possible; teaching subjects practically first and then theoretically; and withholding instruction in logic and metaphysics until the end of the academic program because of their reliance on pure reason rather than sense perception.[18]

Dury also called for the creation of specific institutions and professorial chairs. One of his proposals advocated the establishment of a public agency for universal learning to coordinate the work of the universities and the lower schools. Its functions were similar to those proposed by Hartlib for the office of communication in his office of addresses. Dury favored founding a college dedicated to the teaching of oriental languages, especially Hebrew, with state support amounting to £1000 per annum. His religious convictions were revealed in his call for the establishment of a professorship of practical divinity in every university plus one in London at Sion or Gresham College. He also proposed founding a lectureship in London designed to teach common people how to read and use Scripture.[19]

Dury shared a Baconian concern for the application of knowledge to practical problems with William Petty (1623–1687). In 1650 Petty became Professor of Music at Gresham College, and the following year was appointed Professor of Anatomy at Oxford, where he worked with Boyle on experimental anatomy. He was also Vice-Principal of Brasenose College. His ideas on education were set forth in a tract entitled *The Advice of W.P. to Mr. Samuel Hartlib, for the Advancement of Some Particular Parts of Learning* (1648), a tract which effused Baconian and Comenian ideas.

As had Comenius, Petty insisted that education be utilitarian; no child was to be excluded by reason of poverty from obtaining a good education. He was certain that there were many plowing fields who were better adapted, had they been educated, to direct affairs of state. To remedy the situation he proposed the establishment of *ergastula literaria,* or "literary work-houses, where children may be taught as well to do something towards their living, as to read and write." [20]

As a practical businessman as well as a Baconian, Petty was interested in the advancement of mechanical arts and manufacturing. For this purpose he proposed the erection of a *gymnasium mechanicum,* or college of tradesmen. Included in the college would be a collection of live animals, birds, and fish; a museum with antiquarian objects, architectural drawings, and mechanical inventions; an astronomical observatory; a chemical laboratory; fountains; a select library; an anatomical theater; grounds for agricultural experiments;

galleries for rare paintings and statues; and collections of maps. It was a university of the natural world *cum* vocational school and was equipped for research experiments as well. Petty called it "the epitome or abstract of the whole world." [21]

Related to this was Petty's call for the compilation of a history of trades describing the various occupations. If this history were written, he felt, there would cease to be an abundance of "fustian and unworthy preachers in divinity, so many pettifoggers in the law, so many quack-salvers in physick, so many grammaticasters in country-schools, and so many lazy serving men in gentlemen's houses; when every man might learn to live otherwise in more plenty and honour. . . ." No longer would young scholars spend their time reading difficult Hebrew passages in the Bible or "parrot-like repeating heteroclitous nouns and verbs," but would instead read and hear an exposition of "the history of faculties" and study actual things rather than "a rabble of words." [22] Thus Petty, like others in the Baconian tradition, valued the utilitarian and experimental.

The Baconian tradition in general and the writings of the Comenian school played a significant role in the movement for educational and social reform in Puritan England, helping to create a climate of opinion conducive to an effective evaluation of the academic program and of the social structure of which it was a part. The currency of these ideas in the 1640s and 1650s brought them before the sectaries, whose similar concepts of education have a rightful place beside those of the Puritan thinkers who embraced this tradition.

ATTITUDES OF PURITAN WRITERS

Puritans were not agreed on the nature and function of education. In mid-seventeenth century England the Puritans were in the process of re-evaluating their concepts and methods of education, with the avant-garde embracing Baconian principles. Numerous Puritans, however, persisted in their opposition to the new directions of thought. It is probable that those Puritans who actively supported the new educational thought, with its emphasis on utilitarianism and experimental science, were a minority.

Thomas Hall was typical of conservative Puritans who distinguished between the "superior Arts and Sciences" such as physic (medicine), ethics, and logic and the "inferior Arts" such as mathematics, chemistry, optics, geography, architecture, and stenography.

Among the latter Hall also included such assorted subjects as magic, dactylology (a topic of interest in this period), physiognomy, astrology, pyrotechny, "Pneumatithmy," and stratarithmetry.[23] Hall did not express the Puritan "wholehearted approval of the new science . . ." which one modern writer thought existed.[24] Whatever interest in experimental science was demonstrated by some Puritans, little support could have come from the pulpit if Seth Ward's 1654 testimony was indicative. Ward's complaint was that

> . . . of those very great numbers of youth, which come to our Universities, how few are there, whose designe is to be absolute in Naturall Philosophy? Which of the Nobility or Gentry, desire when they send their Sonnes hither, that they should be set to Chymistry, or Agriculture, or Mechanicks? . . . The desire of their friends is not, that they be engaged in those experimentall things, but that their reason, and fancy, and carriage, be improved by lighter Institutions and Exercises, that they may become Rationall and Gracefull speakers, and be of an acceptable behaviour in their Countries.[25]

If the gentry gave substantial support to the Puritan cause, as is generally believed, it is enlightening to note that their offspring in the universities were sent to obtain social graces rather than experimental and utilitarian knowledge. Such a conservative attitude was contrary to the expected Puritan emphasis on industry, sobriety, and purpose. Ward's observation is further substantiated by the fact that a number of gentry had been opposed to the establishment of the Savilian and Sedleian Chairs. Furthermore, in the 1650s, according to Francis Osborne, the gentry were keeping their sons at home rather than allowing them to become polluted by "the Black Art" of mathematics.[26]

The gentry's attitude as indicated by Osborne was not necessarily Puritan, but was generally embraced by conservative apologists for education. To praise education, as did Thomas Hall, as that which "helps to civilize us, and to mollifie the harshnesse, and mitigate the fierceness of our natures . . ." was not to extol experimental science, but to encourage those who sent their sons to the universities to become "Rationall and Gracefull speakers" and to learn to behave acceptably.[27] Another conservative apologist for education, Edward Waterhouse (1619–1670), asserted that the liberal arts provided the way to virtue. Virtue might "receive some weak impulsions from Nature; but the vigorous, the full seas, and high tides are from

Learning. . . ." Without "Learning & Learned Men, as the Horsmen and Chariots of any Nation," Waterhouse warned, "a People can expect nothing but Barbarity and Bestial Volpiuariness. . . ." [28] The old ideal of higher education with an emphasis on training clergy for the state church and providing a gentleman's education (without in most cases expecting the latter to take degrees) had by no means died out with the Puritan triumph in the 1640s.

In the minds of perhaps most of the Puritan clergy the primary function of higher education and the *raison d'être* for the universities was the advancement of religion, not seeking knowledge by means of experimental research or pursuing utilitarian goals. "What are the Universities appointed for but to fit men thence for the work of the Ministery?" asked Joseph Sedgwick.[29] Arguing in defence of the necessity for learning in the ministry, Henry Thurman, a student at Christ Church, Oxford, asserted that "the Arts and Sciences sharpen our faculties, and proportion them for greater things." By the latter phrase he meant religion, for in his mind the end of all human learning was the study of Scripture. The university statutes were to aim only at enforcing "the study of humane learning, in subordination to divinity. . . ." [30]

An anonymous writer at Christ Church, in a 1659 pamphlet, described the two universities as "the standing seminaries of a ministry" which were evaluated in terms of their success in educating clergy. The importance of religion in education for the same author was illustrated in his proposal for the erection of a new college in which one-third of the fellows were to study divinity for the pastorate, another third prepare to be instructors in divinity, and the final third study the remaining subjects, provided that a third of those studied medicine. Thus of the proposed sixty fellows, forty were to prepare for careers as clergymen and professors of divinity, seven were to study for careers in medicine, and the remaining thirteen were allowed to study in other fields. The professional staff of this college was to be "erected and supplied from Westminster School." It was to include one or two professors of divinity, a professor of civil law and politics, a professor of Descartes' philosophy and mathematics, a professor of Gassendi's philosophy and geography, assistants for the latter two professors to inquire into the "magnetical philosophy" of Gilbert and to give instruction in optics and mechanics, a professor of physic, a professor of anatomy (to be aided by a chemist), and a professor of logic and civil rhetoric. From the standpoint of the professional staff the trend toward scientific studies was well represented, yet of the sixty fellows forty studied divinity and seven physic.[31]

In his Walgreen Lectures Alan Simpson gave a brief description of Harvard College which is equally descriptive of what most Puritans in the seventeenth century expected of Oxford and Cambridge: "The college was to be a school of prophets—learned prophets, certainly, but emphatically prophets. What else would a chosen people expect from its educational institutions?"[32] The religious predominance in the New England Puritans' concept of higher education is paralleled in the thought of the English Puritans. Thomas Hall looked on Oxford and Cambridge as "Nurseries for the Church." In order to refute the arguments of the sectaries he urged the further unification of the work of the church and the universities. Obviously this could not be done unless the universities maintained a principal place for theology in the curriculum.[33] Other Puritans argued in similar fashion, warning the elect that the welfare of the church was dependent on thorough theological instruction in the universities. The removal of that function, they contended, would lead to the decline of the ministry and the destruction of the church. To a people as religiously dedicated as the Puritans it was only natural that teaching divinity was regarded as the foremost function of the universities. "As petty Schooles [are] for private Christians," wrote the Staffordshire Puritan Thomas Blake (1597?–1657), "so are Schooles of a higher nature for the Ministerial Function. . . ."[34]

In pursuing fulfillment of that ministerial function the Puritans modified the medieval concept of education. They altered the medieval emphasis on metaphysics and dialectic, replacing it with emphasis on subjects more utilitarian for the Puritan ministry: Hebrew, Greek, moral philosophy, and rhetoric. At the same time the Puritans retained the medieval notion of the existence of a body of revealed knowledge (now Calvinist instead of Thomist) with which the divinity student was to be familiarized so that he could instruct the laity in religious truth and social responsibilities. For the Puritans theology was superior though not contradictory to the other and subordinate areas of knowledge. Where the Puritans excelled over their Scholastic thirteenth-century counterparts was in their ability to maintain a healthy interest in academic areas not directly related to the "queen of the sciences." The Puritans, as Perry Miller observed, "did indeed subordinate all concerns to salvation, and they did force their social and philosophical thinking into conformity with religious conclusions, but they were incapable of confining themselves solely to dogma or giving over the arts and sciences into the keeping of the unregenerate." [35]

In view of the Puritan's belief in the unity of all knowledge, to surrender any of the arts and sciences (whether conceived in medieval or modern terms) was unthinkable. Thus it was necessary to maintain the supremacy of theology without altogether neglecting the remaining arts and sciences which, with theology, comprised the all-encompassing body of knowledge, divine and human. If he was to make progress in the arts and sciences the Puritan had to divest himself of the deadly assumption that he already possessed the truth, and that the task at hand was confined to its explanation.

Although the conservative concept of education stressed the importance of learning as a divine ordinance to enable men to expound Scripture and defend orthodoxy,[36] there were other values of education. Its role in the preparation of proper gentlemen has already been noted. It was useful in providing improved rational faculties, and in promoting "a sober freedom in a cause that concerns whatever is dear to man, his soul, his eternity, his fame. . . ." Without higher education there would be "Lean and Letterless Parliament men, Pithless Justices, Hair-braind Governours. . . ." Education was necessary for the proper functioning of the English army, for without it "the Souldiers Trade will decay and lose its Reputation; for there is no Military man of place, compleat, but he who is in some measure, though to no high degree, learned: for war can never be well managed without learning. . . ." Education enabled a soldier to select proper methods of combat and discipline, suitable places and times to render battle, adequate reasons to justify participation in or abstention from war, and relevant lessons from the battles of history.[37]

Puritans such as Thomas Hall and Joseph Sedgwick were content with the traditional Puritan concept of education. Others, such as John Wilkins and John Wallis, pressed for a greater place for the experimental sciences in the university curriculum and would have supported Lord Brooke's condemnation of

> Criticall, Cabalisticall, Scepticall, Scholasticall Learning: which fils the head with empty, aeriall, notions; but gives no sound food to the Reasonable part of man. Yea their study is mainly laid out upon bookes, which they prize, and sleight as they please. . . .[38]

The particular target of Greville's criticism was the education of the episcopalian clergy, but it was applicable to training in other areas as well. Wilkins gave voice to the utilitarian criterion embraced by progressive Puritans when he wrote: "Our best and most divine knowledge is intended for action; and those may justly be accounted barren studies which do not conduce to practice as their proper end." [39] Wilkins was intrigued by the possibilities of applying the principles of physics for utilitarian purposes, such as a windmill-driven carriage, the preservation of the spoken word for later playback, and the invention of airplanes, submarines, and engines.

A moderate program of Puritan reform was developed by John Milton, who set himself to the task of "the reforming of Education, . . . the want whereof this nation perishes. . . ." [40] His 1644 tract *Of Education* was elicited by and addressed to Samuel Hartlib. In it Milton made a careful attempt to fuse the ideals of classical humanism with the principles of Puritanism without losing sight of the utilitarian ideal. It was a system of education suited to the preparation of political leaders. Intended essentially for the boys and young men of the nobility and gentry, it dealt with their education from the age of twelve until twenty-one, prescribing a level of academic attainment sufficient to discuss subjects intelligently but probably not in depth.

Milton condemned contemporary university practice. With regard to the traditional method of teaching the arts,[41] Milton accused the universities of maintaining the scholastic tradition: They began instruction not with easy subjects but with "the most intellective abstractions of Logick & metaphysicks. . . ." Such pedagogy provoked students into a contempt for learning because they were "tost and turmoild with their unballasted wits in fadomles and unquiet deeps of controversie. . . ." Those following a professional career rather than living on inherited wealth usually became unprincipled politicians or lawyers whose goals were based "not on the prudent, and heavenly contemplation of justice and equity which was never taught them, but on the thoughts of litigious terms, fat contentions, and flowing fees. . . ." Others were led by their university education "either to an ambitious and mercenary, or ignorantly zealous Divinity. . . ."

Milton's proposed educational plan was less of a reform than a reordering of the existing system. It was "not innovation but renovation." [42] The old subjects remained, though their order in the curriculum was altered. Study of the ancient languages continued; indeed it was intensified. Milton was sufficiently aware of developments in experimental science to give it a place in his curriculum, though he did not recommend any scholarly works or theories to his readers as he did in more traditional areas. It is difficult to avoid seeing some disinterest in scientific developments in his question,

> What if the Sun
> Be centre to the World, and other stars,
> By his attractive virtue and their own
> Incited, dance about him various rounds? [43]

Milton was conservative in his approach to education, though his conservatism accepted some change. His approach was probably typical of what other Puritans would have accepted. Differences undoubtedly would have existed, but Milton's plan of reform, retaining the traditional subjects and gradually integrating the experimental sciences with them, serves as an example of a fairly typical Puritan approach to education. The utilitarian criterion was present but not dominant.

SECTARIAN VIEWS

Sectaries of all types in Puritan England demanded reforms in education. "We desire," wrote William Hartley in reply to Thomas Hall, that "the Universities be well regulated, that they may not (as formerly) be a cage of unclean Birds: For humane Arts, who maintaineth them more then those termed Separatists?" [44] It was not an attack by sectaries on education *per se*, but a demand for the reordering of its goals and methods. The hostility to universities which Perry Miller purported to discover in the sectaries was not motivated by an obsession to destroy the schools but by a concern to reform them in order to make them useful for society.[45] Although the outspoken critic John Webster condemned the "Academick and Scholastical Learning" taught in the universities as "the rotten rubbish of Ethical and Babylonish ruines . . . ," he made it clear that "if Learning were plac't where it ought, and mov'd not above its own sphere, it were one of the greatest blessings that man enjoyes in this fraile life. . . ." [46] According to the sectary Gerrard Winstanley the universities overvalued learning by using it to attain religious knowledge, and confused it by their "traditional, Parrat-like speaking. . . ." [47] The Quaker William Tomlinson insisted, in the Comenian manner, that the purpose of all schools was to provide students with a correct understanding of "things as they are in themselves, . . . and to profit their utterance and demonstration of that truth that is in things. . . ." [48] John Hall, who objected to the strictness of the university statutes because they hindered the introduction of new studies and methods, criticized irrational and uncivil customs and courses of the universities, which tended to "the choaking of all literature." [49] The Bermuda-born alchemist and sectary George Starkey (Stirk; d.1665) contended that schools relied on mere words and notions, "which indeed are nothing, and in application prove but empty shadowes. . . ." They were the bed of sloth and idleness, having as their maxim the esteeming of things which were removed from reality.[50]

For the sectaries in general the function of education was divorced from religious ends. Webster's concept of the goal of education as the enabling of men to fulfill their responsibilities in the Commonwealth was like that of Milton, except that the latter had included religion in his curriculum. For Webster, education was utilitarian and profitable since it prepared men for military and civil tasks, "without which men do not much differ from brute animants. . . ." [51] Winstanley similarly viewed education as that which made young people rational and enabled them to become "good Commonwealths men." [52] Sectarian criticism of the universities aimed at the reformation of the traditional clerical learning used to repress them. "Tyrants very wel knowing," Lilburne warned, "nothing is so likely to destroy their tyrany, & procure liberty to the people, as knowledge is. . . ." [53] Dell, who boasted that the reformation he advocated would produce a twenty-fold increase in the number of students, proposed that education be reformed to improve the students' ability to reason and make them serviceable to the Commonwealth. The Commonwealth of the future, he reminded, would be no better than the youth of the present and the education they received.[54]

Prominent in the sectaries' concept of education was utilitarianism. Knowledge was to be used for the relief of man's estate. Men must become selective in what they study, argued the Leveller Walwyn, and learn "to reject what is uselesse (as most of that which hath hitherto borne the name of learning, will upon impartiall examination prove to be) and esteeme that only which is evidently usefull to the people. . . ." He put his process of utilitarian selection into practice in his personal reading, preferring the Bible, Plutarch's *Lives*, Montaigne's *Essays*, and the writings of William Perkins, Joseph Hall, Richard Hooker, George Downham, Pierre Charron, Lucian, and Seneca. He found Cicero vain and Plutarch's *Moralia* tedious.[55] Dell would have regarded some of these writings, particularly those of Montaigne, less than utilitarian and deserving of condemnation along with the present university practices which filled students "only with empty knowledge and foolish notions; whereby neither can God be glorified, nor their neighbour profited." [56] The utilitarian criterion was used by Webster as the test of whether or not a subject should be included in the curriculum. Webster's utilitarianism led him to reject the academic distinction of dividing subjects into "Speculative and Practick." He contended that the speculative subjects were of no use to mankind unless they were "reduced into practice. . . ." [57] Similarly, John Saltmarsh urged that knowledge be put into practice.[58] Winstanley used the utilitarian criterion to condemn both theological and legal training, which were not practical but led to an idle life. This kind of knowledge was "no knowledg, but a shew of Knowledg, like a Parrat who speakes words, but he knows not what he saith. . . . And from this Traditional Knowledg and Learning rise up both Clergy and Lawyer, who by their cunning insinuations live meerly upon the labor of other men. . . ." [59] George Fox used the utilitarian criterion as the basis of his appeal for the establishment of new schools at Waltham Abbey and Shacklewell, which would provide instruction in useful subjects. Fox himself was described by William Penn as a man who was "ignorant of useless and sophistical science, . . . [and] had in him the grounds of useful and commendable knowledge, and cherished it everywhere." [60]

William Sprigg (*fl.* 1652–1695), a Fellow of Lincoln College, Oxford, and a sectarian in his religious views, used the utilitarian criterion in condemning contemporary university practice as an insider. The universities, he argued, engaged in studies that brought no advantages to the Commonwealth and that were neither pleasurable nor profitable to students. Universities were consequently to end their preoccupation with theological studies and "stoop to a more honest civil notion of Schools of Education and humane literature, for training up the youth of the Gentry in Learning and good manners." Like conservative Puritans, Sprigg highly valued the concept of a gentlemanly education, but he did so on unmistakably utilitarian grounds. "Study such things," he advised, "as are of use, rather than ostentation. . . ." [61]

The sectaries were concerned with the quality of the graduates the schools were producing as well as the educational program. Dell criticized the licentiousness and profanity common at Oxford and Cambridge, "whereby it often comes to pass, that parents sending their children far from them, young and hopeful, have for all their care and cost, after several years, received them back again . . . proud, profane, wicked, abominable, and incorrigible wretches." For Dell, existing university education made youth more worldly than they already were by nature because their "corruptions" were increased by daily contact with classical philosophy and poetry. [62] Students were led to their ruin, bemoaned Walwyn, by professors whose learning deceived the minds of men. The products of English education, as he saw them, opposed the Commonwealth, pled for absurdities in government, supported tyranny, and corrupted their neighbors' judgments. [63] William Penn, a friend of Petty and Dury, later denounced the universities because they fostered idleness, laxity, profanity, prodigality, and even ignorance. [64] Whatever merit in any of these representative accusations, their psychological role in persuading the uninformed to support reforms must be recognized.

The most thorough of the sectarian reformers was John Webster, whose *Academiarum Examen* gave a sweeping and incisive indictment of contemporary education. The colleges and halls in each university, he contended, were bound to one method and to the same authors. Such narrow restrictions hindered instruction and the advancement of knowledge. Webster also objected to the practice of requiring students to spend a specified amount of time at the university before taking their degrees—a practice which assumed that all students were of the same capacity and had the same amount of industriousness. Webster believed the educational program overemphasized theory and disputations and gave insufficient emphasis to practical training and experiments. Logic and philosophy were not taught methodically, and instruction in mathematics was slighted. Effective instruction in all subjects was hindered by the use of Latin, which promoted poor facility in English. Unlike Milton, Webster argued that foreign languages received undue stress. "For Scholars to spend divers years for some small scantling and smattering in the tongues, having for the most part got no further knowledge [of other subjects], but like Parrats to babble and prattle, that whereby the intellect is no way inriched, is but toylsome, and almost lost labour." Besides overemphasizing languages, the universities paid excessive homage to antiquity, as if the ancients had known everything. This was especially true, he felt, of the authoritative position granted to Aristotle. The universities were accused of binding themselves "with the universality of opinions, and multiplicity of voices, as though it were not better to stand single and alone with truth, . . . or as though the multitude could not err, or that the greater number must necessarily be in the truth. . . ." The students, furthermore, performed their academic exercises negligently and were permitted to become ridiculous and vicious "in their histrionical personations in the performance of their exercises, being full of childishness, and scurrility, . . . scoffing and jeering, humming and hissing. . . ." [65] Webster did not appreciate the zest which English students brought to their learning. Nor did John Wilkins, Warden of Wadham College, Oxford, appreciate the criticisms of Webster, whom he regarded as ignorant of the state of the universities in 1654 and of the arts and sciences which Webster undertook to advance. [66]

Webster offered a blueprint for reform, most of which will be discussed later as it relates to specific curriculum changes. Generally, he proposed a new classification of academic subjects into three groups. First, there were arts and sciences which were useful only as tools to advance other disciplines. These subjects included grammar and foreign languages, logic, and mathematics. Second, there were subjects which were not instrumental to others, such as philosophy and metaphysics, politics, ethics, and economics. Finally, there were subjects which were essentially "ornamental," such as oratory and poetry. Having regrouped his subjects, Webster prescribed a new order of study, beginning with mathematics, "which by reason of its perspicuity and certitude would so settle and season the understanding, that it would ever after be sufficiently armed to discern betwixt truth and opinion, demonstration and probability. . . ." Once grounded in mathematics, students were ready to study natural philosophy and science, followed by foreign languages. Then came medicine, logic, and finally metaphysics. [67] In this abbreviated version of prescribed studies Webster omitted such subjects as philosophy and ethics, history, rhetoric, politics, economics, and classics. In part such omissions resulted because the order of study was abbreviated rather than exhaustive.

Other sectaries besides Webster valued experimentalism. Nowhere is the application of the experimental criterion more evident than in the stress they placed on the natural sciences in the curriculum.[68] Even Sprigg's program of higher education for the gentry, which gave less attention to science than did the proposed reforms of other sectaries, gave an important place to experimentalism. Chemistry, anatomy, and medicine were recommended areas of study. "A Labratory for Chymical Experiments," he wrote, "together with frequent Anatomies, would . . . be of . . . use and . . . advantage in Colledges for making new and farther discoveries into the America of nature, and inriching the world with knowledge. . . ."[69] The sectarian emphasis on experimentalism is also apparent in the careers and interests of various leading sectaries. George Starkey and Noah Biggs were alchemists; Thomas Lawson was a botanist; George Fox was interested in natural science, especially botany; Winstanley was interested in the experimental sciences, even to the point of suggesting that lectures on them take the place of Sunday sermons; William Penn became a member of the Royal Society; and Nicholas Culpeper devoted his life to medical science. When these men thought of educational reform, it was natural that they made experimentalism a major criterion in that reform.

Sectarian and Puritan educational reformers alike maintained and propagated the Baconian tradition. As had Bacon, they developed reform proposals that had as their nucleus the empirical approach to the discovery of knowledge and its application to practical matters. Bacon, the Comenian group, and the English reformers reacted against servility to traditional authorities, though their independence from them was never complete. Their emphasis, nevertheless, was upon the structuring of the educational system to provide students with facility of learning and relevance rather than upon mastering a received body of classical or medieval knowledge. Whether or not religious knowledge was to be emphasized or even included in the curriculum was a matter that was hotly disputed. Bacon himself had not been antireligious, but as far as education was concerned he clearly wanted no theological impediments to the advancement of knowledge. Comenius, on the other hand, was concerned that sound religious instruction be a vital point of the educational program, a point with which Puritans but not sectaries agreed. The most signifi-

cant point upon which there was firm agreement among the reformers was the place in the curriculum to be accorded to science and its
practical applications. In this area their empirical and utilitarian ideals
found satisfying embodiment. Their reorientation of education along
these lines exercised immeasurable influence on the development of
modern education.

CHAPTER THREE

Education and the Poor

A primary motive for educational reform was the betterment of the poor. Economic conditions in the 1640s and 1650s produced a climate conducive to reformist thought. Economic depressions had plagued the 1630s; the practice of enclosure created hardships for the poor in the country; the lot of the journeyman worsened as the distinction between bourgeoisie and proletariat sharpened; unemployment increased in the 1640s; and the political crisis of 1648–49 caused another depression. Compounding the difficulty for the poor was the failure of the harvests five consecutive times in the years 1646–50. Food prices fluctuated rapidly; in 1647, for example, rye and wheat sold for more than double their normal prices. Conditions did not significantly improve in the 1650s. The Dutch War brought a depression in the years 1652–54, and another depression occurred in 1659–60 due to the renewed political upheavals.[1]

Broad reforms were called for by the sectaries and liberal Puritans—the proponents of the Baconian heritage—to deal with the plight of the poor in the 1640s and 1650s. With respect to education, these reforms entailed a broad program of technological and agricultural education, an expanded system of schools to educate all children, and the establishment of new programs of financial aid for deserving students. These reforms, unlike those calling for poor relief alone, could have been of lasting value as a means to better the status of the lower classes if they had been widely implemented.

TECHNOLOGICAL AND AGRICULTURAL TRAINING

The existing educational program, particularly at the grammar school and university levels, was wholly unsuited to raising the standard of living for the lower classes. Logic, rhetoric, grammar, and philosophy were gentlemanly studies designed to provide a cultural background for the upper classes. Law was viewed by most sectaries as an instrument of Norman bondage—something to be reformed, not learned. Theology at best provided only for man's soul, and customarily was viewed as an instrument to hold the people in bondage through mysterious awe. Even medicine was regarded with suspicion, primarily because of its professional associations. What the lower classes needed was a program of technological and agricultural education designed to enable them to improve the work in which they were engaged. They needed husbandry, not rhetoric; applied mathematics, not philosophy; agriculture and commerce, not logic and classical grammar. Those in the Baconian-Comenian tradition recognized this fact, and sought suitable reforms.

Bacon's interest in technology had been apparent in his proposal for the compilation of a history of trades. That history was to include scientific reports of experiments carried on in the trades. These reports were to be scrutinized by scholars with a view to discovering principles applicable to the trades for their improvement. The basic idea of such a history was older than Bacon: The Spanish philosopher Juan Luis Vives had published his *De Tradendis Disciplinis* in 1531, which included cooking, clothing, building, agriculture, and navigation as higher studies. In his *Gargantua*, François Rabelais had likewise approved trades as a subject of academic study. According to Walter E. Houghton, Bacon reached his conception of a history of the trades from two premises: "in general, from the first principle of his thought, the inductive study of nature for the use and benefit of man; and in particular, from the groundwork for such a study in a new natural history that would include and emphasize the mechanical arts." [2] In Bacon, then, technology was directly associated with utilitarian and experimental principles.

Bacon's interest in technological education was continued by the Comenian reformers. Comenius included the study of trades and occupations in the second stage (ages six to twelve) of his proposed educational program.[3] At the secondary level (ages thirteen to eighteen), his students were to study the mechanical arts and agriculture as well as medicine, theology, and the arts and sciences. Dury too was concerned with technological and agricultural education. Among the subjects which he recommended for inclusion in the academic curriculum were husbandry and gardening as well as bookkeeping, architecture, navigation, and even hunting and fishing. These would accompany such traditional subjects as classical languages, science, medicine, philosophy, music, and history. Like Milton, Dury recommended classical authors when he singled out special works. In agriculture he recommended the writings of Cato, Varro, and Columella.[4]

Hartlib, in calling for curriculum reform at Gresham College, proposed abolishing lectures in divinity, law, and rhetoric, and establishing lectures in technology. He was especially interested in discovering better practices in husbandry and manufacturing to improve the welfare of the nation. This interest was manifested in his preface to an agricultural treatise by Cressy Dymock and his support for Dymock's proposal to establish an agricultural college—an institution that would have aided the poor. Hartlib's broad plan of educational reform called for the establishment of four kinds of schools, one of which would educate the "Vulgar" students whose occupations would be mechanical in nature.[5] His general concern for the welfare of the poor was revealed in his 1650 tract, *Londons Charity Inlarged, Stilling the Orphans Cry. By the Liberality of the Parliament, in Granting Two Houses by Act, and Giving a Thousand Pound towards the Work for the Imployment of the Poor, and Education of Poor Children.* In that work Hartlib described himself as "a well-wisher to the Nations prosperity, and the Poors comfort."

Like Bacon, William Petty called for the compilation of a history of trades to improve the living standards of all men. His proposed *gymnasium mechanicum* was really a college for tradesmen and farmers, and for their benefit included land on which to conduct agricultural experiments, and mechanical inventions and architectural drawings. Petty urged that children be instructed in such subjects as watchmaking, carving, embossing, engraving, gardening, the making of musical instruments, dyeing, perfume making, the art of a confectioner, the making of mathematical instruments and dials for use in astronomy, the work of a lapidarist, optometry, navarchy, architecture, the making of costume jewelry, and the making of mariners' compasses, globes, and other magnetic instruments. Even children of the highest social status were to be educated in "some genteel manufacture." [6]

Petty's interest in technological and agricultural education influenced Milton, whose classics-oriented program of studies included more utilitarian, experimental subjects. He specifically recommended that students read the agricultural treatises of Cato, Varro, and Columella. These were useful for teaching Latin grammar and introducing better agricultural methods, including social reclamation and improved methods of tillage. Other utilitarian subjects recommended by Milton in *Of Education* were fortification, architecture, and navigation.

The sectaries too advocated instruction in technological, agricultural, and other utilitarian subjects. Webster proposed education in architecture. Penn advocated moderate study of navigation, as did Thomas Lawson, who also suggested that building be included in the curriculum. The study of husbandry was proposed by both Penn and Lawson, with the latter adding arboriculture and forestry, horticulture, agriculture, metallurgy, bee keeping, plant propagation, land improvement, and traffic management (as a branch of economics). William Sprigg advocated the inclusion of agriculture, animal husbandry, and gardening in the academic curriculum of the universities. Furthermore, in their leisure time, students were encouraged by Sprigg to study limning, drawing, painting, carving, engraving, watchmaking, and "other Mathematical practices." Students were exhorted to "become pupill to the Experience of various imployments." [7] The result would have been the transformation of the English university into an institution resembling a modern American land grant college.

The most extensive proposal for an educational system oriented toward technology and agriculture was that of Gerrard Winstanley. It was described in his utopian tract, *The Law of Freedom* (1652). Winstanley, who became a Quaker by faith and a corn chandler by occupation after the failure of his Digger experiment, proposed the establishment of an interim Holy Commonwealth to serve as a preparatory step to divine restoration and the millennium. [8] In Winstanley's schools instruction would be rendered in all arts and languages, history, and the laws of the commonwealth. He was concerned that boys also be taught a trade in order to "prevent idleness and the danger of Machivilian cheats" and promote the welfare of the Commonwealth. "One sort of Children shall not be trained up onely to book learning, and no other imployment, called Schollars, as they are in the Government of Monarchy, for then through idleness, and exercised wit therein, they spend their time to finde out pollicies to advance themselves, to be Lords and Masters above their laboring brethren, . . . which occasions all the trouble in the world." [9]

Winstanley desired that all trades be maintained and improved for the benefit of the Commonwealth. This could be done if *every* boy was trained in a trade. Hence, once a boy had completed his instruction in the normal academic subjects, he commenced the study of one of the five basic trades. Winstanley called the first of these husbandry, which included agriculture, horticulture, brewing, baking, the weaving of linen, rope and harness making, milling, medicine, pharmacy, wine making, and fruit preserving. The second basic trade was metallurgy, which encompassed mining, chemistry, masonry, the making of gunpowder, and smithery. Animal husbandry was the third basic trade and embraced tanning, hat making, shoemaking, the weaving of wool, the making of clothes, tailoring, dyeing, and glove making. Winstanley regarded the fourth basic trade as silviculture, which included carpentry, ship building, plow making, and the making of musical instruments. The last basic trade was the natural sciences, which included astrology, astronomy, navigation, and physical science. "And in all these five Fountains here is Knowledg in the practice, and it is good." [10] There was no clearer manifestation of Baconian philosophy in the seventeenth century.

Girls too were included in Winstanley's educational program, for the Commonwealth must "suffer no children in any Parish to live in idleness, and youthful pleasure, all their days. . . ." Girls were to be trained in reading, sewing, knitting, the spinning of linen and wool, music, "and all other easie neat works, either for to furnish Storehouses with Lynnen and Woollen cloth, or for the ornament of particular houses with needle work." [11]

Winstanley made provisions in his utopia to prevent any person, including scholars, from being idle by requiring that every man be engaged until the age of forty in the trade for which he was trained in school. After that age, except for those convicted of a crime, men were to be freed from working at their trades if they desired, but they were required to fulfil the responsibilities of the offices of the Commonwealth, if chosen, between the ages of forty and eighty. To encourage the advancement of the trades Winstanley specified that no "young wit be crushed in his invention, for if any man desire to make a new tryall of his skil in any Trade or Science, the Overseers shall not hinder him, but incourage him therein; that so the Spirit of knowledge may have his full growth in man, to finde out the secret in every Art." [12] As with the traditional arts and sciences, technological and agricultural education were to be advanced, especially by the application of utilitarian and experimental criteria.

Progress in procuring the acceptance of technological and agricultural subjects—of training students for specific trades—was relatively slow. The old ideal of a classical, gentleman's education continued to have wide acceptance in the 1640s and 1650s. A typical statement of the traditional view appeared in the Anglican Charles Hoole's *A New Discovery of the Old Art of Teaching Schoole*, published in 1660. Hoole (1610–1667), former master of a free school at Rotherham, Yorks., and master of a private grammar school in London in 1660, regarded the schoolmaster's aim as providing instruction in languages, oratory, poetry, and literature.[13] More progressive was a school established at Sunderland, which stressed writing and arithmetic in order to prepare students for the sea and other occupations.[14] The progressive tradition continued in some of the nonconformist schools established after 1662. Some of these schools became somewhat specialized as schools for commerce, navigation, or mathematics (with its utilitarian applications).

THE EXPANSION OF THE EDUCATIONAL SYSTEM

The poor could benefit by a greatly expanded system of education as well as by technological and agricultural instruction. The Comenian group favored universal education, with Comenius himself opposed to the idea that the poor should be excluded from education. The program of education outlined in his *Great Didactic* for children between the ages of six and twelve was designed to "provide a common cultural experience for all children and to substitute a sense of national solidarity for . . . keen class consciousness. . . ." [15] Hartlib favored the establishment of vocational schools for the poor, though he excluded the poor from schools to train the gentry, nobility, teachers, and ministers.[16] Dury was of a similar opinion.[17] Petty likewise did not believe that poverty should exclude any child from an education, hence his proposal for *ergastula literaria*.[18]

Others sought the expansion of the educational system to benefit the poor. In his *Oceana* James Harrington portrayed an educational system which was free, universal, and compulsory, though it may have excluded girls. Henry Robinson, one-time student at St. John's College, Oxford, a member of a leading merchant family, and an influential rationalist, called for the establishment of a state school system to provide free education for all children of both sexes. He was concerned that the children of the poor receive at least enough education to be able to read and write.[19] Seth Ward, the Savilian Professor of Astronomy at Oxford and an opponent of the expansion of higher education, believed that more schools should be erected, especially in the larger towns.[20]

Because education was utilitarian in nature and because it could benefit the poor, most sectaries contended that it should be extended to all children. Winstanley included universal education in his utopian commonwealth, which did away with a class of professional scholars untrained in a trade.[21] The anonymous author of *Tyranipocrit*, perhaps William Walwyn, contended that all children (probably excluding girls) should have equal means on which to live and equal education, "and then one man could not by arts or languages so easily deceive his artlesse neighbours. . . ."[22] The Leveller Richard Overton, a Baptist, a printer by trade and a staunch defender of human rights, proposed in 1647 the creation of a sufficient number of free schools, maintained by the counties, to provide education for the freemen of England.[23] William Dell advocated creating schools throughout England, even in the smaller villages. Godly people— women as well as men—were to be appointed instructors, and children were to be taught to read Scripture. In the larger towns and the cities students were to learn Latin, Greek, Hebrew, and the arts and sciences, though classical authors were to be excluded. Simultaneously these schools were to teach each student a trade.[24]

At the pre-university level positive action was taken to procure the decentralization of education. Many new schools were established, especially in Wales (where sixty free schools alone were founded) and northern England, in accordance with the provisions of the two Acts for the Propagation of the Gospel. Schoolmasters had to be selected and approved by a Committee for Plundered Ministers, but not all Royalists were ejected from their positions. Among those who were not ejected were the warden of Winchester and the headmasters of Westminster and King's School, Canterbury. Parliament in 1649 manifested its interest in pre-university education by approving a grant of £20,000 for elementary education, though the political turmoil of that year resulted in stalemate of the program. Two years later Parliament passed an act appointing trustees empowered to grant funds for the increase of schoolmasters' salaries. In 1658 the Council of State approved a grant of £1,200 to the Scottish schools. At the end of the period there was a proposal for the education of the poorer Irish. It was suggested that they be sent to England at the age of ten where they were to be (much in the manner of the English Poor and Apprenticeship Law of 1601) bound to religious and honest people for the purpose of learning a trade. Yet as much as was accomplished, it was not enough to satisfy the clamor for the expansion of education, especially for more free schools.

There was a decided interest in Puritan England in founding new colleges and universities. The motivating factors were academic, religious, and socioeconomic. Academically those inspired by the Baconian and Comenian heritage sought new colleges in order to train more men for the ministry, while others advocated additional institutions to make it less costly for parents to provide children with a university education. By 1660 the efforts of those who proposed expansion had, in spite of some temporary success, proved fruitless. England waited until the nineteenth century for the permanent expansion of higher education.

The proposals for expansion were numerous and came from various quarters. The city of Manchester, with the support of Fairfax, petitioned for a university in 1641. York petitioned in the same year and again in 1648. In 1641 the Commons resolved to appoint a Committee for the Advancement of Learning, but apparently the resolution was not acted upon at that time. Hartlib proposed, in 1647, the establishment of a university in London and the remodelling of Gresham College to promote the study of the scientific principles involved in the trades. Petty, who also desired a university in London, wrote to Hartlib in 1648 manifesting similar interests in expanded higher education for science and the trades. From 1649 on, the calls for expansion multiplied. Bristol, Exeter, Norwich, Cornwall, and the Isle of Man were all suggested sites for institutions of higher learning. George Snell, in 1649, proposed the establishment of pansophic colleges in every county town, and dedicated his plan to Hartlib and Dury. Ralph Bathurst called for the founding of state-supported teachers' colleges, and Adolphus Speed proposed the creation of a women's academy. A proposal for a college of husbandry at Fulham was put forth by Cressy Dymock and supported by Hartlib. The erection of an academy at London was called for by Hugh l'Amy and Peter le Pruvost, and Balthazar Gerbier (1591?–1667) supported the founding of a similar institution at Bethnal Green. Gerbier, a former diplomatic agent in Brussels for Charles I, actually opened an academy in 1649. Various lectures delivered there were published, and included such subjects as navigation, geography, cosmography, military architecture, oratory, and justice. In Wales, a Merioneth-shire rector, John Ellis (1599?–1665), advocated creating a Welsh university at Ludlow. Sprigg proposed the dispersal of colleges at convenient distances throughout the counties. Interest was so great that Parliament established a Committee for the Advancement of Learning in July, 1653, with Cromwell's friend, the Puritan physician Jonathan Goddard, as one of its members.[25]

Various Puritans led in demanding the expansion of higher education. Some of their proposals have already been mentioned. The Westminster Assembly, with Dury among its members and Wallis as its assistant clerk, advocated establishing a university in London in 1643. Baxter wanted an institution of higher education at Shrewsbury, and Hugh Peter proposed founding colleges in Cornwall, Wales, and Yorkshire to train ministers. Milton favored creating a combined school and university in every city to handle a minimum of 150 students between the ages of twelve and twenty-one. Cromwell not only was associated with the new college at Durham, but he also thought of founding a new college—St. Mary's Hall—at Oxford, where a synopsis of English Protestant beliefs could be formulated.[26]

The government took a positive step toward the expansion of higher education in March, 1650. At that time Parliament passed an act placing control of the lands of the Archbishop of Dublin and the Dean and Chapter of St. Patrick's in a group of trustees whose task was to maintain Trinity College, found a second college, and erect a free school. The Restoration intervened before the new college was actually established.[27]

The most impressive short-range achievement of the movement for expansion was the founding of a college at Durham, which lasted from 1657 until 1660. After the cathedral and collegiate chapters had been dissolved in April, 1649, Durham petitioned for a university and persistently renewed its petition until a college was established.

As early as 1651 Cromwell wrote to William Lenthall, Speaker of the Parliament, informing him that various persons from Durham and northern England in general had approached him concerning the founding of a college at Durham out of the buildings and endowments of the dean and collegiate chapter. Cromwell "willingly and heartily" concurred with the proposal and recommended that the House take favorable action. "Truly it seems to me," he wrote,

> a matter of great concernment and importance, as that which, by the blessing of God, may much conduce to the promoting of learning and piety in those poor rude and ignorant parts; there being also many concurring advantages to this Place, as pleasantness and aptness of situation, healthful air, and plenty of provisions, which seem to favour and plead for their desires therein.[28]

In 1656 Colonel Robert Lilburne, a Baptist, requested approval of the Durham project, and he as well as Hartlib were eventually made members of the committee to establish the college, as were Francis Rous, Thomas Goodwin, Ralph Cudworth, Edmund Calamy, and others. Approval was granted by Cromwell in May, 1657. Although the writ of Privy Seal (May 15, 1657) specified that the college would be of value "as well in reference to the promoting of the Gospel, as the religious and prudent education of young men there . . . ,"[29] Durham was not simply a school of divinity. It offered training in secular subjects, including mathematics and geography. The sectary William Sprigg was one of four "Fellows and Schoolmasters" of the new college, as was Ezerell Tonge, a friend of Hartlib.[30] After Cromwell's death, opposition from Oxford and Cambridge resulted in suspending the grant of university power to Durham, and in 1660 it was officially disbanded.

The socioeconomic factors involved in the call for the expansion of higher education were well illustrated in the writings of William Dell. To him it was not sufficient to have universities at Oxford and Cambridge alone, since the resulting distances sometimes created financial hardships for parents. To remedy the situation, at least one university or college should be founded in every major town and city. Colleges or universities should be established in London, York, Bristol, Exeter, and Norwich. Godly, learned instructors should be maintained by state support channeled through the counties. Once such a program of education was established, parents could keep their children at home while they were attending school and thus reduce educational expenses. The practical effect of such a program would be the extension of higher education to academically-capable children of parents with lower incomes. Dell clinched his appeal with a clever argument *ad hominem:* "If human learning be so necessary to the knowledge and teaching of the scriptures, as the universities pretend, they surely are without love to their brethren, who would have these studies thus confined to those places, and do swear men to read and teach them no where else: certainly it is most manifest, that these men love their own private gain, more than the common good of the people." [31]

In his reply to Dell, Ward stated the case against the expansion of the universities. Using an argument that was later associated with defenders of a large university, Ward wrote: "There is nothing in the world more conducing to the enlarging of the minds of men and the compleating of their Knowledge, then the cōversation with men eminent in all the severall parts of Learning, and the honest emulation of those that doe excell." To make this possible it was essential that there be "great" numbers of students and professors, for the advance of knowledge "encreases alwayes with the variety and eminency of mens wits and learning who converse together." Ward manifested no concern for educating children of parents with lower incomes. Neither did Ward agree with Dell's suggestion that students be permitted to reside at home while attending a college. He contended that such a practice would deter rather than advance learning.[32]

John Hall was also unsympathetic to the expansion of higher education by the founding of new schools. He proposed that Parliament "think of some better way of disposing those few Colledges which are thinly scattered up and downe the land, and make them either collaterall or subservient to this designe. . . ." If everyone was provided with a higher education, the result would be a "Platonicke Commonwealth," the attainment of which would enervate the people, take them from the necessary tasks of tillage and war, and acquaint them with "the artifices of delight." Hall was not, however, speaking in the interests of the upper classes alone, for he insisted that education benefit the public at large and not just be for "the private fostering of many idle Pedantick Brotherhoods." The extent of higher education was to be restricted, but only for the overall benefit of society.[33]

Although Sprigg favored the establishment of more colleges, he agreed with Hall that higher education must be limited—in this case, to the sons of the gentry alone. In Sprigg's mind there was no reason to provide such education for those whose place in life was to be little better than slaves. Men were to receive only enough education to enable them to fulfil their callings as determined by their socio-economic status. It was foolish, Sprigg believed, to spoil a good plowman to create a poor scholar, or to rob shops of capable craftsmen in order to find enough college fellows. Sprigg's disdain for the poor was not, however, typical of the sectaries.[34]

New Fellowship and Scholarship Programs

Men of varying opinions in Puritan England recognized that the program of fellowships and scholarships in the universities needed reformation. The call for reform was sounded at the outset of the period by the anonymous author of *The Curates Conference*, who complained that "Schollerships and Fellowships are bought and sould as Horses in Smithfield." [35] Eight years later John Hall requested that Parliament "reduce those Frier-like Lists of Fellowships into a fewer number . . ." and bestow them on men "excellent in their particular endowments, and peculiar for some use or other, that so the number of the Professours might encrease. . . ." The revenues that remained were to be sequestered by a select committee and used for the purpose of "examining and pursuing experiments, encouragements of honour, compleating and actuating some new inventions, supplying the needy ones that really wanted these wings to take great flights, relieving of strangers; and lastly, provoking some sydereall and flaming souls to display themselves in their full and radiant meridian lustre." [36] Hall's was a challenging program of reform which recognized the needs of the poor.

The most comprehensive program of reforming the fellowships and scholarships in the universities was formulated by one who was not a sectarian—Matthew Poole. Poole began his *Model for the Maintaining of Students of Choice Abilities at the University* with a call for men of means to subscribe to a plan for a minimum of eight years designed to support capable but needy students in the universities. The money collected from the subscribers was to be allocated to deserving students by a committee of sixty trustees, "whereof 36 to be Gentlemen or Citizens of eminency, and 24 to be Ministers in or within five miles of the City of London. . . ."

The students were to be of godly character, "or at least, hopeful of Godlinesse," and "of eminent parts, of an ingenuous disposition, and such as are poor, or have not a sufficient maintenance any other way. . . ." The conservative Puritan ideology which motivated Poole's plan was evident in its stated purpose, which was "the bringing up of Schollers of eminent parts and learning, and the supplying of the Church with choyce Ministers. . . ." Consideration would be given to nonministerial students, but they would be at a disadvantage in competing for the grants. Poole's motivation was largely due to his belief that "there is still a great famine of the Word in divers places; especially in Ireland, Wales, &c. . . ."; that need could only be met by graduates trained in divinity. The conservative nature of the scheme was further revealed by Poole's insistence that students study Latin, Greek, Hebrew, and oriental languages as well as the arts and sciences, "so far forth as their Genius's will permit." Except for the nondivinity students, the last three years of study were to be devoted to theology. Poole made provision in his plan for assistance to non-English-speaking scholars to help them learn English in order to read the English divines. To convince the wealthy to support his plan, Poole held forth this promise: "It may be a notable and sound discovery of a lively faith, . . . and a serious and true desire of salvation. . . ." [37] This was one way for a Calvinist preacher to help the saints find assurance of election. Poole's plan was put into operation and some £900 was raised. The plan had the support of such leading intellectuals as Ralph Cudworth, Benjamin Whichcote, and John Worthington, but it did not survive the Restoration.

As late as 1659, William Sprigg criticized the practice of assigning fellowships to counties because it often resulted in preferment to unworthy persons and the exclusion of the qualified. [38] Sprigg's criticism reflected a concern for academic ability, whereas Poole was basically interested in providing assistance for needy ministerial candidates. Throughout this period and thereafter it was customary for divines to recommend university scholarships for needy students, a practice upon which Poole had elaborated. Hall's plan of reform clearly reflected Baconian objectives, ranging from the support of scientific experiments to financial aid for needy students. In him there was no narrow preoccupation with ministerial training, which was Poole's principal motivation.

Poole's interest in ministerial education was linked to Hall's charitable objectives in Hugh Peter's proposed reform. Believing that "colleges properlie are the meeting of men for the hearing Lectures, and improving their parts, not wals to contein monastick drones . . . ," Peter proposed that if there were sixteen colleges in Cambridge, eight should be set apart solely to train men for the ministry. Students of those eight colleges were to be chosen for their godliness and tractability. Socioeconomic factors were to have no bearing on their selection. The two subjects specifically mentioned by Peter for their study were logic and foreign languages. In addition to this "all the rest of the Fellowships and Scholarships revenue [was to be] laid up in a stock, to maintein these young Preachers, when sent out, till they bee setled in the Countrey. . . ." To make certain of the religious indoctrination of the students, every college was to have its own church. The Comenian tradition was reflected in Peter's belief that tutors should teach students in the shortest way possible.

The other eight colleges were condescendingly treated by Peter: To them "all Gentlemen whatsoever may resort, and there may . . . have whatever anie out-landish Academie can teach. . . ." He was concerned that the finances of these colleges be so managed that they could send some students to travel abroad. Peter's Puritan view of education, evident in his proposals concerning ministerial scholarships, was expressed in 1647 when he was an army chaplain. Education, which he then limited to the nobility and gentry, was to emphasize piety and righteousness as well as gallantry and "Courtship"; be provided in the shortest time possible; and be given to godly youth wherever feasible.[39] Peter's concern for the poor in other areas of social reform was not strongly manifested in his philosophy of education. In general, however, the poor would benefit by the proposed reforms of fellowships and scholarships, as they would by a broadened educational system embracing technological and agricultural training.

The reflection of the needs of the poor in the proposals of the educational reformers was a manifestation of the aroused social conscience in the 1640s and 1650s concerning the plight of the lower class. The natural and most obvious reaction to that plight was the establishment of programs for poor relief. The educational reformers, however, realized that a primary key to the *permanent* betterment of the lower class was education. The first step was to revise the curriculum of the schools to provide practical training rather than gentlemanly refinement. Sons of the poor needed education in technology and agriculture, not classics and philosophy. The second step was to expand the educational system to provide training for all children and to decentralize it at all levels in order to make schooling less expensive and schools more accessible. Some progress in this direction was actually made by the Cromwellian government, but it was only of a token nature. The final step which reformers advocated was the establishment of new fellowship and scholarship programs to aid deserving and needy students to obtain a university education. In all of these areas the reformers proved to be in the vanguard of modern education and contributed to the eventual fulfilment of their proposals.

CHAPTER FOUR

Educational Reform
in the Sciences

Imbued with Baconian and Comenian principles, sectarian reformers proposed specific changes in the university curriculum. Some of these proposals were acceptable to the Puritan reformers, who had already begun a more limited plan of reformation. Sectarian criticism placed Puritan reformers in an awkward position by forcing them to defend a curriculum which they found unacceptable and were in the process of altering. Rather than ally themselves with radicals who often embraced mysticism, astrology, and magic, the Puritan reformers followed an uneasy *via media*, sometimes resorting to descriptions of the universities more as they would have liked them than as they were, and sometimes ignoring unanswerable sectarian criticisms. Others replied to the sectaries by the simpler expedient of ridicule: A piece of doggerel misquoted sectaries as saying:

> Reform each University,
> And in them let no Learning be,
>   A great Eye-sore;
> From hence make Romes Arminians flee,
> That none may have free-will but wee,
>   Wee'll ask no more.[1]

THE SPIRIT OF REFORM IN THE SCIENCES

The most positive aspect of the reform program of both progressive Puritans and sectaries was their healthy interest in the sciences and the discoveries which characterized those fields in the sixteenth and seventeenth centuries. Such an interest did not conflict with their religious convictions. Because they believed that within the creation something of the Creator was revealed (a common Christian conception), it behooved them to study the natural world empirically, systematically, and rationally to obtain further knowledge of the Divine.

The mental attitude requisite to the acceptance of experimental science may have been fostered in Puritans and sectaries partially by their religious beliefs. Their faith demanded systematic, methodic labor, and careful, persistent diligence—attitudes required in experimental science. They were accustomed to the anatomical analysis of their conversion experiences in order to determine their validity. The application of this method, based on the careful recording of actual experience and the formulation of conclusions on the basis of the findings, was little different *in principle* from the use of the inductive method in science. There is perhaps more than a superficial resemblance between scientific works based on the inductive method and the spiritual autobiographies that appeared after 1640. In the latter, typically represented by John Bunyan's *Grace Abounding to the Chief of Sinners,* "Bunyan and his like, socially inferior to the Presbyterian and Independent clergy and without formal education for the ministry, attempted to justify themselves and to establish their special calling by detailed accounts of the work of grace upon their souls." [2] The key to knowledge—in this case knowledge concerning one's spiritual state—was experience. That the sectaries and Puritans commonly sought knowledge in this way provided them with a familiar point of reference (if they wished to use it) when and if they contemplated a study of natural phenomena undertaken *ad gloriam Dei* by the inductive method.

It must be emphasized that the comparison between the experimental method in religion and the inductive method in science is only suggestive. Robert Merton wisely cautioned that

> it may very well be that the Puritan ethos did not directly influence the method of science and that this was simply a parallel development in the internal history of science, but it is evident that through the psychological compulsion toward certain modes of thought and conduct this value-complex made an empirically-founded science commendable rather than . . . reprehensible or at best acceptable on sufferance. [3]

There were important differences between the experimental method in religion and the inductive method in science. The former studied metaphysical data, the latter physical phenomena. Metaphysical data could not be measured, nor could it be re-examined at first hand at a later date by qualified, impartial personnel, as could scientific phenomena. In religion there was considerable subjective involvement of those attempting to analyze the data—an involvement essentially absent in scientists. Yet the fact remains that it was an experimental method which both scientists and adherents of the Puritan tradition valued as the means to attain knowledge.[4]

Not all Puritans were enthusiastic about the sciences. There were many Puritans at Cambridge before the 1640s, yet John Wallis (1616–1703), who received his B.A. (1637) and M.A. (1640) from Emmanuel College and became a fellow of Queens' in 1644, complained that mathematics was barely regarded as an academic subject. Wallis himself made it a point to study physic, anatomy, astronomy, geography, and natural philosophy as well as mathematics in his student days. According to Samuel Morison the first man to propound the new scientific philosophy at Cambridge was Isaac Barrow (1630–1677), who went to Cambridge in 1647 and became a fellow of Trinity College in 1649. Once there he complained that mathematics was neglected by all and unknown to most. Barrow, who later became the first Lucasian Professor of Mathematics at Cambridge (1664) and the teacher of Newton, was opposed by James Duport, Regius Professor of Greek and Fellow of Trinity College, and Edward Davenant. The latter feared that admission of a new philosophy would soon lead to admission of a new divinity.[5] Barrow's contributions to mathematical science occurred in the Restoration period, and until then the University did not rival the scientific advancements made at Oxford in the 1650s. The scientists who graduated from Cambridge in the 1640s and 1650s were mostly self-taught.[6]

Throughout most of the 1640s Oxford fared no better than Cambridge in the sciences. The triumph of the New Model Army brought about the purge of Oxford in 1648–49 and the appointment of men imbued with Baconian and Puritan ideals. From the "invisible college" in London, which met in the chambers of Gresham College's Professor of Astronomy, Samuel Foster, came John Wilkins to become Warden of Wadham College in 1648. His colleague, John Wallis, followed in 1649 as Savilian Professor of Geometry. In 1651

Cromwell appointed his physician, Jonathan Goddard (1617?–1675), Warden of Merton College. Goddard would later serve simultaneously as Professor of Physic at Gresham. Another Baconian, though not a member of the London circle from which Wilkins, Wallis, and Goddard came, was appointed to an Oxford post; he was William Petty, appointed Professor of Anatomy in 1651.

All of these men are commonly regarded as Puritans, though Wallis, a decoder of Royalist cyphers during the Civil War and the assistant clerk of the Westminster Assembly of Divines, became a chaplain to Charles II in 1660. Wilkins' sympathies were with the Puritans in the 1650s, yet in the Restoration period he became a bishop in the Church of England. A grandson of the Puritan preacher and pamphleteer Decalogue Dod, Wilkins had studied at Magdalen Hall, Oxford, under John Tombes, who later attained fame as a scholarly Baptist apologist. Wilkins became Cromwell's brother-in-law in 1653, and later served as an advisor to Richard Cromwell. Wilkins' Puritan leanings brought his ouster at the Restoration from his position as Master of Trinity College, Cambridge, a post he had held just eleven months. The Royalist diarist John Evelyn (1620–1706) thought enough of Wilkins to hear him preach in 1656, when he noted that Wilkins "took great pains to preserve the Universities from the ignorant sacrilegious commanders and soldiers, who would fain have demolished all places and persons that pretended to learning." [7]

The presence of these men at Oxford was either unknown to the universities' principal critic, John Webster (apparently a Cambridge man), or deemed insufficient to rectify the traditional lack of scientific interest in the universities. His ignorance of the changes is a possibility since prior to the end of the Civil War he had become vicar of distant Mitton, Yorkshire. Yet he was in London at All Hallows, Lombard Street, in 1653 or 1654, just prior to the publication of his *Academiarum Examen*. On that occasion it seems unlikely that he would not have learned something of the recent developments at Oxford and the continuing work at Gresham College in view of his interest in higher education. At Gresham College the lectures were free of charge to the public and were presented in English (other than those intended primarily for foreigners, who heard lectures in Latin). The close association existing between the new men at Oxford and the London group centering at Gresham College makes it very unlikely that knowledgeable men in London were unaware of contemporary events at Oxford. Those attending the Gresham lectures should consequently have been made aware of the work of Wallis, Ward, Wilkins, and Goddard, and should have been able to tell Webster something about it even if he did not go to any of the lectures himself. In all likelihood, then, Webster was at least dimly aware of the changes at Oxford but did not regard these as sufficient. In any case Cambridge had yet to embrace fully the new science and the Baconian philosophy.

An important point in Webster's criticism of the universities was a plea for the use of the inductive method and the condemnation of Aristotelianism. "We know nothing in nature," he wrote in his *Academiarum Examen*, "but *a posteriore*, and from the affections and properties of things must seek forth their causes. . . . And whereas the best point of Logick for that purpose is Induction, . . . yet that hath been altogether laid aside, while the glory of Syllogisms hath been highly predicated. . . ." To advance the natural sciences scholars must follow the Baconian method, accepting no axioms until proved by diligent observation and experiment. The results had to be recorded in a general history of the natural sciences (akin to the *Pansophia* of Comenius and the review of the sciences called for by Bacon), thereby enabling future generations to continue the advancement by following the same principles. To scholars with a penchant for theories rather than experiments Webster advised: "Be [not] ashamed to cast off thy fine clothes to work in a laboratory, for without this thou mayest wax old in ignorance. . . ." Yet research alone in the natural sciences was insufficient for the advancement of knowledge; they had to be introduced into the curriculum of the schools, where they were to be grounded upon sensible, rational, experimental, and scriptural principles. For the general study of natural philosophy Webster recommended Plato, as methodized by Francisco Patrizzi (1529–1597), an anti-Aristotelian and forerunner of Bacon's experimentalism, and Marsilio Ficino (1433–1479), a Florentine protégé of Cosimo de' Medici; Democritus, as refined by Descartes and others; Epicurus as he was taught by Pierre Gassendi; Philolaus, Empedocles, and Parmenides, as revived by Bernardino Telesio (1509–1588), a critic of Aristotelian science, and Thomas Campanella (1568–1639), a Dominican philosopher who foreshadowed scientific empiricism; Hermes, as revised by the Paracelsan school; and William Gilbert.[8]

In his reply to Webster, Seth Ward agreed that the Baconian

method should be embraced by the universities. Simultaneously he recognized that there were improvements to be made in the use of that method and the experimental work it entailed. But he also made it clear to Webster that instruction in induction as well as the syllogistic method was already available in the universities. As a mathematician he reminded Webster that "Logick is universally subservient to the enquiry of all truths; Induction is ridiculously applyed to Mathematicall truths, and Syllogisme is to be applyed to Physicks. . . ." As far as Aristotle and the natural sciences were concerned, Ward informed his adversary that Aristotle's *Organon* was no longer read to Oxford students. Ward did, however, defend Aristotle's writings on the "Historicall parts of nature," and found it necessary to reject only his physics, "it being founded upon either false, or not intelligible Principles, referring all things to that System, and modell of the World, which time and observation have manifested to be untrue: the Astronomy depending thereon (upon that System of foure elements, and a Quintessentiall solid Heaven) falls necessarily upon the removall of his Physicks, or rather the Physicall part of that Astronomy." [9]

Modern scholarship has demonstrated that the trend away from Aristotle in the sciences (a trend reflected in the writings of both Webster and Ward) was well developed a century before Webster denounced Aristotelian influence. Francis Johnson, who sought to prove that the English scientific tradition was more against Aristotle than for him, demonstrated that in Renaissance England "the philosophical background of the chief scientists was predominantly Platonic, and . . . they emphasized the Pythagorean element in Platonism which sought to interpret nature in mathematical or quantitative terms and thus provided the philosophical sanction of the new experimental method." [10] Webster's recommendation of Plato and his strong interest in mathematics were part of this trend of English thought. That trend was strengthened in its reaction to Aristotelianism by its hostile attitude to accepted authorities and its insistence on the verification of hypotheses by observation and experiment. The inculcation of this attitude in persons interested in the natural sciences was accomplished throughout this period by popular scientific treatises which bred suspicion of authority unconfirmed by personal observation and experimentation. In view of the anti-Aristotelian trend in the natural sciences what is surprising is the survival of Aristotelianism in the universities, which generally remained bastions of scientific conservatism.

The explanation for the scientific conservatism of the universities may partially be found in the fact that before the founding of the Savilian and Sedleian professorships at Oxford in 1619 and 1622 respectively, leading scientists left the universities. They included the mathematicians Robert Recorde (1510?–1558), John Dee (1527–1608), Thomas Hood (*fl.* 1578–1598), Edward Wright (1558–1615), and William Gilbert (1540?–1603).[11] That such men did not remain in the universities left the field to the sterile Aristotelianism which Webster found so objectionable in the 1650s.

MATHEMATICS

With respect to mathematics, which Webster thought more excellent than other sciences because of its lucidity, certitude, and utilitarian value, the universities were accused of handling it superficially in terms of "definitions, divisions, axiomes, and argumentations, without any solid practice, or true demonstrations, either artificial or mechanical; or else the most abstruse, beneficial, and noble parts are altogether passed by. . . ." Arithmetic, Webster claimed, was neglected as valueless, and left to merchants and mechanics rather than university professors. Geometry was treated with the same lack of respect, its practical application being left to masons, carpenters, surveyors, and other craftsmen. To substantiate his point that the universities should do a more thorough job of teaching mathematics because of its utilitarian value, Webster cited John Dee's preface to Henry Billingsley's translation of Euclid (1570), which had been republished in 1651. The same preface, containing a pre-Baconian statement of utilitarian ideals and the value of experimentation, was also quoted with approval by Samuel Hartlib in 1655. Webster's acquaintance with Dee's preface raises the possibility that he had read other of the mathematician's writings. Webster was aware of recent mathematical thought, and spoke approvingly of the advances made by the Scottish theologian and nobleman John Napier (1550–1617), who invented logarithms; the Gresham Professor of Astronomy Henry Briggs (1561–1631), who developed logarithmic tables; and the mathematical rector William Oughtred (1574–1660).[12]

Other sectaries were also concerned about the teaching of mathematics. Dell thought that mathematics should be held in good esteem because it was devoid of wickedness in its content (as the classics were not) and because of its utilitarian and social value.[13] William Penn approved the moderate study of mathematics as profitable, and his fellow Quaker, Thomas Lawson, was of the same opinion. Penn, in fact, recommended that a library of modest size include the writings of the London mathematician and land surveyor, William Leybourn.[14] John Hall, a friend of Hartlib and the translator of some of Comenius' works, berated the universities because they had "hardly Professours for the three principall faculties, and these but lazily read, and carelesly followed." It was no excuse to plead that a man was unable to learn everything, for a university must teach all things to all men, if necessary by luring experts from abroad by good salaries or establishing a program of professorial exchange. In the area of mathematics, he asked, "where [have we] any manuall demonstrations of Mathematicall Theorems or Instruments? Where a promotion of their experiences?"[15] Hall, as a friend of Hobbes, may have derived his interest in mathematics from the Malmesbury philosopher, who regarded the scientific method as acceptable only when grounded in mathematics.

In defense of the universities Ward asserted that arithmetic and geometry were being taught, though "not so much and earely as is fitting. . . ." Although he divulged that "my clamour is against the neglect of Mathematics in our method of study . . . ," he insisted that the study of mathematics had advanced considerably since the Cromwellian triumph. Ptolemy (whose *Almagest* embodied the principal outlines of plane and spherical trigonometry), Euclid, and Apollonius of Perga (whose principal contribution related to conic sections) were read. Mathematical scholarship in the universities, observed Ward, had led to "the promotion of the Doctrine of *Indivisibilia,* and the discovery of the naturall rise and management of Conic Sections and other solid places. . . ."[16]

The mathematical progress described by Ward at Oxford was basically due to the work of John Wallis, who, when he came to Oxford, brought with him knowledge of recent mathematical thought. Wallis was acquainted with the work of the Jesuit Bonaventura Cavalieri (1598–1647), the Professor of Mathematics at the University of Bologna and a former pupil of Galileo's, whose principal contribution was the theory of indivisibles. That theory became the basis of a germinal calculus. The year following the publication of Webster's *Academiarum Examen*, Wallis published his *Arithmetica Infinitorum* (Oxford, 1655), in which he unsuccessfully attempted to use Cavalieri's theory of indivisibles to determine the quadrature of curves. Wallis' *Arithmetica Infinitorum* embodied the rudiment of the differential calculus, and was later used by Isaac Newton in deriving his binomial theorem.

Wallis was also acquainted with the mathematical thought of Descartes, whose appendix to the *Discours de la méthode* of 1637 developed analytical geometry and the idea of co-ordinates. It was a signal achievement for Oxford scholarship that this contribution was not only understood by Wallis but also synthesized by him with the concepts of Cavalieri. Credit also goes to Wallis for recognizing the importance of negative and fractional exponents, for the systematic application of Cartesian methods to conical geometry, for the first general statement of the logarithmic series, and for the introduction of the mathematical symbol for infinity. Later, in 1673, Wallis made the first serious attempt in England to write a history of mathematics (*De Algebra Tractatus: Historicus & Practicus*).

The force of Webster's criticism of the universities for their failure to provide adequate instruction in mathematics loses some of its thrust in the light of Wallis' achievements at Oxford. Yet the publication of Wallis' principal works postdated Webster's attack. The latter's criticism was somewhat vindicated by the case of another Cambridge graduate (B.A., M.A., King's College) who became a noted mathematician—William Oughtred. Both Boyle and Newton acknowledged a debt to him. A member of the Gresham College circle and a teacher of Wallis and Ward, the mathematical rector invented rectilinear and circular slide rules and contributed to mathematical notation. His published works, which Webster recommended, included *Clavis Mathematicae*, a short treatise on arithmetic and algebra published in 1631; *Trigonometrie, or, the Manner of Calculating the Sides and Angles of Triangles*, published in 1657; and probably the "Appendix to the Logarithmes" published with the English translation of Napier's *Mirifici Logarithmorum Canonis Descriptio* in 1618. Yet Oughtred was not a professor of mathematics at Oxford or Cambridge, and in light of his interest in teaching mathematics it is not likely that he would have declined such a post had it been offered to him. Instead Oughtred spent the last fifty years of his life as rector of Albury, Surrey.

Isaac Barrow, credited with introducing the new philosophy to Cambridge and a man who, in the Restoration period, achieved recognition as its Lucasian Professor, left his position as Fellow of Trinity College in 1655 prior to publishing editions of Euclid's *Elements* (1655) and *Data* (1657). Thus of the three leading mathematicians in Puritan England, only one was at a university post when he made his contributions to mathematics. Prior to 1649, when Wallis received his appointment to Oxford and Barrow became a Fellow at Trinity, Webster's criticism was valid; the situation was only beginning to be rectified when his criticism was published in 1654.

Astronomy

In astronomy Webster's disapprobation of the university curriculum was no less incisive. Astronomy was taught, he contended, as if it could "render the true causes, grounds, and reasons of the motions, and effects of all the Caelestial Bodies, and as though no fault, exorbitancy, or defect could be found in this . . . structure." University scientists took for granted the outmoded concept of a geocentric universe and continued to accept the mistaken notion that "the heavenly bodies remain still in the same state wherein they have been observed to be many ages before. . . ." Furthermore, scientists continued to maintain that "the heavens or Orbs are as hard as Steel, and as transparent as glass. . . ." [17] Webster strongly condemned the Ptolemaic system.

John Wilkins, Warden of Wadham College, whose work in astronomy did much to popularize the theories of Copernicus and Galileo, ridiculed Webster in his preface to Ward's apology (*Vindiciae Academiarum*) as one who "urges such pittifull arguments as are enough to fright a serious man from the beliefe of it [the Copernican theory], & to breed a prejudice against it in such as are that way indeed." Contrary to Webster's accusation, Wilkins claimed, the universities discussed the Copernican system. Ward, who as Savilian Professor of Astronomy was a Copernican himself, informed Webster that astronomers had already accepted the Copernican theory and were advancing knowledge by their "inventions and applications on Gnomonicks and picture Astronomy in polishing, and indeed perfecting the Ellipticall hypothesis, and rendring it Geometricall. . . ." [18]

Discussion of the Copernican theory had been under way in England since the time of Robert Recorde in the mid-sixteenth century. Before the publication of Galileo's discoveries in 1632, English astronomers were engaged in telescopic observations of the heavens and demonstrated an eagerness to confirm Galileo's findings when they were announced. So great was the interest shown in the new system that Francis Johnson concluded that "among scientists of recognized standing in England, the old Ptolemaic system was completely discredited from the end of the first decade of the seventeenth century onward." [19] Its replacement was not always the Copernican theory, however, but the geocentric system proposed by the Danish astronomer Tycho Brahe (1546–1601). English astronomers who would not embrace the Copernican theory accepted the Tychonic system, but modified it in accordance with the findings of Gilbert to include the diurnal rotation of the earth due to magnetic force. Webster, however, rejected the Tychonic system because of its geocentricity. Yet he wanted the universities to study not only Copernicus, Kepler, and Galileo, but also Tycho Brahe. Aristotle and Ptolemy were to be rejected.[20]

Precisely what kind of astronomy was taught at Oxford prior to the appointment of the Copernican Ward in 1649 is a matter of dispute. The first Savilian Professor of Astronomy, John Bainbridge, has been recently labeled a Ptolemaic, though Johnson earlier regarded him as an advocate of the heliocentric hypothesis.[21] Bainbridge did reject the Aristotelian concept (later opposed by Webster) of the solid orbs: "That conglomeration of solide orbes was with the Aries or engines of Astronomicall observations battered and demolished. . . ." [22] Bainbridge's successor as Savilian Professor, John Greaves, was a Ptolemaic. Webster's criticism concerning astronomy would generally have been valid prior to Ward's appointment,[23] but not afterwards.

Ward's friend, John Wilkins, was also a Copernican. As early as 1638, at the age of twenty-four, Wilkins demonstrated an interest in astronomy by writing *The Discovery of a World in the Moone*, which attempted to prove the probability of a habitable world of rational creatures on the moon and the possibility of man's getting there. In this work he anticipated Newton's theory of gravitation (first announced in 1666) by some twenty-eight years. The treatise, published while he was a student at Oxford, also discussed the theories of Bacon, Kepler, and Galileo, and attacked the authority of Aristotle. In 1640 Wilkins made a detailed reply to the anti-Copernican treatise *Commentum de terrae motu circulari* (1634) of Alexander Ross, the Scottish master of the Southampton Grammar School. Wilkins' reply was entitled *A Discourse Concerning a New Planet: Tending to Prove, That 'Tis Probable Our Earth Is One of the Planets;* it was published with the third edition of his 1638 treatise. Wilkins' astronomical thought was symbolized by the title page portrayal of Copernicus, Galileo, and Kepler.

The Cambridge Platonist Henry More was also attracted to the Copernican theory, which he praised in a canto of the second of his four poems, published as *Psuchodia Platonica: Or a Platonicall Song of the Soul* (Cambridge, 1642). Milton, who had met Galileo c.1639, spoke well of him in *Paradise Lost,* though Milton was less than enthusiastic about the Copernican theory.[24] Copernican thought was not accepted by all Puritans; William Prynne, for example, attacked it.[25] Slowly, however, the Copernican theory made its way into the universities. Tutors might introduce their students to the new theory through guided readings, though they also might not. Milton apparently had left Christ's College, Cambridge, in 1632 before he seriously began the mathematical studies which led to his awareness of the systems of Tycho Brahe and Copernicus.[26] Webster, who must have been at Cambridge while Milton was there (if at all), must not have fared any better. But by the 1640s Copernican thought had begun to make its way in the universities, making Webster's criticism of 1654 belated.

That the Tychonic philosophy was being discussed in its modified English form necessitated that there also be discussion of William Gilbert's "Magneticall Philosophy." This, Ward informed Webster, was in fact the case. Webster had expressed concern that the universities render instruction in Gilbert's magnetical theory and in the treatments of that theory in the works of Marke Ridley, Nathanael Carpenter, William Barlowe, and others.[27] Ridley (1560–1624), a Cambridge M.A. (1584) and a member of the College of Physicians, used the phenomenon of magnetism to explain planetary motions and the axial rotation of the sun. Barlowe (d.1625), Archdeacon of Salisbury, published a treatise on magnetism (*Magnetical Advertisements,* 1613) in which he discussed much of the same material as Gilbert, with whom he corresponded. Although he rejected the hypothesis of the earth's rotation on scriptural grounds, he developed an improved method of suspending a compass needle and distinguished between the magnetic properties of iron and steel. Carpenter (1589–1628?), known primarily as a geographer, was a Fellow of Exeter College, Oxford, and a friend of Archbishop James Ussher. Like Gilbert, Carpenter accepted the diurnal rotation of the earth and attributed it to magnetism, though at the same time he rejected the Copernican theory of the earth's revolution around the sun.

In addition to stating that the "Magneticall Philosophy" was not neglected in the universities, Ward revealed that "it is a real designe amongst us, wanting only some assistance for execution, to erect a Magneticall, Mechanicall, and Optick Schoole, furnished with the best Instruments, and Adapted for the most usefull experiments. . . ." [28] Gilbert's work on magnetism was recognized to have important ramifications for problems other than those strictly related to astronomy. The English, commercially and scientifically interested in the discovery of a northeast or northwest passage to Asia, were aware of the fact (first discovered in the fifteenth century) that in navigating in polar regions the magnetic compass deviated from true north. Working on the problem, Gilbert had theorized that it was the presence of land masses which caused the deviation, not the longitude of a particular position. Correct latitude, he thought, could be determined by the dipping of a magnetic needle, as Henry Hudson proved on his voyage to North America. But the problem of longitude continued to perplex navigators until the following century. It was only natural, therefore, that Baconian reformers such as Ward wished to continue research in magnetism and its practical implications for navigation.

OPTICS

Webster critically scrutinized optics as it was taught in the universities. He complained that no further progress had been made in optics other than the continuation of "verbal disputes, and some Axiometical institutions and doctrines. . . ." The universities should study the optical works of Galileo, Christopher Scheiner, F. Aguillon, and Johann Hevelius.[29] Galileo actually made little contribution to optics, either in practice or in theory. He improved upon the Dutch telescope with its convex and concave lens, and attempted to prove that light traveled with a finite velocity. Scheiner (1575–1650), one of the earliest scientists to observe sun spots (1611), improved the telescope. Aguillon (d.1617) was a Brussels Jesuit whose work on optics (*Opticorum Libri Sex*, Antwerp, 1613) included material on optical illusions and the theory of projection. Hevelius (1611–1687), a Danzig astronomer, designed a telescope 150 feet in length. Galileo, Scheiner, and Hevelius all were noted more for their optical instruments than their optical theory, and it is curious that Webster did not recommend the works of the two leading optical theorists, Kepler and Descartes.

Ward retaliated to Webster's criticism by asserting that recent advances had been made at Oxford leading to "more solid knowledge of all sorts of radiation or vision, then ever were here, or indeed elsewhere before, and that such things are ordinary now amongst us. . . ." "Opticks and Perspective," he felt, had been considerably furthered since the Oxford purge.[30] The Oxford scientists were undoubtedly working on the basis of recent advances in optics made by Kepler and Descartes, both of whom were read at the University. Kepler had worked on the variance of light intensity (formulating the law of photometry), the refraction of light, the properties of lenses, and the theory of vision. The correct theory of the refraction of light had been discovered in 1621 by Willebrod Snell (1591–1626), Professor of Mathematics at Leiden, who did not publish his findings. Descartes, who was the first to publish the law (in his *Dioptrique* of 1637), possibly saw Snell's manuscript setting forth the discovery. The *Dioptrique* and also the *Principia Philosophiae* contained further discussion by Descartes of the nature of light, its reflection and refraction, and the anatomy of the eye and its vision. Research on the basis of the various Cartesian optical theories at Oxford in the 1650s meant an awareness of contemporary thought on the subject, though the verbal disputes complained of by Webster were partially due to the fact that Descartes himself had developed two theories of light. The kind of progress Webster longed for, however, did not come until the publication of Robert Hooke's *Micrographia* in 1665 and the culmination of Newton's optical research in his treatise on *Opticks* in 1704.

Cambridge, where Descartes was not yet read c.1650,[31] deserved the full brunt of Webster's comments on optics. Godfrey Goodman (1583–1656), one-time Bishop of Gloucester and certainly no Puritan, thought the Cambridge curriculum sufficiently inutilitarian in 1653 to offer the University his collection of optic glasses as well as mathematical instruments, herbals, and items relating to chemistry.[32]

PNEUMATICS

Webster also accused the universities of neglecting such mathematical sciences as architecture, statics, pneumatics, and stratarithmetry (placing men in the form of a geographical figure or estimating the number of men in such a form). In these areas Webster recommended the works of John Dee, Roger Bacon, Galileo, the Bohemian professor of medicine Marcus Marci (1595–1667), Cardinal Nicholas of Cusa (1401–1464), and Guido Ubaldi.[33] There was some significant work in pneumatics under way in this period, though it is doubtful that Webster knew anything about it. Galileo's pupil, E. Torricelli, created a primitive barometer in 1643, which was subsequently used in an experiment by Pascal and his brother-in-law, Perier, in 1648. Later, c.1659, Boyle proved that the height of the fluid in a barometer depended upon external pressure. John Wallis discussed Torricelli's barometer in his writings. Boyle made use of the air pump invented by Otto von Guericke in Magdeburg no later than 1654, a model of which was subsequently built in England in 1658 or 1659 by Robert Hooke. In 1660 and 1661 Boyle conducted the experiments leading to the formulation of "Boyle's Law." That Webster knew anything of the work of Torricelli, Pascal, and von Guericke is improbable; his inclusion of pneumatics with the other mathematical sciences was simply part of a general censure of the universities for ignoring these subjects.

COSMOGRAPHY

Webster criticized the teaching of cosmography in the universities. He admitted that cosmography and its composite subjects—geography, hydrography, topography, and chorography—were usually taught, but he objected (as had John Dee, whom he cited) that little had been done to perfect these subjects, "especially in the mutual correspondence and application of the heavens, and earth. . . ." In Baconian fashion he observed that "Cosmography is the whole, and perfect description of the Heavenly and also Elemental part of the world, and their Homologal application, and mutual collation together, and so is no small or simple art, but high and of manifold use. . . ." Thinking of cosmography's value, Webster deplored the lack of practical application, particularly of the theorems of hydrography in navigation. With reference to geography Webster noted the contributions of Nathanael Carpenter, the leading English geographer of the Tudor-Stuart period.[34]

Other sectaries voiced similar approval of cosmography and related subjects for their utilitarian value. Lawson commended geography, and Dell thought geography and other mathematical sciences were to be esteemed.[35] Progressive Puritans would not have disputed the value of these subjects.

CHEMISTRY

Debate over chemistry provided one of the most interesting aspects of curriculum reform in Puritan England. Webster enthusiastically wrote of chemistry: "One years exercise therein to ingenious spirits, under able Masters, will produce more real and true fruit, than the studying Aristotelian Philosophy hath brought forth in many centuries." [36] John Hall proposed that the universities establish chairs of chemistry and endow research in mathematics and the sciences. Hall contended that chemistry had "snatcht the keyes of Nature from the other sects of Philosophy. . . ." [37] William Sprigg thought that "a Labratory for Chymical Experiments, together with frequent Anatomies, would . . . be of more use and greater advantage in Colledges for making new and farther discoveries into the America of nature, and inriching the world with knowledge, then those many fruitless wrangling Disputations in which Scholars are trained up, that tend to nothing but strife. . . ." With anatomy, chemistry was regarded by Sprigg as one of the two keys able to unlock the cabinet containing the secrets of nature.[38]

Webster recommended writings on chemistry by Paracelsus, Basilius Valentinus, and Isaac Hollandus. The writings attributed to the latter two men were cribbed from Paracelsus. Webster, therefore, was really advocating Paracelsian chemistry alone. Theophrastus Paracelsus (d.1541) was a controversial Swiss physician, chemist, and alchemist who had a wide following among sixteenth and seventeenth century men of similar interests. Essentially an iatrochemist, Paracelsus firmly believed in the alchemical theory of transmutation. His theory (which became a distinguishing mark of Paracelsians) of the three basic principles—sulphur, mercury, and salt—influenced Webster. The latter criticized the universities for being ignorant of the "admirable, and soul-ravishing knowledge of the three great

Hypostatical principles of nature, Salt, Sulphur, and Mercury . . . ," into which all other substances in the universe could be reduced. "By that introversion," he enthusiastically wrote, "is the secrets of nature more laid open than by all the Peripatetitk Philosophy in the world. . . ." [39]

Another admirer of Paracelsus and Valentinus and an ardent champion of chemistry was George Starkey. The son of a Scottish minister, Starkey was a Harvard M.A. (1646) who had practiced medicine in the New World before returning to England no later than 1650. Like Webster, Starkey believed in pyrotechny, and dedicated a 1658 work on that subject (subsequently translated into Dutch and French) to Robert Boyle. Starkey's interest in chemistry was primarily from the medical standpoint, and specifically concerned iatrochemistry, as is apparent from his definition of chemistry as "the Art of preparing Simples, Animal, Vegetal, and Mineral, so as their crasis or virtue being sequestred from its superfluities, and its virulency overcome, its crudities digested, it may be an apt medicine to perform what God and nature hath granted to it, and this in reference to the healing of the infirmities of man or beast, or metals." [40]

Starkey had apparently studied chemistry under the tutelage of John Winthrop, Jr., the first governor of Connecticut, the first astronomer in America, and the first colonial member (1663) of the Royal Society. Winthrop had taken "chemical bookes" and equipment with him to Massachusetts as early as 1631, and subsequently received additional volumes from friends in the Old World. His collection included alchemical volumes from the library of John Dee, some of which were adorned with Dee's own notes. Among the authors with whom Winthrop was acquainted—and with whom, therefore, he presumably acquainted Starkey—were Paracelsus, Basilius Valentinus, Isaac Hollandus, and Jean-Baptiste van Helmont. Once Starkey began publishing his own works, Winthrop added copies of at least two to his personal collection: *Natures Explication* and *Pyrotechny Asserted and Illustrated*, the latter dedicated to Robert Boyle. [41]

Christopher Hill has suggested that chemistry was associated with artisans and religious radicals, and mathematics and astronomy with London merchants and Gresham College (which had no chair of chemistry). Furthermore, "the Parliamentarian scientists who 'Greshamized' Oxford had no thought," Hill contends, "of introducing chemistry there," nor did chemistry have, as long as it was excluded from the university curriculum, any success "in shaking off either its lower-class subversive aura, or its alchemical and magical fancies." [42] Yet in his reply to Webster, Seth Ward, one of those Parliamentarian scientists to whom Hill refers, specifically stated that chemistry was *not* neglected in the universities. Ward was displeased at the concern of the nobility and gentry to have their sons exposed to "lighter Institutions and Exercises" rather than "Chymistry, or Agriculture, or Mechanicks." [43]

When various Parliamentary scientists left London for Oxford, Robert Boyle, who transmuted alchemy into chemistry, likewise moved and established a private laboratory for his research in Oxford. At his behest the Prussian scholar Peter Sthael was invited to the University in 1659 to lecture on chemistry, an event regarded as the introduction of that subject to the University. After a slow start Sthael's lectures became very popular and were attended by such notables as Wallis, Christopher Wren, and John Locke. [44] It would seem reasonable to conclude, then, that the Parliamentary scientists who came to Oxford were interested in chemistry, that (in view of Ward's reply to Webster) they engaged in some rudimentary instruction in chemistry or recommended relevant readings to their students, but that they took no effective action to establish a chair of chemistry because of the prevailing interest in gentlemanly rather than scientific studies.

ASTROLOGY, ALCHEMY, AND MAGIC

The principal weakness in Webster's critique of the universities was his defence of astrology and magic. Although acquainted with various writings of the intellectual giants of his era, he fell prey to the superstitious beliefs of the charlatans of pseudoscience. In the fifth chatper of his *Academiarum Examen*, which he devoted to the mathematical sciences, he praised astrology as a "noble and beneficial . . . Science" which was in "no way offensive to God or true Religion." In the following chapter, devoted to an examination of scholastic philosophy, he wrote of "that noble, and almost divine Science of natural Magick. . . ." He made it clear that he would not defend that kind of magic which was "impious and execrable Magick, that either is used for the hurt and destruction of mankind, or pretends to gain knowledge from him who is the grand enemy of all the sons of Adam. . . ." He defended the magic which was the "sublime knowledge whereby the wonderful works of the Creator are discovered, and innumerable benefits produced to the poor Creatures." This was achieved, he contended, by the operations of magic, which were "fitly and duly to join and connex agents to their patients, masculines to faemines, superiours to inferiours, Caelestials to Terrestrials, and thereby nature may act out her hidden and latent power." [45]

Webster recommended the astrological writings of Robert Fludd (1574–1637) and Jacob Boehme (1575–1624), whom he quoted frequently throughout his tract; Nicholas Culpeper (1616–1654); the Puritan astrologer William Lilly, who was a friend of Oughtred; Richard Saunders, who had attempted to refute Thomas Collier's *Pulpit-Guard Routed;* Elias Ashmole; and John Booker (1603–1667), maker of the annual almanac *Telescopium Uranium* and famed for predicting the deaths of the Elector Palatine and Gustavus Adolphus from a solar eclipse. Webster believed that the universities ignored subcelestial, meteorological, mineralogical, botanical, and anthropological physiognomy, which he defined as the science of studying external objects to determine their internal nature. In pursuit of this occult study he recommended the sixteenth century writings of Paracelsus, Oswald Croll, Quercetanus, and Giovanni Battista Porta. [46]

Webster's detractors were contemptuous of this unscientific aspect of his reform. Ward wrote with fervor of "that ridiculous cheat, made up of nonsence and contradictions, founded only upon the dishonesty of Imposters, and the frivolous curiosity of silly people. . . ." He noted that Webster recommended the works of Robert Fludd, who viewed chemistry as a search for God and whom Ward denounced as one who depended "upon mysticall Ideal reasons," and Jacob Boehme, the German mystic. Wilkins too noted these views of Webster: Because the latter "doth assent unto the highly illuminated fraternity of the Rosycrucians," of whom Fludd was a member, and because he respected the writings of Boehme and his "judiciall Astrologie," Webster must be "a kind of credulous fanatick Reformer. . . ." [47]

Fludd, a disciple of Paracelsus, freely mixed science and the occult to the point that nature became a mystery and magic a science. Van Helmont and Gassendi, whom Webster also recommended, disapproved of Fludd. Fludd's numerous writings approved magic, alchemy, cabala, Pythagorean arithmetical divination, onomancy (divination from the letters of a name), astrology, geomancy (divination by figures or lines formed by dots or points), physiognomy of the face, and chiromancy of the hands. Fludd was also interested in the dissection of bread by fire and the occult qualities of bread. His medical interests included the examination of urine and other excrement, and the pulse. His *Philosophia Moysaica* (Goudae, 1638; published in London in 1659 as *Mosaicall Philosophy*) depicted a thermoscope based on information from an old manuscript, thus making him one of the earliest scientists to write about a thermometer. One of his scientific experiments, conducted in 1617, involved a study of combustion in an inverted glass vessel held over water. Like Webster he uncritically mixed science and pseudoscience, taking care only to distinguish (as Webster later did) between good and evil magic.[48] In 1616 his apology for the Rosicrucians, entitled *Apologia Compendiaria Fraternitatem de Rosencruce Suspicionis . . . Maculis Aspersum*, was published in Leyden.

Webster's admiration for Boehme was not particularly unusual in Puritan England, for a Boehme cult existed as early as the 1640s. All of Boehme's writings were circulated in England in book form between 1645 and 1662, and his manuscripts had been circulated before that. In 1644 the anonymous *Life of One Jacob Boehmen* was published in London, after which there was a quickening of interest in his message. The title page described Boehme as a common man who had attained deeper knowledge in natural and divine things than any man since the time of the Apostles, but without reading it in the writings of another man. Boehme's principal translator was the mystic John Sparrow (1615–1665), whose career included service as an officer under Cromwell and membership of the bar. Sparrow probably knew Hartlib, who mentioned Sparrow in a letter to Boyle.[49] Another of Boehme's English translators was one of Sparrow's relatives, John Ellistone of Essex (*fl.* 1651–1654).

In Boehme's writings there was a strong emphasis on the "Supersensuall" life, which could be attained only "when thou canst throw thy selfe but for a moment into that, where no creature dwelleth, then thou hearest what God speaketh." In true mystical fashion communicating with the Divine was possible only when the seeker abandoned all thinking and willing. Foreshadowing the thought of various English sectaries, Boehme spoke of *the* original language which existed prior to mere human languages. Men, though humanly uneducated, were encouraged to understand "thy Mother Tongue aright; thou hast as deep a Ground therein, as there is, in the Hebrew, or Latine: Though the Learned elevate themselves therein, like a proud arrogant Bride; it is no great matter, their Art is now on the Lees, or bowed down to the Dust." Men must attempt to gain a knowledge of the "Signature, or Figure" of the spiritual world; the visible world was a Signature of that inner world. Knowledge of the Signature was impossible without the aid of the Spirit: All that was taught of God was, without a Spirit-inspired knowledge of the Signature, void of understanding.[50]

The similarity of Boehme's epistemological views to those of Webster and other sectaries is striking, possibly indicating direct influence, though perhaps stemming from the carrying of Protestant principles to their logical conclusion. The remarks of John Ellistone in his preface to the 1651 edition of the *Signatura Rerum* contained several of the basic contentions used by the sectaries in the debate on education. Ellistone warned that the mysteries of philosophy, divinity, and theosophy were not to be profaned by being subjected to the criticism of "outward Astral Reason," which would turn religious truth to covetous, envious, and cunning ends. Therefore "a parabolical or Magical Phrase, or Dialect is the best, and plainest habit, and dress that Mysteries can have to travell in up and down this wicked world. . . ." All men were not capable of knowledge of the mysterious operations of the eternal and temporal nature, which had been locked up by God in his treasury, to be given only to those who asked. Like some sectaries Ellistone admitted that although "I have been trained up in the Schools of learning, and have made some progress in the Tongues, and Arts, according to my mean capacity, yet I do acknowledg my self to be but an unlearned A.B.C. Scholler in Sophia's School, that would fain learn to read her Christs Cross line."[51]

Boehme's name was commonly associated with alchemy, astrology, and magic in England.[52] Webster's recommendation of Boehme provoked the former's critics to ridicule him for his adherence to pseudoscience. The increasing tendency among educated Puritans was to follow Bacon[53] in regarding alchemy, astrology, and magic as fanciful belief, not rationality. Yet not all denunciation of pseudoscience came on scientific grounds; some of it was religiously motivated. Edward Leigh, in his *Treatise of Religion & Learning*, opposed astrology because its study was not commanded in Scripture.[54]

The Quaker Thomas Lawson rejected astrology because it depraved people and led them "into an uncertain Airy State." [55] Similar objections to astrology were made by the Quakers George Fox, Edward Burrough, and Richard Farnworth.[56] The educational apologist Edward Waterhouse, on the other hand, was not ready to reject astrology. Although admitting that it was incapable of foretelling the future, he did not wish to "depretiate naturall Astrology as it is a piece of Astronomick Philosophy. . . ." Astrology was an ancient branch of knowledge and was to be lauded as long as the ultimate purpose was the glorification of God "in a modest observing [of] the language of the Stars and Heavens. . . ." [57] The sectaries were not alone in their acceptance of the occult. Nor should it be forgotten that Webster himself later attacked the credulity of Henry More and Joseph Glanvill, both reputed rationalists, and Meric Casaubon in his *The Displaying of Supposed Witchcraft* (1677).[58]

BIOLOGICAL AND MISCELLANEOUS SCIENCES

In the sciences there were other areas which interested the sectaries. The biologist Thomas Lawson thought students should study zoology, ornithology, ichthyology, geology, and mineralogy. George Fox was interested in botany, and wanted to purchase a piece of land in London (in conjunction with Penn and others) to build a school and botanical garden. He subsequently bequeathed a plot of land to the Quaker meeting in Philadelphia for a botanical school.[59] Webster complained that botany was ignored by the universities. Nothing new, he contended, had been discovered in that subject since Dioscorides Pedanius and his *Materia Medica* of the first century A.D., other than the discovery of some new plants and species, and "their cuts and figures more perfected. . . ." Nothing new had been added to botanical knowledge, in his opinion, by observing the properties of plants, which would be useful in medicine.[60]

Sectarian criticisms were being remedied. About the time that chemistry was being introduced at Oxford in the 1650s, a small group of herbalists formed (independently of the Faculty of Medicine) to study botany. Research into plant growth was made by the most noted of these herbalists, Robert Sharrock (1630–1684).[61] A Fellow of New College, Sharrock published his research in *The History of the Propagation & Improvement of Vegetables* (Oxford, 1660).

Botany was also one of many interests developed by John Wallis, others being geology, physiology, and physics.

MEDICINE

Medical education was a matter of interest to various sectaries. William Penn regarded the study of medicine as a commendable and profitable endeavor.[62] Thomas Lawson approved training in chirurgery (surgery).[63] George Fox was interested in medicine, and found time in 1657 to formulate some queries concerning the origins of disease and other medical matters. In fact, as a young man he had contemplated becoming a physician himself.[64] Even the sectary Samuel How, noted for antirational and antiprofessional views, sanctioned medical studies.[65] William Dell approved the study of medicine in the universities, but only in accord with "that Reformation which a wise and godly Authority will cause . . . [it] to pass under . . . ," inasmuch as medical studies were "now exceedingly corrupt and out of order, both for practice and fees." [66] Dell's words were echoed by Webster, who charged that professors of medicine primarily sought popular applause and esteem with the rich and mighty, hoping to procure larger fees. Consequently the poor were unable to receive adequate medical care. "Must these things have the countenance of Law, and confirmation by Charter?" Webster asked.[67]

One of the most thorough critiques of medical education came from Noah Biggs (*fl.* 1651), whose sweeping plan of reform was outlined on the title page of his treatise: *Mataeotechnia Medicinae Praxeos. The Vanity of the Craft of Physick. Or, a New Dispensatory. Wherein Is Dissected the Errors, Ignorance, Impostures and Supinities of the Schools, in Their Main Pillars of Purges, Blood-Letting, Fontanels or Issues, and Diet &c. and the Particular Medicines of the Shops. With an Humble Motion for the Reformation of the Universities, and the Whole Landscap of Physick, and Discovering the Terra Incognita of Chymistrie* (1651). Biggs was influenced in his zeal for reform by John Hall, who had inspired his call for reformation. Biggs wrote of the universities:

> Where have we any thing to do with Mechanical Chymistrie the hand maid of Nature, that hath outstript the other Sects of Philoso-

phy, by her multiplied real experiences? Where is there an examination and consecution of Experiments? . . . Where have we constant reading upon either quick or dead Anatomies, or an ocular demonstration of Herbs? Where a Review of the old Experiments and Traditions? . . .[68]

Two years earlier Hall had asked:

Where have we any thing to do with Chimistry, which hath snatcht the keyes of Nature from the other sects of Philosophy? . . . Where have we constant reading upon either quick or dead Anatomies, or ocular demonstration of herbes? . . . Where a promotion of their experiences? . . . Where an examination of all the old Tenets? [69]

Biggs called on the universities to cease reliance on classical authors and seek new experimental knowledge in medicine. The study of Galen and Aristotle was to cease. Biggs would have agreed with Hall's proposal to endow research in medicine as a means of achieving new knowledge.[70]

Another man with sectarian leanings concerned with reforming medical studies was the apothecary Nicholas Culpeper, who served as a doctor in the New Model Army. Like Dell and Webster he was concerned that the poor receive adequate medical treatment, blaming the lack of it on the monopolistic College of Physicians. He denounced the College for refusing to publish medical knowledge in the vernacular, and likened this practice to that of the Papists who kept the Scripture in Latin. Culpeper found a partial remedy for this, issuing in 1649 an English translation of the *Pharmacoepia Londinensis* (1618), which he entitled *A Physicall Directory, or a Translation of the London Dispensatory Made by the College of Physicians in London. Being That Book by Which All Apothecaries Are Strictly Commanded to Make All Their Physicke.* The translation was popular and useful, though Culpeper's defiance of the existing system resulted in his condemnation as an atheist in the conservative paper *Mercurius Pragmaticus* (Sept., 1649). Undaunted, in 1651 Culpeper published *A Directory for Midwives* in which he attacked scholars for imprisoning the people by withholding knowledge.[71]

Like Webster, Culpeper was addicted to credulity, especially with respect to homemade medicine. This was evinced by his translation (published posthumously in 1656) of the *Medicina Pauperum* of

Jean Prévost (1585–1631), a Swiss professor at Padua. Prévost's medical remedies included various herbs, among them tobacco, and such things as millipedes, excrements, and antimony. His cures were even more unorthodox. To remove splinters and weapons he prescribed the use of a fox tongue which had been torn out in March and subsequently dried, soaked in wine, and heated. In view of Culpeper's interest in midwives he must have been intrigued by Prévost's suggestion that an eaglestone, jasper, or coral fastened to the thigh would aid in delivery, as would a magnet held in the left hand.[72] Culpeper's interests were also reflected in the titles of his *Semeiotica Uranica. Or an Astrological Judgment* (1651), *Opus Astrologicum* (1654), and *Culpeper's Astrological Judgment* (1655).

Webster's recommendations for the reform of medical education entailed banishing Galen, as Biggs had earlier advocated, and embracing theories concerning the causes of disease advanced by Paracelsus and the Flemish scientist Jean-Baptiste van Helmont (1577–1644). Galen was criticized by Webster for his reliance on Aristotle. He disapproved the Aristotelian theory (still widely held as late as the sixteenth century) that bodies were composed of four elements. He also rejected the concomitant idea of the four humors or bodily juices (phlegm, blood, black bile, and yellow bile), altering the balance of which supposedly caused disease.[73]

Paracelsus, whose theories Webster recommended, had been a reform-minded physician who inaugurated his medical lectures at Basle by burning the writings of Galen and Avicenna. To him the human body was basically a chemical system composed of mercury, sulphur, and salt, the improper balance of which produced illnesses. The remedy was the use of mineral medicines (the science of iatrochemistry). Concerning diseases, Paracelsus believed that each was specific in its action and therefore must have a specific chemical cure rather than the traditional cure-all, catchall remedies. The result was a renewed study of diseases and research into the effect of specific remedies. Paracelsus also was on the verge of realizing that diseases were entities in themselves and not diseased states of the body—a prerequisite to the later discovery of the germ theory of disease. His interests included mental diseases, concerning which he published a treatise anticipating modern psychopathology. His work in iatrochemistry led him to believe that certain chemicals (e.g., mercury, ammonia, and arsenic) could be used in treating mental illnesses, but he also believed in the use of psychotherapy. Paracelsus has been aptly described by George Sarton as "a reckless experimentalist" whose "sounder views were crudely mixed with metaphysical and magical ideas," and whose "rational cures could not always be separated from miraculous ones," but nevertheless "an exciter, a catalyzer, the outstanding medical prophet of the Renaissance."[74] Webster's advocacy that his works be included in the medical curriculum was no discredit to the English reformer.

Van Helmont, also recommended by Webster, was a Brussels nobleman devoted to medical aid for the poor. His principal work, the *Ortus Medicinae* published posthumously in 1648, was not translated into English until 1662 (as *Oriatrike or, Physick Refined,* trans. J. Chandler). Like Paracelsus, van Helmont proposed that diseases, which he regarded as living beings, be treated by specific remedies, not general cure-alls. Each disease had a specific cause, effect, and location, and was to be treated by an appropriate remedy. Unlike ancient doctors, van Helmont cautioned, care was to be taken to distinguish between the actual disease (the *causes* of which were to be treated) and the symptoms. In other areas of medicine, a study of the chemistry of digestion led him to the conclusion that digestion was basically a process of fermentation. He also undertook detailed research into the properties of urine, and recognized the usefulness of the thermoscope to measure body temperature. Van Helmont did not follow Paracelsus' injunction to keep astrology and medicine separate. He believed that one skin disease was caused by the influence of the planet Mars. The remedy, therefore, was a planetary one; but failing this, one might try applying to the afflicted part the hand of one who had died a slow death, until a great chill was felt. Van Helmont's cure for warts was to cut an apple in two, rub its pulp on the warts, then sew the apple back together. As the apple rotted, the warts supposedly disappeared. Van Helmont believed in sympathetic medicine, natural and human magic, and witches.[75] Yet his scholarly research, especially in chemistry, led to his esteem by Boyle and other scientists and to indirect praise from Hartlib, who, in 1661, referred to a recent German immigrant as "an excellent Helmontian physician."[76] It is, therefore, not surprising that Webster recommended his writings for study in medicine.

Webster complained that for centuries the schools had not discovered more certain, safe, or easy ways to cure diseases than had been known to Hippocrates and Galen. Chirurgery had been advanced by anatomy in its "manual operation" and the use of medical instruments, but it was still defective in its ability to cope with lupus, cancer, fistulas, carcinoma, elephantiasis, strumae, and virulent and malign ulcers. Without the use of mineral and chemical elements, such as were prescribed by Paracelsus and van Helmont, Webster felt little improvement could be expected. He did acknowledge that medical science had been advanced in anatomy, an area which appeared "to be growing, and arising towards the Zenith of perfection . . . ," especially because of William Harvey's discovery of the circulation of the blood. Nevertheless, Webster insisted, little had been done to apply this theory in medical practice. He praised Paracelsus, van Helmont, and Fludd for their endeavors in mystical anatomy, which he defined as the attempt to discover the "signature of that invisible Archeus or *spiritus mechanicus*, that is the true opifex, and dispositer of all the salutary, and morbisick lineaments, both in the seminal guttula, the tender Embrio, and the formal Creature. . . ." [77]

In his reply to Webster, Ward pointed out that medicine would always be defective in its ability to achieve complete knowledge, but simultaneously he noted that advances in medicine were being made. "The Colledge of Physitians at London," wrote Ward, "is the glory of this Nation, and indeed of Europe, for their Learning and felicity, in the cures of desperate Ulcers and diseases, even of the Cancer, and those he (ignorantly) mentions, which have been diverse times performed, by D. Harvey and others." But, Ward cautioned, some recent advances in medical science, including Harvey's discovery of the circulation of the blood, had not been put into practice by the universities because that practice had to be grounded on sufficient experience and observation. [78]

Ward was correct in asserting that medical reserach was advancing, though the universities played little role in attaining that progress. Oxford did not even have a hospital for clinical research. The most revealing fact pertinent to the evaluation of Ward's praise of English medicine is the succinct observation of a modern historian of science: "The ablest men in the medical profession, if they had a strong scientific bent, turned their chief attention to subjects other than medicine. . . ." Harvey turned to biology, Gilbert to physics, Petty to demography, and, later, Locke to psychology and philosophy. [79]

Three years after the Webster-Ward controversy a lengthy attack was made on English medical education and practice by George

Starkey, a disciple of Paracelsus and van Helmont. Of van Helmont he wrote: "From Helmont's Writings I have reaped more real Benefit (as to solid Learning) then from any that I have read, or met with, either Ancient or Modern. . . ." Starkey was probably sympathetic toward the religious concepts of the sectaries in view of his belief that medicine did not "come to the knowledge of any, but by the special gift of the most high." Viewing himself as "a Physician created of God and not of the Schools," he argued that healing the sick was "the grand mark of a real and true son of [medical] Art, it is his diploma by which he appears to be one created of God, and not by the Schools; for their creatures they adorn with titles, God graceth his with real abilities." Starkey believed in the necessity of medical study, though not in ancient tomes but in actual experimentation. Through the latter God granted medical abilities and revealed medical knowledge. Starkey was nevertheless careful to guard himself against the accusation of academic ignorance commonly hurled at his fellow alchemists. He reminded his readers that as a Harvard M.A. he had received a thorough training in languages, philosophy, logic, and the other arts, though these he found useless in the practice of medicine.[80]

Starkey condemned Aristotle and Galen, though he praised Hippocrates. He regarded what he had learned in the medical writings of Jean Fernel of Amiens, Daniel Sennert of Wittenberg, Galen, Leonhard Fuchs, and Avicenna as valueless in the light of practical experience. He criticized all of the Arabic writers because of their reliance on Galen. Those writers whom he approved in addition to Paracelsus and van Helmont were Basil Valentinus; Joseph Duchesne (Quercetanus), a physician to Henry IV of France; John de Suchten, a physician to the Polish court; and Bernard of Trevisan (Treves). Among his contemporaries he commended Jonathan Goddard, Ralph Bathurst, and others for having "chosen the Chymical for the true way" in medicine.[81]

Because medicine was the highest of all the arts or spheres of knowledge for Starkey, it was natural that he was concerned about its instruction. He was especially critical of the "*Hocus pocus* Rhetorique" of the London College of Physicians. He regarded all contemporary academic instruction in medicine as valid only insofar as the doctors had managed to learn things of value from old wives and good folk. He viewed the Galenical theories of the doctors as foolishness. "Our modern Goosquil Doctors" were taught in such a way that medicine had "become the Engine of oppression, cruelty, and butchery, the prop of pride, and ambition, covetousness and idleness." Medicine had become monopolistic; this was a deterrent to the advancement of medical knowledge and a hinderance to medical care of the poor. Doctors were censured by Starkey for their steadfast adherence to outdated medical theories; "they alone in the world have the priviledge to murther innocent persons, provided they do it according to a methodical way of Art." True medicine, which Starkey considered a serious, secret, and sacred art dependent upon divine revelation and human experimentation, was to be practiced only for charitable ends *ad gloriam Dei.*[82]

Starkey proposed specific remedies to better medical education and practice. Most of them involved the use of chemical medicines and more attention to the causes of diseases rather than their symptoms and haphazard treatment. The traditional theory that some diseases were incurable was rejected, as was the prevailing medical treatment of diseases. Starkey was convinced that all diseases could be cured if the proper chemical remedies were prescribed. But, Starkey complained, a contemporary doctor was unconcerned with the proper preparation of medicines, "his Theory consisting only in turning over of leaves [i.e., of Galen's writings], and his Practise in tossing of Pisse-pots and writing of Bils. . . ." He challenged such doctors to a contest to determine whose methods were more fruitful. Such a contest was based on his belief that conflicting medical methods should not be judged in an oratorical war but by concrete results. The proper use of experience made medicine a science, he argued, not opinions. Furthermore, it was not just any kind of experience: "Fie on all positive conclusions drawn from *negative* experience, which is indeed but ignorance. . . ." Starkey was thus firmly in the reformist tradition with his denunciation of antiquity and his adherence to empiricism.[83]

Others besides the sectaries were interested in the state of medical studies in Puritan England. Milton included medical studies in his curriculum and recommended learning from the experience of apothecaries and anatomists. Hartlib advocated further medical research in his utopian *Macaria*, and Petty's educational tract addressed to Hartlib gave much space to medical education and research. Petty was able to observe contemporary medical education first-hand. While he was lecturing on anatomy at Oxford, the Regius Professor of Physic was Dr. Clayton, whose lectures consisted merely of reading the ancient medical classics, including Hippocrates. In his proposed medical school, Petty recommended that the steward be skilled not only in mathematics but also in "judicial astrology, which he may apply to calculate the events of diseases, and prognosticate of the weather. . . ." [84] Observation and experimentation were stressed, but Petty did not recommend medical authorities other than Hippocrates. Petty's descriptions of the duties of the various personnel of the medical school are precise, but do not reflect a particularly advanced level of medical knowledge. Webster was probably as knowledgeable of modern medical theory (with the exception of anatomy) as Petty. Webster's concern for the slow rate of progress in English medical education was reasonable, and reflected a sectarian belief that people deserved both better and less expensive medical care.

Both Puritan and sectarian educational reformers gave considerable attention to the role of the sciences in the curriculum and to their methodology and content. In an age in which major strides were being made in the sciences it was significant that the reformers consciously and consistently sought both a greater role for the sciences in the educational process and the inclusion of recent scientific thought and method. Unquestioned adherence to classical or Scholastic authorities was condemned in the strongest of terms. Galen and Aristotle were subjected to the severest criticism. The use of the inductive method was both encouraged and practiced, and emphasis was placed on the study of mathematics. The criticism of the sectaries tended to lag behind the reforming endeavors of the progressive scientists, especially at Oxford, but the sectarian demands focused attention on the necessity for curricular improvement in the sciences at the universities and helped create an intellectual milieu more conducive to the acceptance of scientific advances. The reformers, particularly the sectarian reformers, did not restrict their interests to scientific theory alone; they sought its practical application for the betterment of man's estate. Nowhere was their concern for the beneficial application of scientific knowledge more evident than in their proposals relating to medicine. Science could better their living conditions; medicine could improve their physical well-being. Improvements in both areas, the reformers believed, would enable them to live a more productive life *ad gloriam Dei.*

CHAPTER FIVE

Educational Reform in Linguistics and the Humanities

Men who valued scientific education because of its utilitarian worth and potential for the betterment of man's estate could logically be expected to subject other academic subjects to the same criteria. This the sectaries and liberal Puritans did. Languages were to be studied for utilitarian ends, with linguistic pedagogy reformed to attain those ends as rapidly and thoroughly as possible. Although the Puritan and sectarian reformers disagreed on the details of the reform proposals for linguistic study, they agreed on the general tenor of those reforms. They also insisted that philosophy be critically examined, especially its compatibility with Christian principles, without which its study was thought to be a vain and inutilitarian effort. The role of Aristotle received special attention. Logic was scrutinized as a means of obtaining knowledge; John Webster anticipated John Stuart Mill's later critique of the syllogism for its inability to produce new knowledge. The revolt against the Ancients was exemplified in the attack of the reformers on logic, the pagan classics, and the Aristotelian predominance in ethics. Historical studies were encouraged, and Webster lamented the decline of serious musical studies in the universities.

LINGUISTIC STUDIES

The application of the utilitarian criterion to linguistic studies was thoroughly in the Baconian tradition. Bacon had regarded the

Idols of the Marketplace, or linguistic difficulties, as the most trouble-some of all the Idols which plagued the mind and obstructed learning. Language hindered cognitive progress because it confused knowledge of natural phenomena by its inaccuracy and gave birth to ideas that had no corresponding existence in reality. Man's understanding was obstructed by the unfit choice of words and was led into fruitless controversies and idle fancies. The tragedy in the minds of Baconians was the gulf they found between the world of reality and the world of terminology. Language could not be fully trusted. Fortunately, during the early stages of the scientific revolution it did not have to be, for the Baconian call was for a return to nature, to observation and experiment. The classical treatises on science could be laid aside as unnecessary or even undesirable in the acquisition of knowledge. But as the scientific revolution developed, it became apparent that attention had to be paid to linguistic studies, for there had to be a reliable means of communication to record and transmit the knowl-edge obtained by the use of the inductive method. The sciences and language were therefore closely related in the seventeenth century. Reform of one ordinarily led to attempts to reform the other, often by the same men.

Comenius was especially interested in deriving new methods of teaching Latin, which he regarded as the language of science and the proper language for international communication. His interest in Latin pedagogy, therefore, was not directed toward stylistic finesse but toward Latin's utilitarian value, much as Milton later insisted. Adapting Bacon's principle of inductive methodology to linguistic pedagogy, Comenius stressed not words but actual things in his teaching of Latin. This concept he set forth in his *Janua Linguarum Reserata*. To encourage students to concentrate on the study of natural objects while engaged in their linguistic training he published his *Orbis Sensualium Pictus*, a Latin text which taught the language by illustrating natural objects and briefly describing them in Latin. Comenius opposed using the ancient classics in teaching Latin. Pagan authors, except possibly a few moralists whose writings were unobjectionable, were to be banned from the curriculum.

Like Comenius one of Samuel Hartlib's principal interests in education involved Latin pedagogy, concerning which he wrote *The True and Readie Way to Learne the Latine Tongue* (1654). In it he criticized "the Grammatical Tyranny of teaching Tongues . . ." and proposed that students should learn to read and write a foreign language before they learned its grammatical rules. His reason was that "languages were not first devised by the Rules of Grammar, but the Rules of Grammar were framed according to the common practice of Speech. . . ." [1] Hartlib's adoption of Comenian proposals for the reform of linguistic study was typical of the Comenian reformers in England.

Both Puritan and sectarian reformers emphasized the application of the utilitarian criterion to language study. John Dury, as a leading spokesman in England for the Baconian-Comenian tradition, imposed subordinate and utilitarian criteria on linguistic study when he observed that "Tongues are no further finally usefull then to enlarge Traditionall Learning; and without their subordination unto Arts and Sciences, they are worth nothing towards the advancement of our Happiness." [2] In a similar vein, William Penn asserted that languages were not to be despised or neglected, but neither were they to be preferred to the study of "things." [3] The sectaries, who saw no necessity for linguistic study in Hebrew and Greek for the clergy, applied a utilitarian criterion to the question of the value of studying foreign languages. The Puritans, on the other hand, had to give an important role to the study of foreign languages in the academic curriculum if for no other reason than their belief in the necessity of knowing Hebrew and Greek in order better to understand the divine revelation in Scripture. It is surprising to find the Quaker Robert Barclay approving academic study in foreign languages for the purpose of reading Scripture in Hebrew and Greek. But like his fellow Quaker Thomas Lawson, he also recommended linguistic study as beneficial for carrying on foreign commerce and international relations. [4] Winstanley was of the same mind. [5] Webster cautioned that there was little profit from linguistic study other than being able to read works in a foreign language, and to converse with foreigners in order to carry on foreign trade and international relations. [6]

Concern for the function of linguistic studies in education led to proposals for pedagogical reform, inspired largely by Comenius' desire to simplify grammatical study and to place an emphasis on things rather than words. Through the minds of various reformers echoed the question posed by John Hall: "Where [can one find] a ready and generous teaching of the Tongues? Free from Pedantisme, and the impertinencies that that kind of learning hath been pestered with?" [7] The pedantry which Hall and others found so objectionable was that associated with learning a language by a strict grammatical approach. Edward Leigh, a Puritan defender of the conservative approach to linguistic studies, defended that approach when he wrote: "The way to learn the Hebrew tongue, is to inure ones self to one methodical and compleat Grammer." [8] The progressive attitude toward such an approach was expressed by Thomas Grantham (d.1664), rector of Waddington, Notts. (ejected, 1656), who ridiculed the attempt to learn a language by the use of grammars as "a taske passing the patience of an Asse." [9] Grantham, who was also a schoolmaster, invented a scheme for speedy instruction in Hebrew, Greek, and Latin. The sectary Thomas Lawson regretted that grammars were so tedious, for "the great heaps of Rules, Exceptions, Criticisms and Nicities therein are a discouragement to many. . . ." [10]

Webster offered suggestions as to how a language should be taught, though admonishing that all arts and sciences were to be taught in English, not Latin. Foreign languages were to be taught by use rather than by grammatical rules. Webster felt the value of teaching rules was questionable since many learned to speak a language without knowing its grammatical principles or having "followed the wayes of Conjugations, and Declensions, Noun or Verb." It should be observed, Webster pointed out, that "many unletter'd persons . . . understand some languages in far shorter time than any do learn them by method and rule. . . ." Those who learned a language without first memorizing its rules, he felt, would be more at ease in speaking than those who first stopped to think about the rules. Webster believed that emphasis should be placed, as Comenius advocated in his *Janua Linguarum Reserata* (which Webster cited), on learning "both words and matter, names and things" together. He encouraged instructors to make certain that students had a firm knowledge of English grammar before they embarked on a study of Latin. In this regard he recommended the pedagogy practiced by John Brinsley (*fl.* 1633), the Puritan master of the public school at Ashby-de-la-Zouch, Leicestershire, and the author of several works on grammar schools. [11]

Ward's reply to Webster was in effect a reply to all sectarian critics of education. He made it clear that he was acquainted with the theories of Comenius and that he regarded them as useful. But he pointed out to Webster that instruction in basic Latin grammar was not undertaken in the universities. Webster should, he argued, have directed his criticism to schools at the preuniversity level. Most of

Ward's comments concerned Webster's advocacy of learning foreign languages by use. "The way of Conversation," Ward wrote, "makes men ready and confident, but that alone will never make them accurate, an instance whereof we have, in that none that have no skill in Grammar, can ever amongst us . . . attaine the true writing of our English Tongue. . . ." Overlooking the fact that any foreign language could be learned by conversation with an Englishman knowledgeable in that language as well as with one whose native tongue it was, Ward wanted to know where a student could travel to learn ancient languages such as Latin, Greek, and Hebrew by conversation. With regard to suggestions by Webster and other sectaries that modern languages were best learned by travel to the respective countries, Ward, combining practicality with a little absurdity, noted that "if any man make it his businesse to comprehend them all, he must either hire men of all sorts to be with him as Conversers, or must apply himselfe to all, (travelling till he meet with them) so that the result will be that instead of some daies in his study, a man spends many years in travell or conversation, and all for saving the expence of time and charges." [12]

The sectary William Sprigg had ideas of his own for reforming language study. He proposed that in the universities students should reverse the prevailing pattern of speaking English and composing in Latin, "since when they come into the world [upon leaving the university], they have greatest use of elegant English to write, and a promptitude in familiar Latine for travail and converse with strangers." This was not the same sort of pedagogical reform suggested by other sectaries, but the goal was still Baconian utilitarianism. Another suggestion of Sprigg's involved a proposal for establishing an "English Colledge" at Chelsea to refine the language and to educate the better sons of the gentry "in a more Generous and Noble way, and [with] less curbed studyes, then are commonly, though with little profit, taught in our other Colledges and Universities. . . ." With the ancient languages, the arts, and the sciences—including history, politics, and law—the curriculum of this English college was to include French, Italian, and Spanish. The college's goal was training men to be more useful to the Commonwealth.[13]

Sprigg's proposals were criticized by an anonymous writer whose views on education and religion were those of a progressive Puritan writing from a ministerial point of view. This writer saw no need for a college at Chelsea or anywhere else apart from those at Oxford and Cambridge, where the English language was being refined and all learning was being advanced. With respect to Sprigg's plea for speaking Latin in the universities, the anonymous respondent retorted that university students did or *should* speak Latin.[14] The interest expressed by Sprigg in refining the English language was, however, shared by others. The most concerted effort to bring about such a reformation was later undertaken by a committee of the Royal Society, motivated largely by the French Academy. In the end the project was abortive.[15]

It would be difficult to overemphasize the role allotted to linguistic training in the grammar schools, where the aim was a mastery of the contents of classical works in Latin, Greek, and Hebrew.[16] Hebrew had been added to the curriculum of some grammar schools in the sixteenth century, and by the following century it was taught at such leading schools as Westminster, St. Paul's, and Merchant Taylors'. At Westminster students composed orations and verses not only in Hebrew, but also in Arabic and other oriental languages. At Winchester and Eton, however, Hebrew did not win much acceptance. Latin was the principal language in all grammar schools, and instruction was customarily rendered in that language, which students were required to speak. Some knowledge of Latin was required before boys could be admitted to Winchester. Greek was becoming increasingly important due to men like Richard Busby, headmaster of Westminster from 1638 until his death in 1695. Busby, a noted Greek scholar, required his students to read from a Greek text without the aid of the customary parallel version in Latin, and he insisted that the Greek accents be observed. At Merchant Taylors' students commenced the study of Greek in the fourth form and Hebrew in the sixth. In learning Greek and Latin the grammar schools continued to use the ancient classics, which the students were encouraged to imitate in their exercises.[17]

Sectarian criticisms of linguistic study applied to the teaching of languages in the grammar schools as well as in the universities. This was also true by implication of the criticisms of Thomas Grantham and William Sprigg. The former, whose concern was with free rather than grammar schools, opposed linguistic instruction by the use of grammars and instead favored teaching children languages from the beginning of their education. Grantham proposed sending students abroad for linguistic study at the age of seven or eight.[18] Sprigg urged that arts and languages be taught together rather than separately, and that schools be annexed to colleges in order to avoid "the conclusion of many Methods" (as well as to make it possible to teach the basic principles of mathematics to children).[19]

There was a wide interest in Puritan and Restoration England in developing a universal language. Comenius had urged reforms in Latin pedagogy because he believed in the utilitarian value of Latin as a language of international communication for all affairs—diplomatic, commercial, and scholarly. In scientific circles in Puritan England and, in some cases, even outside it, however, there was a growing tendency to consider Latin inadequate as a universal language. Wilkins was to express in 1668 a very critical view of the defectiveness of the Latin language because of its irregularities and complexities.[20] Yet if Latin would not suffice, another universal language was to be sought for several reasons. First, there was a need for a common medium to transmit advances in knowledge from one country to another. Second, the difficulty in learning Latin caused the scientist to spend too much time on linguistic studies instead of productive research. Third, the attack on the ancients had come to involve, by implication, an attack on Latin, the utilitarian efficiency of which was open to question. Fourth, there was a growing desire, in part born out of scientific curiosity, to develop a language that would avoid the defects of existing languages, including Latin. Finally, the Comenian school, in emphasizing things, inspired a desire to make words correspond to them so that a word revealed the nature of a thing rather than serving simply as a symbol of it.[21]

There were numerous attempts to develop a universal language. One of the earliest was Hartlib's *Common Writing* (1647), which concentrated on the problem of developing a character for a universal language. In a letter to Hartlib dated March 19, 1647, Boyle spoke enthusiastically of a universal character as helping to make amends for what mankind lost after the "Tower of Babel." More important, he spoke of the words of a universal language as being akin to universally understood mathematical characters.[22] Webster wrote of a universal language in his *Academiarum Examen* of 1654, as did Ward in his *Vindiciae Academiarum* of the same year. In 1655 the *Sun Theo. Lingua Linguarum* of Henry Edmunson was published. Cave Beck (1623–1706?), master of the free grammar school at Ipswich (1655–1657), in his *Universal Character* of 1657 also took a mathematical approach to the development of a universal language, proposing that numbers be substituted for letters and syllables. If such a language were developed, avoiding all superfluous synonyms, anomalies, and equivocal terms, it would be of great assistance, he asserted, in propagating learning.[23]

Interest in a universal language continued into the Restoration era. George Dalgarno (1626?–1687), master of grammar schools in Oxford and Guernsey, in 1661 advocated a universal language in his *Ars Signorum.* In the development of that language he had received the assistance of Ward, Wilkins, Wallis, Boyle, Petty, and Ralph Bathurst (1620–1704), a practicing M.D. in Oxford and a Fellow of Trinity College. In 1668, Wilkins, who had expressed interest in a universal language as early as 1638, published his *Essay towards a Real Character and a Philosophical Language.* As did Dalgarno, Wilkins formulated a symbol for each thing in the universe. He ended with approximately three thousand symbols and classes which he expected that an ordinary man could learn in about a month's time. Those who mastered the language were supposed to be able to communicate with anyone else who had learned it, irrespective of his native tongue. Wilkins was aided in the classification of mathematical and physical items for this universal language by Wallis. The language was viewed—as all proponents of similar schemes had viewed theirs—as a utilitarian means for the advancement of knowledge.[24]

Webster, like others interested in a universal language, advocated its formulation in order to repair the ruin inflicted on man as a result of the "Tower of Babel." At the same time he urged a return to the language of nature as it was propounded by Boehme and the "highly-illuminated fraternity of the Rosie Crosse" (i.e., the Rosicrucians). Presumably a return to this language of nature would not obviate the need for a universal language, for the latter would be necessary to express *outwardly* the *inner* communication of the former. Webster explained his Boehmist concept in this way:

> The mind receiveth but one single and simple image of every thing, which is expressed in all by the same motions of the spirits, and doubtlessly in every creature hath . . . the same sympathy in voice, and sound, but men not understanding these immediate sounds of the soul . . . have instituted, and imposed others, that do not altogether concord, and agree to the innate notions, and so no care is taken for the recovery and restauration of the Catholique language in which lies hid all the rich treasury of natures . . . secrets.[25]

This concept of Webster's was logically compatible with sectarian epistemology, though embracing such a radical view detracted from his more rational plan of educational reform.

In his reply to Webster, Ward rejected the former's advocacy of a language of nature. Ward did, however, render assistance to Dalgarno in 1661 in the formulation of a universal *tongue* which used a single symbol to represent each thing. This was quite different from retaining existing languages but adopting a universal *character* in which to write them. Ward's interest in a universal language derived from his knowledge of recent advances in mathematical symbols as developed by such men as the French mathematician François Viète (1560–1603), the English mathematician Thomas Harriot (1560–1621), who was responsible for the symbols > and <, Oughtred, and Descartes. To formulate a universal language, taking advantage of the assistance of logic and mathematics, Ward proposed that all discourses be resolved into sentences, and the sentences into words signifying simple ideas or resolvible into simple ideas. Then a single symbol was to be assigned to each simple idea. He did not expect these ideas to be numerous. Once this was accomplished one could begin joining appropriate symbols to produce compound ideas, which would become words. Every word (or combination of symbols) would thus be a definition in itself. This would be possible only "if the first & most simple things & notions are so few as is the nūber of consonants, & the modall variations so few as may be expressed by Vowels and Dipthongs. . . ." Homonyms and synonyms had to be avoided. Such a universal language, he informed Webster, might justly be regarded as a legitimate natural language.[26]

In the course of his discussion of a universal language Ward also criticized those who attempted to find such a language in Hebrew. The latter attempt was common in the seventeenth century, with some arguing that Hebrew was the oldest language and the only one which existed before "Babel." Others thought the original "pre-Babel" tongue had been lost, and that Hebrew had been one of the languages which subsequently came into existence. The former position was accepted by the Puritan Edward Leigh, who contended that "the Hebrew tongue kept its purity, and remained uncorrupted, though other tongues were added to it, and derived from it." [27] Others asserted that Hebrew should consequently be made the universal tongue, sometimes adding that all the secrets of nature were hidden in Hebrew. Such a position was held in Ward's time, for he made a point to rebuke it, but its classic expression came in the publication of a treatise by the Baptist sectary Francis Bampfield late in the Restoration period.

Bampfield urged Christian princes to promote the Hebrew alphabet as the only universal character. But he wanted more than that. "There is in all Languages," he wrote, "a well-agreeing Harmony, with the Hebrew Tongue, which is the Mother of all the rest, which cognation of Consanguinity, and Affinity should be preserved and propagated." To do this, Hebrew should be made the universal language and "all Places and offices of Publick trust [were to be] more thoroughly studied and researched in Scripture-words and Phrases, collected and well put together. . . ." This applied not only to princes but also to statesmen, generals, soldiers, admirals, ambassadors, judges, and everyone else that had anything to do with the welfare of a nation. Too much good could not be said of Hebrew, the very letters of which Bampfield saw as revelations of their divine origin, "there being no other Tongue in the world, that hath such natural Characters, so evidently to be known by the motion of the Mouth and Tongue, and other Organs . . . ; by observation whereof, those who are born Deaf, may yet be taught the knowledge, and use of Speaking, Writing, and Printing." [28]

Bampfield's concern for communicating with the deaf was part of the Baconian heritage and the interest in a universal language. Bacon himself had been interested in the use of signs to communicate with the deaf. John Wilkins subsequently took up the problem in his *Mercvry, or the Secret and Swift Messenger* (1641). Wilkins' friend, John Wallis, whose writings included material on physiology and sound, has been credited as being "the first successful English teacher of the deaf. . . ." [29] Another English pioneer in this field was the physician John Bulwer (*fl.* 1644–1654), whose *Chirologia* of 1644 discussed the possibilities of communication by the use of the hands. In his *Philocophus: or, the Deafe and Dumb Mans Friend* (1648) Bulwer called for the establishment of an academy for the mute where instruction would be given by the use of signs, gestures, and lip-reading, and where music would be enjoyed through the transmission of impulses through the teeth. [30] This interest in finding satisfactory means of communication for the deaf and dumb was another manifestation of the Baconian application of knowledge for the betterment of man's estate.

Webster, whose ideas on educational reform were nearly boundless, had yet another idea relating to linguistic study in the universities. Nothing at all, he believed, was being done toward instruction in and advancement of cryptography, secret hieroglyphics, and symbolical and emblematic writing, all of which he thought were pleasant and useful.[31] Wilkins, in reply, informed him that the universities were far from ignorant of the art of cryptography. Ward, with patience and a touch of humor, pointed out that hieroglyphics and cryptography had been invented (as Webster obviously knew) for the concealment of things, to be used to cloak mysteries in religion or to meet the exigencies of war and other occasions demanding secrecy. Grammar, on the other hand, was "one of those Arts and Language one of those helps, which serve for explication of our minds and notions. . . ."[32] The two were not to be mixed, even in the name of utility.

PHILOSOPHY, LOGIC, AND ETHICS

The Baconian revolt against antiquity in science was integrally related to the revolt against antiquity—specifically Aristotelianism—in philosophy, logic, and (for the sectaries) the classics. The sterile philosophy of Scholasticism with its dependence on antiquity had been verbally repudiated by the Puritans, though they embraced the Scholastic spirit and retained its emphasis on antiquity. The figure of Aristotle continued to loom large—a man of many abilities whose writings contained much that the Puritan abhorred, particularly the Puritan imbued with Baconian philosophy, but they also embraced much that he could accept. For the moderate reformers, the task before them was not a rejection of Aristotelian thought *in toto*, but a careful examination of Aristotle's writings to preserve the valid and discard the worthless. The guiding principle was that "what illustrates the doctrine of the Gospel, and shews . . . its consonancy to naturall light, can in no sober sense be called vain Philosophy."[33] This principle was a logical outgrowth of the Puritan concept of the relation of natural to revealed knowledge.

Furthermore, what mattered to the moderate reformers was not that Aristotle was fallible, but that his universal approach to the scope of human knowledge provided a starting point for academic work. They believed that his scientific methodology was wrong, but the deductive method could not be discarded, nor could the rules of logic. There was much in Aristotle and in other ancients from which men could learn. Seth Ward, who regarded Aristotle's works as "the best of any Philosophick writings," expressed the moderate view when he wrote: "Now the chiefe reason as I conceive, why Aristotle hath been universally received as *Magister Legitimus* in Schooles hath been [and is]; The universallity of his Enquiries; the brevity and Method of them; fitting them for Institutions, and not the truth or infallibillity of his Workes. . . ." [34]

As late as 1660, Oxford, the more progressive of the two universities in the 1650s, still retained its traditional ties to Aristotle, though they had been weakened by substantive criticism. That criticism had begun before the sectaries mounted their attack on the university curriculum in the 1650s. One of the most persistent anti-Aristotelians had been the Calvinist Nathanael Carpenter (1589–1628), a Fellow of Exeter College, Oxford, and later chaplain to Archbishop James Ussher in Ireland. Carpenter had attacked Aristotelianism in his *Philosophia Libera*, originally published abroad in 1622, and reprinted at Oxford in 1636 and 1637.[35] Criticism of Aristotle was part of the Baconian heritage and of English progressive thought in general. Such diverse writers as Sir Walter Ralegh, Thomas Hall, and William Dell criticized the Greek philosopher. Hall regarded it as "the folly of many young wits, that they prefer Aristotle before Paul . . . ," and Dell complained that Plato and Aristotle were given more respect in the universities than Moses and Christ.[36]

Webster, the author of a vigorous attack on Aristotle, revealed the basic cause of sectarian antagonism to the proto-Peripatetic when he criticized him as a non-Christian who was "distant from the knowledge of the true God, who is the primary verity: . . . what he hath written was rather by a Diabolical than a Divine instinct. . . ." Webster's attitude toward Aristotle was governed by his Spirit-centered epistemology and his belief in the fundamental distinction between revealed and natural knowledge. There were, according to Webster, other reasons to doubt Aristotle. Here Webster relied heavily on the earlier criticisms of the French philosopher and scientist Pierre Gassendi (d.1655). Much of what Aristotle wrote, Webster asserted, was superfluous or false; the authorship of some of his works was questionable; and the style of his writing was so obscure "that to fish out his meaning there is need of a Delian Urinator." Webster did, however, concede that not all of Aristotle's philosophy had to be eliminated from the curriculum. His principle was that "the throne [not] be yielded to Aristotle alone, nor his Philosophy onely adored, and admitted. . . ." Webster commended Epicurean philosophy, particularly as it was propounded by Gassendi.[37]

With respect to the university curriculum Webster was highly critical of philosophy, which he said was "meerly Aristotelical" in content. The apostles, as far as he could ascertain, had not taught philosophy but had warned Christians to beware of human wisdom. Yet he believed universities should examine the philosophy (especially aspects dealing with politics and economics) of Plato, Bodin, Machiavelli, and Hobbes.[38]

The area of philosophy that most troubled Webster was metaphysics. As it was taught in the universities he defined it as an abstract consideration of things by way of foreknowledge, or the cutting of one's mind off from all concomitant thinking in order "to weigh and examine the things nudely and barely under the respect of their being, all other notions there about being [having to] remain separate from it. . . ." He regarded the weakness of this approach to metaphysical knowledge as the total reliance on the "weak and bare operation of the Intellect," which was phantasy. It was phantasy because professors believed that the soul was a *tabula rasa* "in which nothing is insculpt, and that Science comes not by reminiscence, or resuscitation, but meerly acquisitively de novo. . . ." If there was nothing in the mind that was not acquired by the senses, argued Webster, then any operations of the mind alone were "but weak means to produce Scientifical certitude, and so Metaphysical learning [is] but barren and fruitless." Metaphysics had neither established nor assumed any principles necessary or helpful to the promotion of knowledge, nor had it succeeded in teaching anything true about metaphysical phenomena. The proper remedy, Webster contended, was not to dispense with metaphysics entirely, but to reconstitute it so that it would hold forth "certain grounds and principles, from whence demonstrations might be drawn, that men might proceed with some certainty. . . ." This would not be difficult: It entailed, said Webster, the adoption of the philosophical principles of Descartes.[39]

Wilkins rejected Webster's accusation (also made by Hobbes) that the universities were bound to the philosophy of Aristotle, and asserted that Aristotle was respected but not regarded as infallible in the universities. On the contrary, Wilkins stated that he could not hope for more liberty to discuss the validity of Aristotle's philosophy than already existed in the universities.

Ward, whose respect for Aristotle has already been noted, reacted strongly to a suggestion of Webster's that the universities pay more attention to the philosophy of Hobbes, whom Webster regarded as being as profound a philosopher as Aristotle. Ward, who was not an admirer of the Malmesbury philosopher, caustically retorted: " 'Tis true our Theologues say he [Hobbes] is bottomed in the great Abysse." To Hobbes' complaint that Aristotle was the only philosopher studied in the universities, Ward sarcastically replied: "The only thing which paines him is the desire that Aristotelity may be changed into Hobbeity. . . ." But the Savilian Professor of Astronomy did agree with Webster that metaphysics needed reformation.[40]

Distrust of philosophy was rampant among the sectaries, who would have disapproved of Edward Waterhouse's citation of "Divine Plato" as proof of a religious point.[41] Dell was typical of the sectaries when he stressed that Jesus had not taught philosophy "in his School." Christians were to emulate the apostles who discoursed only of Jesus and resurrection from the dead. To substantiate his point, Dell recounted the story of the pagan Emperor Julian, who preferred philosophy more than the Gospel because of the tutoring of Libanius. And that, said Dell, "may be a fair warning to all Christians, that they suffer not their children to be so educated, lest at last, with Julian, they . . . loath and reject the Gospel. . . ." Philosophy, therefore, was not a fit subject of study for Christians.[42] Oxford students must have been with John Evelyn in St. Mary's in July, 1654, when he heard similar thoughts enunciated in the pulpit.[43]

One of the strongest denunciations of philosophy came from a Cambridge-educated Arminian minister famed for his skill in oriental languages. One would have expected an educated Arminian to value philosophy. The Arminian clergyman was John Horne (1614–1676), minister at All Hallows, Lynn Regis, Norfolk, until his probable ejection in 1662. Horne had no sympathy for those in "a Pulpit with their worldly rudiments, and humane Divinity." He sneered at philosophy as the observations of a purblind mind and the deductions and inferences of a perverted reason. Philosophy, being only speculation about the nature of creatures and their relation to God as creator and governor, led men to pry into the divine essence and actions, climbing "up into Heaven to him by his Metaphysical Scales to bring us down an infallible discovery of him. . . ." Metaphysics was condemned because it served (as did oratory) to obscure the truth of the Gospel.[44] George Starkey was also critical of the "totally rotten" philosophy taught in the universities. Philosophy was to be taught only if its practical end was kept in mind, which was "Agriculture and all Mechanicks, for the use of Mankinde as to the conveniency of life. . . ." [45]

Instruction in logic, too, came under attack from the sectaries, who were concerned that logic might be applied to questions of divinity. The criticisms of Webster were more substantive than those of other sectaries. Logic as it was taught in the universities was, in his opinion, a civil war of words in which the only criterion was victory over one's opponent, not truth. With regard to the subject matter Webster found basic flaws. The principal defect was that logic taught "no certain rules, by which either notions may be truly abstracted and gathered from things, nor that due and fit words may be appropriated to notions. . . ." Logic absurdly demanded that one begin with universal axioms and from those derive particulars, whereas one should proceed from particulars to generals. Apparently Webster regarded metaphysics as an exception to this principle. He admitted that "Syllogistical disputations" produced conclusions, but these, he said, were bare opinions, in no sense infallible. Thus everything remained conjectural, not certain. At best logic could only restate what was already known, not produce new knowledge.[46] Webster's criticism of logic in view of his recommendation of the Cartesian method initially appears contradictory, but his limitation of Descartes' philosophical method to metaphysics acquits him of the charge of inconsistency.

Ward firmly vindicated the teaching of logic in the universities. He rejected Webster's accusation that logic led to a civil war of words by asserting that a system of logical rules that directed students to a knowledge of the truth produced "no intestine warre, no humming, hissing, nor obfuscation." Logic was defended as a valuable discipline that taught the rules of abstracting notions by a thorough examination of the agreements and disagreements of things. If those notions had been rashly abstracted, the fault was not due to the methods of logic but either to the difficulty of the nature of the thing examined, or to inherent faults in the philosophers. "The notions of things being rightly abstracted they are rightly assigned to words by Definition." As long as logic was kept free from physical and metaphysical doctrines, as it was in Oxford, contended Ward, it was a valid tool for achieving knowledge.[47]

Sprigg's critique of logic was as vehement as that of Webster. Disputations according to the rules of "the Moon-shine light of

Logick" seldom produced new knowledge. Instead, "in the Cloud and dust of a wrangling Disputation" knowledge was more often obscured than discovered. Syllogisms were criticized as "Fetters and Shackles of Reason" which drowned out rational argument in a "Jangling of *Ergoes*." Similarly, the rules regarding logical fallacies were condemned as "the Art of Jugling truth out of Reasons pocket by playing *Hocus Pocus* with the Understanding." [48] Clearly, Sprigg was incensed more with the abuses of logic than with the discipline itself. Dell was not as critical of logic as Webster and Sprigg. He spoke of it as a *Gladius diaboli* when used in divinity, but an art of reason when properly applied to knowledge in areas other than divinity.[49] Locke, later in the century, took a far more critical view of logic when he observed that he had "seldom or never observed any one to get the Skill of reasoning well . . . by studying those Rules, which pretend to teach it . . ."; consequently he "would have a young Gentleman take a view of . . . [logic] in the shortest Systems [which] could be found. . . ." [50] The Puritans nearly half a century earlier had been more laudatory in their regard for logic. Thomas Hall, a typical conservative Puritan in his approach to education, spoke of logic as the mistress of methodology to all the sciences. No one could rationally reject it since it was nothing more than reason regulated by method.[51] John Gauden, a rather vascillating Anglican, praised logic because it disentangled all truths by methodical reasoning, and Giles Firmin observed that the Puritans used no logic other than that which was divinely created and used by the Spirit.[52]

Ethics, according to Webster, as it was taught in the universities needed reforming. The difficulty with ethics in his opinion was its dependence on Aristotle. "He that understands not the real, and true end, cannot teach the indubitate means that leads to that end, and therefore must needs be a blind guide, especially to Christians. . . ." Ethical principles were not to be derived from Aristotle but from the principles of Christianity. Yet some attention was to be paid to the writings of Socrates, Plato, Zeno, Seneca, and Epictetus. Pedagogically ethics would better be taught (as Locke later said) by precedent and practice than by examining ancient treatises. Webster recommended the writings of Philip Melanchthon and Descartes for ethical instruction, and he quoted approvingly from Lambert Daneau's treatise on Christian ethics.[53]

Ward's reply to Webster pointed out that the ethical writings of

Aristotle were not preferred at Oxford before those of such Christian writers as Thomas Aquinas, William Ames, Abraham Scultetus, and Lambert Daneau, or any of the classical authors mentioned by Webster.[54] The Puritan attitude toward Aristotelian ethics was stated by Baxter in 1676: "There are things in Aristotle's Ethicks, and in the Ethicks of the Stoicks and some other Philosophers, of great worth and use to Christians, to shew us what by natural evidence may be discerned: But they are all poor, defective, spiritless Doctrines and Precepts, in Comparison of the Gospel of Christ. . . ." [55] Baxter's statement was representative of the Puritan tendency to scrutinize antiquity in order to preserve the good and reject the bad. Such a tendency reflected Puritan acceptance of the idea that Spirit and reason bore united witness to one truth.

LITERATURE

Criticism of Aristotelian philosophy and logic was part of a broader criticism by sectaries of the use of pagan writings in the universities. Dell accused the universities of making human learning prevail for the first seven years on the assumption that students must be made good heathens before they could be made good Christians. The results, he said, were obvious to all, for nowhere was there more enmity to the Gospel than in the universities. There must be a reformation to cast out the "dirt and dung" from the university curriculum, for there was no need for Christians to seek knowledge from heathen writings when all wisdom had been given to man by Christ. "It is enough for Christian Schools," he proclaimed, "to be taught to know Christ, by the Ministration of the Spirit. . . ." Not only must Plato and Aristotle be abandoned, but also Pythagoras, Thomas Aquinas, Duns Scotus, and the other Scholastics.[56] Equally outspoken in his condemnation of heathen writings was Henry Stubbe, who called for their removal from the schools so that they could become "the Well-springs and Nurseries of true Learning and Godliness." In his zeal he gave various reasons to support his position, all of which were based on the assumption that the Scripture alone was sufficient for religious instruction. Other writings would be allowed to teach other subjects, but only insofar as they were warranted by Scripture and only if they would be of use to the understanding and propagation of Christianity and the betterment of the Commonwealth.[57]

This attitude had repercussions for the teaching of literature in the universities. Penn spoke disparagingly of those who were delighted with romances, love sonnets, and plays.[58] Obscene books and heathen authors, lascivious poems, comedies, tragedies, frivolous fables, and heathen orations were condemned by Lawson.[59] Another Quaker condemned the classics for this reason:

> Thus People are your Children taught the reason of the names of the dayes and moneths from the Latin and Greek Authors; Now consider whether you can plead for it, that your Children should be taught to name the dayes after the names of these gods of which these things are related in honour of such gods as these, of which such filthy things and idle foolish fictions are sung by their Heathenish Poets and worshippers; If ye deny it, then why do ye your selves teach them to name the dayes and months after them in English? [60]

Dell attacked the universities for asking students to read not only philosophy but also classical poetry.[61] According to Webster the universities were spending too much time on poetry and rhetoric, which were ornamental rather than essential arts.[62] The gulf between conservative Puritans and sectaries is apparent when one compares these ideas with those of Leigh, who wrote in glowing terms of poetry as "the quintessence or rather the luxury of Learning." Painting as a form of silent poetry was included by Leigh in this quintessence.[63]

Because of sectarian disapprobation of antiquity and the deprecation of its literature it was natural that some sectaries called for the abolition of classical readings in linguistic study. This was the Quaker position, and it was accompanied with warnings that reading the classics to learn the ancient languages would corrupt the good manners of the students, to say nothing of what it would do to them religiously.[64] Others besides the Quakers felt the same way. Dell proposed that Latin and Greek be learned from Christian literature only, and that students be urged to forget the names of pagan gods and muses, those "devils and damned creatures," and all their mythology and "fabulous inventions. . . ." It was better, he believed, to be ignorant of a language than to learn it by reading classical fables, with their lasciviousness, idolatry, and wickedness.[65] It was as if the sectaries wished to block out antiquity entirely except for that part of it that recounted the origins and development of Hebrew history.

HISTORY

Historical studies were not at a high level in Puritan England, though chairs of history had been established at Oxford by William Camden and at Cambridge by Fulke Greville, Lord Brooke. An examination of the historiography of the period has revealed that "scholarship consisted in the exhibition of a great deal of information which was often grotesque erudition." [66] Whether or not the sectaries realized this, they expressed an interest in the place of historical studies in the academic curriculum, as had college tutors in the preceding half century.[67] In spite of the basic disregard for antiquity by the Quakers, Penn urged students to read the best histories of ancient times.[68] Lawson regarded the study of "sound" history as useful and necessary.[69] John Hall, who worked on a translation of the writings of the Byzantine historian Procopius, proposed establishing a library of historical manuscripts. Hall, author of the treatise *Of the Advantageous Reading of History* (1657), criticized the neglect of historical studies in the universities. "Where," he asked, "is there a solemn disquisition into History? . . . Where a survey of Antiquities, and learned descants upon them?" [70] Such views were indications of a growing interest in history in the seventeenth century, a trend typified by Cromwell's recommendation to his son to read Sir Walter Ralegh's *History of the World*. By the end of the century Locke could write: "History . . . is the great Mistress of Prudence and Civil Knowledge; and ought to be the proper Study of a Gentleman, or Man of Business in the World. . . ." [71]

MUSIC

Music in the seventeenth century had not yet freed itself from its traditional association with mathematics and the medieval quadrivium. Leigh, for example, distinguished between pure mathematics such as geometry and arithmetic, and mixed mathematics such as astronomy, optics, and music.[72] Dury regarded music as a branch of mathematics.[73] When Webster discussed the teaching of music in the universities he did so in his chapter on the mathematical sciences. There was nothing unusual about this; scientists periodically interested themselves in music (usually from the mathematical standpoint) as a theoretical rather than a practical discipline. An excellent example of such a scientist was John Wallis, a trained musician and the author of an original book on music. He was, in addition, editor of the Greek texts of Ptolemy's *Harmonics*, Porphyry's commentaries on the *Harmonics*, and the *Harmonics* of Manuel Bryennius (*fl.* 1320), commonly regarded as the last Greek musical theorist. In 1677 Wallis made advances in the understanding of the acoustical properties of the overtone system. John Wilkins was another scientist with musical interests, particularly the revival of instrumental music.[74]

When Webster discussed music in his *Academiarum Examen*, he complained that the only aspect of music that was being advanced was "that vulgar and practical part, which serves as a spur to sensuality and voluptuousness, and seems to be the Companion of Melancholicks, Fantasticks, Courtiers, Ladies, Taverns, and Tap-houses. . . ." Simultaneously he lamented the lack of interest in the theoretical or "mysterious" aspect of music, by which he meant the attempts to discover "the nature, quality, distinction, sympathy, dyspathy, significancy, and effects of all sounds, voices, and tones that are in nature. . . ." He was also interested in knowing to what extent music might be useful to the sciences "and the laying open of the universal Harmony of the whole Mundane Fabrick. . . ."[75] There was an affinity between his speculation concerning music as a key to the harmony of the universe (which would essentially be, it should be remembered, a mathematical key) and his Boehmist advocacy of a universal language and an inner, spiritual natural language. In both cases there was a touch of the mystical and hidden.

Ward's rejoinder to Webster was that the universities were not neglecting the theory of music. At the same time, he admitted that "the Musick meeting, by the Statutes of this University, appointed to be once a weeke, hath not of late been observed, our Instruments having been lately out of tune, and our harpes hanged up. . . ."[76] It was not as bad as Ward reluctantly admitted, for Evelyn recorded in his diary that in July of the same year that Ward wrote (1654) he was at All Souls College, Oxford, "where we had music, voices, and theorbos, performed by some ingenious scholars." On the following day he heard "that famous musician" Christopher Gibbons (1615–1676), elder son of Orlando Gibbons, play an impromptu concert on the double organ in the chapel of Magdalen College.[77] The historian Anthony Wood, a keen music lover, took violin lessons at Oxford as early as 1653, and by 1656 had progressed sufficiently to take part in weekly meetings of musicians.

At Cambridge some interest in music continued. Henry More was a music lover and played the theorbo. Nicholas Hookes, who took his B.A. at Trinity College in 1653, published in the same year two books of poems (*Amanda; Miscellanea Poetica*) commending the level of musical instruction at the University and praising his own instructor. And as in the case of science, there was also a genuine interest in musical instruction in London as well as at the universities.[78] The level of musical attainment in the universities may not have been all that Webster wished, but musical instruction and interest continued, stressing instrumental technique.

The concern of the Puritan and sectarian reformers for a utilitarian education was reflected in their proposals for reform in the teaching of language, philosophy, logic, ethics, literature, history, and music. As in other aspects of their reform program, these proposals embodied the fundamental elements of the Baconian-Comenian tradition. Languages were to be studied only if they were of direct practical value. There was recognition of the need to reform linguistic pedagogy to enable language instruction to proceed as rapidly as possible and produce the greatest possible benefit for the pupils. There was, furthermore, interest in developing a universal language to facilitate the spread of knowledge. Philosophy and logic were subjected to special scrutiny. There was sharp disagreement on the question of including the philosophy of Hobbes in the curriculum. The sectaries were especially critical of philosophy because of its Aristotelian character, its deductive emphasis, and its tendency to concern itself with knowledge of little practical value. Logic and ethics were acceptable to the sectaries only if the former was divorced from religion and the latter purified of its non-Christian (especially Aristotelian) elements. Classical literature was criticized by the sectaries both because of its pagan content and because of its lack of utility. The Puritans were more moderate on these issues, preferring to prune out only the unsatisfactory material. History was not widely discussed, though it was generally accepted as a useful subject of study. Music was regarded with some suspicion because of the frivolous use to which it could be put,[79] though Webster was interested in its study as a key to understanding the natural world. In short, if an academic subject had utilitarian value and did not hinder religious faith, it was a fit subject study for the reformers.

CHAPTER SIX

Education and Religion

In their zeal to reform education and their defiance of university-trained clergy and professors of divinity the sectaries consciously based their arguments on religious premises. Those premises involved the opposition of Spirit to reason in the epistemological realm, of Spirit-infused knowledge to knowledge derived through rational methods in the cognitive realm, and of Spirit to divinity in the educational and ecclesiastical realms. Usage of these premises by the sectaries stemmed from genuine religious convictions, not from class antagonism, antiprofessionalism, or political motivation. Yet at the same time these religious premises convinced sectaries that opposition to the state church with its university-trained clergy, to the educational system with its stress on "scholastic" theology and pagan classicism, and to the social ills of the seventeenth century, was part of a spiritual crusade against the forces of evil. Enlistment in this holy war was motivated by religious reasons first, but they were bolstered by strong feelings of class antagonism and resentment against the professionals who appeared as pillars of the *status quo*.

RELIGIOUS STUDIES IN THE CURRICULUM

THE PROBLEM OF EPISTEMOLOGY

In a brief analysis of the conflict between religion and higher education in Puritan England, Richard Schlatter summed up the religious arguments in the following words: "The debate was part of the eternal controversy about reason and faith, rational and intuitive epistemologies: the sectaries put the emphasis on inspiration, and the more conservative Puritans, although recognizing the importance of inspiration, wanted it tested by reason." [1] Puritan epistemology was not truly rational, neither was it truly intuitive. It was an attempt to juxtapose Spirit and reason, at times going so far as to identify the Spirit in man with man's rational faculties. Such a juxtaposition was the essence of an epistemological ideal which enabled the Puritan to retreat to spiritual intuition when the dictates of reason clearly opposed his position; yet the same ideal gave him recourse to rational arguments when intuitive claims threatened his theological, ecclesiastical, or social edifice.

The juxtaposition of Spirit and reason was the fundamental characteristic of Puritan epistemology. The precise delineation of their relationship, however, was a matter on which there were varying shades of opinion, ranging from a virtual conjunction of Spirit and reason to a concept of reason as markedly inferior to Spirit. As representative as any statement can be of Puritan epistemology is Richard Baxter's assertion that "the Spirit and reason are not to be . . . disjoined, much less opposed. As reason sufficeth not without the Spirit, being dark and asleep; so the Spirit worketh not on the will but by the reason. . . ." [2] If the Spirit dealt with man rationally, as Baxter said, then what the Spirit revealed to man was not contradictory to reason. The Scottish Presbyterian Samuel Rutherford (1600?–1661), in a work directed against the teaching of such sectaries as William Dell and John Saltmarsh (d.1647), stated that the nature of the knowledge gained from the Spirit and that gained from reason was the same, though the acquisition of the knowledge differed: Knowledge from the Spirit came as if one were reading a book by sunlight, while knowledge gained by the use of reason came as if one were reading the *same* book by candlelight. [3] Joseph Sedgwick, a defender of the universities and the clergy, was surprised that sectaries such as Dell were "offended" because religious knowledge was rational. Sedgwick told a Cambridge audience in 1653 that he would be dissatisfied with a gospel that was irrational and with knowledge revealed by the Spirit if it contradicted knowledge gained by natural means. Although such a view coming from a Puritan may sound extreme, it logically followed from Sedgwick's belief that knowledge gained by natural means was the result of divine revelation. [4]

The Puritans were aware of the dangers of a rationalist epistemology to their ideology, for the unhindered use of reason led to freedom of inquiry and moral choice, and hence to a life of self-determination.[5] Puritanism never became that liberal, though throughout its history it spawned rationalists who did and were consequently condemned. Instead Puritanism clung to that aspect of its Protestant heritage which maintained a distrust of reason, a distrust seized upon by the sectaries and pushed to its logical extreme. Although when attacked by the sectaries the Puritans defended reason, they were on other occasions often chary of reason lest it be elevated beyond its proper place. Such chariness appeared frequently in the writings of the Independent Thomas Goodwin (1600–1680), an Oxford Doctor of Divinity (1653), one of the Dissenting Brethren in the Westminster Assembly, a Chaplain to the Council of State in 1649, and President of Magdalen College, Oxford, commencing in 1650. No radical, Goodwin nevertheless asserted that "all the wisdom and reason in man is against the way of faith." Without such faith, which for every Puritan was a work of the Spirit, all of the conclusions drawn by reason alone would hang on uncertainties and ultimately fail. In Goodwin's Calvinist thought, divine omnipotence would be threatened if reason could work unaided by the Spirit.[6]

Other Puritans likewise found it necessary to warn against the abuses of reason. The author of *The Marrow of Modern Divinity* (1645, 1649), known to history as E.F., was concerned that the use of reason in religion not be abused. Strongly disapproving of Christians engaging in the discussion of "curious questions and discourses," he urged his readers so to subdue reason that it became one with their faith, promising that then they would be ten times more "reasonable" than they previously had been. As he carefully explained,

> I do not contemn nor despise the use of reason. Only I would not have you to establish it for the chief good; but I would have you to keep it under. . . . I would have you more strong in desire than curious in speculation; and to long more to feel communion with God than to be able to dispute of the genus or species of any question, either human or divine; and to press hard to know God by powerful experience.[7]

Without the aid of the Spirit, this kind of knowledge was thought to be impossible. According to an earlier Puritan writer, even reason, without the help of the Spirit, could not enable a divine with only "notional" and "discoursive" knowledge to know more about true divinity than an illiterate man illumined by the Spirit.[8] Even the staunchest defenders of the educational system in Puritan England admitted that reason had its bounds. Thomas Hall said: "Wee must not bring down the mysteries of Religion to be scorned by Philosophy, but we must make Philosophy wait and submit to Divinity." Hall, in fact, threatened the traditional Puritan concept of the juxtaposition of Spirit and reason when he added that philosophy and divinity could contradict each other, and that many things that were true in divinity were not true in philosophy.[9]

For the Puritans a primary function of reason in man was to perceive the knowledge revealed by the Spirit. In this sense reason was like a candle of God in man, and revealed his nature to him. It was necessary for reason to set forth "rational evidence" to persuade heathens that the knowledge revealed by the Spirit was divine. This explains why one finds in the bulk of Puritan sermons a strong emphasis upon the use of rational means rather than emotion or even experience to persuade hearers and readers of religious tenets. To be sure, effective use was made of appeals to experience, yet that experience was subjected to rational analysis. The Puritan believed that just as the reality of his experience could be rationally analyzed and demonstrated, so could the reality of the divine truths revealed to him by the Spirit. Faith was a prerequisite to knowledge —the Puritan accepted the axiom *credo ut intelligam*—but once the act of faith was undertaken it was his duty to seek to know rationally all that could be discovered. He was strengthened in this endeavor by an assurance that natural and revealed religion pointed to the same infallible truth. Therefore, when the sectaries objected to his use of reason in religion on the grounds that the apostle Paul had condemned philosophy, the Puritan could retort that the philosophy Paul condemned would be condemned by any man reasoning correctly, and furthermore that Paul would have accepted "genuine Philosophy proceeding upon true principles of nature, i.e. God's discovery of himself to our understandings by the light of Reason and works of Creation." [10]

In the preceding quotation is implicit the Puritan contention that divine knowledge was revealed by the Spirit mediately rather than immediately as most sectaries maintained. In the debate on religion and higher learning the Puritans made much of the argument that the Spirit no longer immediately infused wisdom into the elect.

There was no denial that immediate infusion had taken place in New Testament times, but it was generally agreed that such a practice had discontinued with the completion of the Scriptures and that there was no longer any "new light" revealed by the Spirit. The knowledge itself remained the same; only the means used in attaining that knowledge had been altered. The Spirit's present function was not to enable believers to know more (quantitatively) than nonbelievers, but (qualitatively) to know it better.

The epistemology of the sectaries was based on the belief that religious knowledge came only from the Spirit and not through the use of human reason. Unlike the Puritan, the sectary "sought to associate the Holy Spirit less with reason or conscience and more with a spiritual perception analogous to the physical perception of the senses and given in 'experience' as a whole." [11] The sectary, not the Puritan, could unqualifiedly say, "I preached what I felt, what I smartingly did feel. . . ." What he felt was what the Spirit had revealed to him through grace and faith, which for the sectary involved a special element of mystical, infused knowledge. What need of a university education was there for a tinker-preacher like John Bunyan whose grace-bestowed faith gave him a sense of contemporaneity with the events about which he preached:

> Me thought I saw . . . the wonderful work of God in giving Jesus Christ to save us, from his conception and birth, even to his second coming to judgement: me thought I was as if I had seen him born, as if I had seen him grow up, as if I had seen him walk thorow this world, from the Cradle to his Cross. . . .[12]

For the sectary grace was like a tide which swept over the believer, instilling in him not only love and joy but also knowledge. Perhaps the most sensitive to this phenomenon were the Quakers, who confidently asserted to their audiences that what they were saying had been received directly from God himself. Yet the Quaker had no monopoly on such assurance; the Leveller John Lilburne (1614?–1657) told his readers: "I am a yong man and noe Scoller, . . . yet . . . I speak to you in the name of the Lord, . . . for I did consult with my God before I came hither. . . ." [13]

Although English doggerel of the mid-seventeenth century often caricatured or misrepresented sectarian beliefs, on occasion it was reasonably accurate, as was the following verse:

> Then I perceive that wit they have
> They gather in by Inspiration,
> No Books they need to learn to read,
> If all be true of their relation.[14]

In actual practice the sectaries often used religious books—more often, in fact, than they admitted. The successful but uneducated preacher John Bunyan disparagingly spoke of learned religious writings and haughtily informed his readers, "I am for drinking water out of my own cistern." [15] Yet he is known to have read Luther's commentary on the Epistle to the Galatians, Arthur Dent's *The Plaine Mans Path-Way to Heauen*, Lewis Bayly's *The Practice of Pietie*, Edward Burrough's *The True Faith of the Gospel of Peace Contended for*, Edward Fowler's *The Design of Christianity*, Thomas Paul's *Some Serious Reflections*, Henry Danvers' *Treatise of Baptism*, Thomas Grantham's *St. Paul's Catechism*, and William Penn's *The Sandy Foundation Shaken*. Undoubtedly Bunyan read other works as well,[16] but in sectarian fashion he was loath to admit it, for scholarly endeavor in religion was ordinarily rejected by the sectaries.

Sectarian literature abounds with passages attributing the attainment of religious knowledge to the infusing work of the Spirit. Although there was disagreement between the sectaries on the precise work of the Spirit, all were agreed that spiritual knowledge was not attained by rational means. The Quakers and men such as the Digger Winstanley asserted that the Spirit was in every man as an Inner Light, whereas the more conservative sectaries argued that the light in every man was a natural one and that the special work of the Spirit was undertaken only in believers.[17] The radical Independent Peter Sterry (d.1672), preaching before the Long Parliament in 1645, made the basic sectarian position clear: "To seek out spirituall things by the s[c]ent and sagacity of reason: were to plough with an Oxe & an Asse. . . . You cannot understand spirituall things Rationally." [18]

Sterry's last phrase clearly underlines a sharp epistemological difference between Puritanism and sectarianism. Francis Rous (1579–1659), a mystical Presbyterian who in 1649 switched to the Independents and whose career included positions as Provost of Eton and Speaker of the Nominated Parliament, was so convinced of this conception that he published, in 1638, his *Academia Coelestis: The Heavenly University: Or, the Highest School, Where Alone is That*

Highest Teaching, the Teaching of the Heart. This work fore-shadowed the basic religious concepts that motivated men such as John Webster and William Dell to attack the universities in the 1650s. Clearly there was no need of a university program in divinity if one heeded Rous' admonition concerning the acquisition of religious knowledge: "When thou goest up, to get a Spiritual Mind of the great Father of Spirits, remember to put off thy Carnal Wit and Wisdom, which must be stript off, before thou canst put on the other."[19] Webster echoed these ideas in his *Academiarum Examen* when he asserted that the Scripture was given so that man could abrogate his reason in religion inasmuch as those who believed something on rational grounds rather than the testimony of the Spirit had a faith which was "statuminated upon the rotten basis of humane authority. . . ." Having in mind something akin to Rous' distinction between earthly and heavenly universities, Webster challenged the clergy of his day: "Dare you presume to aver that you are Christs Ambassadors, and know not the Message that you should deliver, but have it to frame, and hammer out by your study, cogitations, devices, and the working of your carnal wit, and corrupted Reason?"[20] These words are frequently paralleled in sectarian writings, especially those of the Quakers. The Puritan answer to such challenges was caustic: They too could preach without academic preparation if they were lazy or if they had not had sufficient time to study.[21]

The sectaries were very critical of reason. The Welsh Independent, Morgan Llwyd (1619–1659), viewed reason as a "thief within . . . which locks the door of every mind against the waft of the Holy Spirit."[22] Webster rejected any suggestion that rationality was the *imago Dei* in man, or that reason was the essential difference between a man and an animal.[23] The sectaries refused to identify (as some Puritans did) the Spirit with reason. But as soon as they felt they had safely barred reason from use in religion, the sectaries regarded it more respectfully. One radical Independent, Walter Cradock (1606?–1659), admitted that many New Testament duties were based on reason, which was a light in the soul and a relic of the brighter light that originally was in Adam.[24] Even Webster for practical purposes had to give some place to reason if he expected his university reform to be carried out, though he carefully stated that in the realm of human learning "the immediate concourse of Gods Spirit" was essential if knowledge was to be attained.[25]

THE NATURE OF RELIGIOUS KNOWLEDGE

Puritans and sectaries disagreed on the relation between spiritual and temporal knowledge. Whereas sectaries regarded spiritual knowledge as possessing a special metaphysical quality which opposed it to human wisdom, Puritans attempted to show that although the two could not be regarded as identical, neither were they opposed to one another. Spirit and reason bore witness to one supreme truth, not to two mutually opposed bodies of knowledge. In this sense they were united. On this basis Puritans joined in one massive and neoscholastic system faith and reason; science and religion; the liberal arts and theology; piety and accumulated human wisdom. The sectarian attempt to drive a wedge between spiritual knowledge and human knowledge threatened to split this structure.

Because God was the God of all truth, the Puritan found it inconceivable that truth in the human realm could be despised because it was not spiritual. Truth was truth—and therefore God's—wherever it was discovered. It was impossible for truth to conflict with truth, even if one was spiritual and the other natural. Because knowledge was not bestowed in a miraculous way by the extraordinary means of the Spirit did not mean that such knowledge was to be despised, for the Spirit used natural means, including reason and education, to bring men to an awareness of the truth. Truth which came by ordinary means, as in science, philosophy, and the arts, would not contradict but enhance revealed truth. "Our Physicks, which is a great part of Humane Learning, is but the knowledge of Gods admirable works; and hath any man the face to call himself Gods Creature, and yet to reproach it as vain Humane Learning? . . ." [26] At best human erudition was so full of God's truth that its only enemy in Puritan eyes was ignorance; it was so closely related to God as the author of all truth that it tended toward the perfection of the human mind.

The acceptability of temporal knowledge and its joint witness with spiritual knowledge to the truth did not imply, in Puritan minds, the equality of the two bodies of knowledge. Human learning was subordinate to spiritual knowledge, though the teaching of the Spirit through temporal learning was included within the latter. Cognition attainable by man through reason and experience was subservient to spiritual knowledge and formed a substratum to or foundation for it. If this relationship was properly maintained, both kinds of knowledge would work together in maintaining a unified witness. As Thomas Hall expressed the Puritan belief, "wee must . . . bring humane learning home to Divinity, to be pruned and pared with spirituall wisedome, and then it may lawfully and profitably be used. . . ." [27]

The Puritan concept that Spirit and reason bore witness to one truth was not shared by the sectary. In his concern to glorify the Spirit and repudiate human endeavor the sectary depreciated knowledge attained by human effort. Most sectaries had the common sense to look disparagingly upon natural knowledge only as it related to religion, though there were radicals who sought the complete destruction of all learning and the universities. Part of the distrust of earthly erudition was not simply theological but socioeconomic. William Dell suspected that Sidrach Simpson tried to convince people that divinity was "wrapped up" in temporal learning in order to deter common people from studying it and consequently make them dependent on the clergy. [28] The accusation was probably justified. Similarly, the Quaker Edward Burrough (1634–1662) warned that the government of the Beast had established itself in the world through deceit, oppression, and human knowledge. [29] Winstanley called for men to "cast off the shadow of Learning, and . . . reject covetous, subtile proud flesh that deceives all the world by their hearsay, and traditional preaching of words, letters and sillables, without the spirit. . . ." [30]

From the theological standpoint the basis of the sectaries' belief in the contradistinction of spiritual and human knowledge was a conviction that in religion truth came through the inward working of the Spirit. The sectaries stressed that an ignorant man could learn more in a few minutes if taught by the Spirit than an educated man could learn in years of study without it. Stated in the proper context Puritans would have agreed. What disturbed the Puritans were the practical results of such preaching, as was revealed in the reputed remark of one of Anne Hutchinson's followers to the New England Puritan Edward Johnson: " 'Come along with me . . . I'le bring you to a Woman that Preaches better Gospell then any of your blackcoates that have been at the Ninneversity, a Woman of another kinde of spirit, who hath had many Revelations of things to come, and for my part,' saith hee, 'I had rather hear such a one that speakes from the meere motion of the spirit, without any study at all, then any of your learned Scollers, although they may be fuller of Scripture.' " [31] The acceptance of such a notion by a Puritan would threaten his socioreligious authority by placing in the hands of the common man the power to interpret the divine will as each individual saw fit.

The sectaries objected to the Puritan tendency, in practice more than in theory, to rely upon human wisdom as a subsidiary authority for use in propagating and defending religious knowledge. For the sectaries human traditions and philosophical arguments were to be rejected as unscriptural authorities. Whereas the Puritans praised learning as a means of defending the Gospel, the sectaries argued that the Gospel needed to be defended only by the Gospel itself. "All true Divinity is contained in God and his word. . . . All the Learning in the world doth not contain in it self, neither can it reveal to us aright, the least thing of God. . . ." [32] Knowledge discoverable by man alone was not suitable to defend the knowledge revealed by the Spirit, for in the eyes of the sectaries the Scripture condemned the wisdom of man as foolishness so it could never be compared with the divine wisdom revealed by the Spirit. Knowledge gained by man alone was no better than the corrupt source from which it originated. John Webster, a harsh critic of the use of human knowledge in religion, relented from his opposition long enough to use two syllogisms to make his point:

> Every tree that is evil, hath also its fruit evil. But every man by nature is an evil tree. Ergo, every man by nature hath also all his fruit evil.

> All the wisdom of the flesh is enmity against God. But all acquired learning is the wisedome of the flesh. Ergo, All acquired learning is enmity against God. [33]

Apparently logical forms such as the syllogism, though not satisfactory in explaining the faith, might be used to refute attacks by those who found a wider use for logic in religion.

Another point raised by the sectaries in opposition to the Puritans was that human knowledge was not equal to the superior knowledge gained by personal experience—experience equally available to the ignorant and the educated. In Francis Rous' heavenly university students obtained an "experimental Knowledge" of what was taught, and this knowledge was superior to that gained in traditional universities. [34] Winstanley argued that cognizance of the liberal arts enabled one to speak methodically of what had transpired in the past and to conjecture about what might happen in the future, but the man who could speak "from the original light within, can truly say, I know what I say. . . ." Voicing the expectations of every sectary, Winstanley anticipated the time "when wise men after the flesh shall become fools and scholars become ignorant, and when the ignorant become learned in the experimental knowledge of Christ." [35]

The sectaries stressed the gulf that separated spiritual and human knowledge, yet what really concerned them was the use of human knowledge in religion. Webster, for example, asserted that human learning was unadvantageous to the propagation of the Gospel and "lustfull and destructive unto the said end. . . ." [36] Others believed that human erudition *per se* was useful, though it would be condemned by God whenever it impinged on the revelatory work of the Spirit. Any pretensions of human knowledge to aspire to spiritual wisdom would result in misdirected endeavors and harm to misguided souls. According to Winstanley this was precisely what transpired in seventeenth century England. He struck out against the dominant Calvinism as a superstructure of thought invented by crafty clerical minds to maintain their oppression over gullible multitudes:

> Many times when a wise understanding heart is assaulted with this Doctrine of a God, a Devil, a Heaven, and a Hell, Salvation and Damnation after a man is dead, his spirit being not strongly grounded in the knowledge of the Creation, . . . He strives and stretches his brains to find out the depth of that doctrine and cannot attain to it; for indeed it is not knowledg, but imagination: and so by poring and puzling himself in it, loses that wisdom he had, and becomes distracted and mad. . . .[37]

To Winstanley as to all sectaries, divinity did not advance truth, as its adherents claimed, but destroyed knowledge of God.

Most sectaries did not condemn human knowledge without qualification. Like the Puritans, they condemned the abuse of natural knowledge rather than the actual body of knowledge itself. Yet there was a decided difference between the positions of the Puritans and the sectaries because of the latter's denunciation of the use of temporal cognition to support, explain, or achieve religious knowledge. Human learning was compared to a fire which was useful in the fireplace but deadly when it spread into the room. In the doggerel of the Fifth Monarchist preacher Anna Trapnel:

For in the Chimny the fire is
    useful and precious,
But when the rafters it doth reach,
    it sets on fire the house.

And so is Learning, when you keep
    it within its true bound,
But when you joyne it unto Christ
    he wil then it confound.[38]

Learning had its place and was not to be disparaged unless it stepped beyond its bounds into religion. Nevertheless, if a man learned religious truth by spiritual infusion and if that truth made earthly erudition appear to be foolishness, then there was no reason to require a minister to have a university education.

EDUCATION AND THE MINISTRY

A significant psychological element in the Puritan stress upon an educated clergy was the assumption that the congregation of elect would not question the authority and orthodoxy of the church if the congregation had been properly instructed by the clergy. To allow uneducated ministers to assume the homiletic task was to invite the undermining of the whole social, political, and ecclesiastical system upon which English society was founded. Ministers or laymen lacking suitable education would instill in the minds of their unsophisticated listeners erroneous ideas and assumptions, which in turn would lead to questioning the validity of the existing ecclesiastical and political powers. The only preventive to such social suicide was a strong university program able to train men in divinity in preparation for guiding the masses in the ways of political and religious orthodoxy.

The apologists for a learned ministry dealt mostly with the sectaries, though as early as 1637 the accusation of an ignorant clergy was leveled by one Puritan against the Anglican ministry. The author of that protest, written from the Gatehouse Prison, was John Bastwick (1593–1654), a practitioner of medicine (M.D., Padua) and a conservative Presbyterian. Writing in words intelligible to those without higher learning, Bastwick castigated the clergy: "So full of ignorance, vanity, and superstition their discourses are stuffed withall, as it brings a nausiousness to the hearers. . . ." [39]

The Puritans were generally agreed that university education was not a *sine qua non* for the ministry, but was instead for the well-being of a preacher. Those with competent knowledge and sound judgment in matters of religion might be ordained to the ministry without a university degree. Furthermore, in cases of necessity, as when no university-trained men were available, others could be ordained. As John Collinges wrote, "better [to] have preachers that can preach other mens Sermons and Expositions, then no preachers at all. . . ." [40] It was not a matter of learning making men ministers—the Spirit working through the church did that—but of more fully qualifying them. Under ordinary circumstances the most that a layman without university education could hope for was the opportunity to interpret some of the easier passages in Scripture in a weekday meeting in a private home. This practice was advocated in a treatise entitled *The Private Christians Non Vetra, or, a Plea for the Lay-Man's Interpreting the Scriptvres* (Oxford, 1656), written by Francis Osborne and containing a commendatory epistle by John Owen (1616–1683), Dean of Christ Church, Oxford, and Vice-Chancellor of the University.

Under normal circumstances the Puritans were agreed that university education was to be a prerequisite for the ministry. It was not a question of whether or not the Spirit was sufficient to teach immediately, nor was it a question of whether or not the Scripture in translation was simple enough for any believer to obtain the essentials of its doctrine without higher education. "But the Question is, whether the emphasis and fullnesse of particular Scriptures can be found out, and the difficulties of dark places opened, without these outward helps; or rather, whether a spirituall Christian, furnished with the additionall help of Learning, cannot bring forth more of the sence and meaning of Scripture, and give a better accompt of the same, then another that has not Learning. . . ." [41] If the answer was affirmative, as it was for Puritans, then human learning was requisite to the ministerial calling by virtue of its utilitarian potential.

Joseph Sedgwick admitted that the Scripture did not require university training for the clergy, but he pointed out that there was no reason to regard everything not specifically mentioned in Scripture as objectionable. University education for ministers was a matter of common prudence. Because circumstances had varied since New Testament times, the practices of the church also had to vary. Thus matters relating to order, including the education of ministers, had been left to the judgment of the church and its officers. The church, as part of a larger civil society, Sedgwick argued, had the right to rationally deduce from the nature and practices of society things which might be useful to the church, though only on the provision that such things were not contrary to Christian principles. Upon these premises higher learning was established as a prerequisite for preachers.[42]

For the Puritan it was a clear case of making ministers only of those who could distinguish between a birthright and a mess of pottage. This only the university-trained could do since the Spirit no longer infused knowledge by extraordinary means. As one author aptly noted, "if I could hear Fishermen or the like, preach or write like the Apostles, and likewise speak all languages by the Spirit as they did; who of no scholars were suddenly changed into greater scholars, and better Orators then ever the World bred up, in the best Universities, I would submit to their judgment." [43] Since most Puritans never observed such a phenomenon, they were concerned that education be a prerequisite if the blind were not to lead the blind.

Experience was not a substitute for education. Experimental knowledge was rejected as insufficient to qualify one for the ministerial role. Looking carefully into Scripture the Puritan found a number of things that a minister had to explain but could not experience. Even with respect to things that could be experienced, a theoretical knowledge of them enabled a minister better to explain them to others. Furthermore, in experience one could mistake the true intent of Scripture, depending on previous experience and knowledge. In this case experiential truth would differ from truth obtained by the use of rational faculties. A continued attempt to obtain truth experientially on such grounds, the Puritan argued, would render academic attempts to seek the truth useless. This was exactly the conclusion drawn by the sectaries with respect to the universities' attempts to grasp religious knowledge by the use of rational discourse and research.

A basic difference between the Puritans and many sectaries was the Puritan idea that what enabled a man to be a Christian did not at the same time enable him to be a minister. It was a case of properly interpreting the traditional but enigmatical Protestant doctrine of "the priesthood of all believers." The Puritans rejected the idea that in every believer there was sufficient teaching of the Spirit to enable him to be a minister. Without denying the pedagogical work of the Spirit in all believers the Puritans refused to accept the principle that such teaching was sufficient qualification for the ministry, essentially because of their belief that the Spirit customarily taught through rational means. It was not proof enough for the sectary to produce Jesus and his disciples as examples of the sufficiency of the Spirit's teaching, for those disciples were taught by Jesus himself. Lacking that firsthand encounter in the seventeenth century, the sectaries could not therefore claim to follow in the steps of the disciples. Nor were mere holiness and an exemplary life enough to qualify the sectaries as ministers, though Thomas Hall admitted that in a minister holiness was more important than education. Referring to ministers lacking in holiness, Hall acidly remarked: "A Religious dunce is better than he. . . ." [44]

Some Puritans placed such emphasis on education that they were willing to countenance ministers in the church who were academically trained but not regenerated. Such ministers were acceptable as a conduit which channeled life-giving water to others without themselves absorbing any. One's office as a minister was not null and void if he were not one of the elect, for the Puritan saw him as a man who still served a utilitarian function. "Christ's sending out of Judas is sufficient ground for calling to and receiving into the Ministery men of abilities, whom we have no presumption of in regard of reall grace." [45] It was an advantage for a minister to have experienced grace, though this was not regarded either as an indispensable requisite or as a sufficient qualification for the ministry. Experience could add life, enthusiasm, affection, and power to one's ministry, yet on many occasions, the Puritan pointed out, only the preacher himself would be aware of his unsanctified state. "A notional knowledge is sufficient to a verball declaration: and may in many things be clearer and safer, while it follows Scripture-revelation. . . ." [46] Other Puritans, however, insisted that both regeneration and education were necessary. One anonymous Presbyterian, who regarded educated but unsanctified men as enemies of Christianity, warned of the two extremes which had to be avoided: "As he that is skilled in Arts and Tongues, without the light of the holy Ghost, cannot universally interpret & apply Scripture according to the minde of Christ, so a man that is destitute of skill in Arts and Tongues, and hath nothing in him, but that light which proceeds from Gods Spirit, cannot on the other side expound according to the originall, for God workes by meanes. . . ." [47]

In the study and in the pulpit the Puritan minister generally found higher learning indispensable, and occasionally he did not bypass the chance to chide the sectary about the inferior quality of his preaching because of his lack of education: "If you had been trained up in the Universities, and had as much Learning Divine and Humane, and as much Grace and natural parts and gifts of God, as Gods faithful Ministers have, you might preach as well as we. . . ." [48] There is, however, a story, perhaps apocryphal, that relates how John Owen, then the former Vice-Chancellor of Oxford, was asked by Charles II how he could stand to hear the uneducated tinker John Bunyan preach. The learned Doctor reputedly replied: "May it please your Majesty, could I possess the tinker's abilities for preaching, I would most gladly relinquish all my learning." [49]

If, as sectaries believed, the Spirit infused knowledge in believers by immediate means and if that knowledge was not in fundamental agreement with man's best efforts to achieve religious knowledge, then it was logical to reject the Puritan principle of the necessity of university training for the ministry. If the unaided human mind was incapable of grasping religious truth but was forced to depend on the inner workings of the Spirit, then it was not necessary, the sectaries believed, to require years of expensive training in logic, rhetoric, philosophy, divinity, and other arts and sciences. The justification for this belief was primarily a theological one. That the sectaries succeeded in persuading men to accept their tenets was due in part to the simplicity of their theological arguments, which appealed to the strong sense of lay piety among the lower classes. It was also due in part to the sectaries' criticism of the clergy on socioeconomic grounds, which appealed to the anticlerical, anti-intellectual, and antiupper-class feelings of the masses. And finally it was due in part to the unique ability of sectaries such as Bunyan and Fox to popularize their ideas by the use of fiery enthusiasm, personal appeal, a strong sense of divine mission, and a sense of persecution and martyrdom. The Puritans unwittingly contributed to the popularity achieved by the sectaries by their campaign of invective and their attempts to restrict the preaching of the sectaries. The campaign of invective was probably more successful than has been realized, for the Leveller William Walwyn, a defender of the sectaries, observed that any man who became a minister without a university education faced "such an odium in the hearts of most of the people against him, that a thief or murderer cannot be more out of their favour then he." [50]

Other writers were less pessimistic, depending in part on their political and religious views. Time was also a factor, for Walwyn made his observation in 1644 when the Presbyterians were dominant, but by the 1650s Cromwell's dominance brought about new conditions. Cromwell's position is enigmatic. Although he favored an established state church, he also included within it Presbyterians and Baptists, moderate Episcopalians and Independents. Although he supported education and approved the establishment of a new university at Durham, one of the principal functions of which was to train men for the ministry, he also noted with approval that "God hath, for the Ministry, a very great seed in the youth 'now' in the Universities; who instead of studying Books, study their own hearts." That remark was made in a speech delivered to Parliament in September, 1656. Earlier, in February, 1651, in a letter to the Vice-Chancellor of Oxford, Dr. Greenwood, he referred in his capacity as the new Chancellor to "that seed and stock of piety and learning, so marvellously springing up amongst you. . . ." In July, 1654, he wrote to the Lord Mayor of London in regard to the appointment of a vicar for Christ Church, Newgate Street, recommending one Mr. Turner, of whom he said: "I can assure you few men of his time in England have a better repute for piety and learning. . . ." [51]

Cromwell's respect for higher learning in divinity coupled with a tolerance which allowed approved men to preach without that learning was representative of those Independents whose views were in the transitional state between Puritanism and sectarianism. Epistemologically these moderate Independents agreed with the sectaries that the Spirit infused knowledge, but they also agreed with the Puritans that such knowledge usually came through the use of rational means. Whereas the Puritan customarily limited the attainment of religious knowledge to rational means in the postapostolic period, the Independent in the transitional stage would not agree that the infusion of knowledge by extraordinary means had ended. The natures of the knowledge revealed in either case, however, had to coincide. Thus men such as Cromwell, Hugh Peter (1598–1660), and John Owen could regard university training as an excellent means of preparing ministers but not as an essential one, even in ordinary circumstances. Theirs was an attempt to maintain the traditional respect of Puritanism for religious education, and yet give full play to the working of the Spirit, of which Puritan theology seemed to them to say much but lack sufficient provision for realization. This position was responsible in the 1650s for the encouragement of education and the limited toleration granted to sectaries.

The Spirit was of fundamental importance to the sectaries, even to the extent that they preferred an uneducated minister with the Spirit to an educated one without it. Those without the Spirit were regarded as false prophets whom the faithful were to abhor, following the biblical injunction to reject the letter without the Spirit. To preach without the Spirit would bring the people to an unsatisfactory external knowledge of religion. Such preaching was not based on the true meaning of Scripture, the sectary claimed, but on the mind of the preacher, who was concerned more with his own attainments than with the welfare of those to whom he preached. No matter how great his knowledge of academic subjects or how proper his ordination, inwardly his evil nature remained unchanged. Learning was of no more use to him in preaching than eyeglasses were to a blind man. What he preached would no more save those who listened than it had saved him. "You must," sectaries believed, "be dead to your customs before you can run into the sea of truth." [52]

Some sectaries went so far as to regard education as a distinct hindrance to the ministry in that God ordinarily selected the poor and the ignorant as his servants. Sometimes the Spirit chose women, such as Anna Trapnel and New England's Anne Hutchinson. The gifts of the Spirit were bestowed "as soone upon a Cobler, Tinker, Chimney-sweeper, Plowman, or any other Tradesman, as to the greatest learnedst Doctors in the world." [53] In preaching, what mattered was not the fancy trimmings which higher education could provide but the meat itself, which was available only through the Spirit. Jesus himself, the sectary pointed out, chose mostly illiterate men to be his disciples and then provided them with knowledge through the indwelling Spirit. "Is not the Gospel of John as bad Greek as any Quaker's English? I say nothing of the difference betwixt Isaiah and Jeremiah, &c." [54] Dell asserted what no Puritan would ever admit when he claimed that Jesus "exercised no worldly witt, Wisdom, Reason, Learning, Parts, nor any thing that might commend him to the World. . . ." [55]

Less radical sectaries were not as deprecatory of learning, and simply pled for tolerance of uneducated ministers because God often used the ignorant as the vehicles of his message. God chose to do this, they argued, because the revelation of divine knowledge in ignorant men could be credited only to the Spirit, whereas the same revelatory work in educated men would commonly be attributed to university training. In the words of John Lilburne, "the Lord many times doth great things by weake meanes, that his power may be more seene, for wee are to [*sic*] ready to cast our eye vpon the meanes and instrument. . . ." [56]

To contend that the ignorant could be used by the Spirit necessitated in the epistemological sphere the continuing use by the Spirit of extraordinary means for infusing knowledge. The use of extraordinary means made it possible for the sectaries to contend that laymen as well as clergy were equally capable of attaining religious knowledge, thus destroying any pretence of a clerical monopoly of religious wisdom. Divinity was not swaddled in human learning as the Puritans asserted, for if it were, plain people without leisure and money could not attain religious knowledge other than from the second-hand accounts that might be gleaned from the clergy. Because of the work of the Spirit no such monopoly of knowledge and clerical bondage had to exist.

Higher education did not render a man a preacher of spiritual truth but a "worldly Virtuoso." A principal task of the preacher was the ability to adapt his message to the needs and conditions of the people. University education was not always useful for this; a tinker, not a Bachelor of Divinity, could best preach to other tinkers and shoemakers.

> Wee'l have no cushon-cuffers to tell us of hell,
> For we are all gifted to do it as well.[57]

Restricting the preaching of the gospel to "cushon-cuffers" with their knowledge of arts, sciences, languages, and scholastic divinity meant that the people would be deprived of the truth. Spiritual knowledge that would satisfy the people's craving for truth could not come on the basis of training in academic subjects. Hence the sectaries proposed the removal of religion from the academic curriculum.

RELIGION AND ACADEMIC TRADITION

Various sectaries attacked what they regarded as abuses in academic tradition. Their motivation was primarily religious and stemmed from their opposition to the necessity of higher education

for the ministry, though it also reflected the presence of socioeconomic resentment. Academic degrees and dress, as they were associated
with divinity training, were condemned. There was even suspicion
of the use of academic titles, especially the title of doctor of divinity,
which smacked of Popery. Much of this criticism came from the
Quakers, but other sectaries and even some Puritans were also
critical.

Edward Burrough, a leading Interregnum Quaker, rejected "the
very Habits and Degrees of Schools" as unapostolic and therefore
unacceptable.[58] The degree of doctor of divinity was deplored by
Henry Stubbe because it was as Popish as the divinity to which it
referred—"A Divinity erected in 1220, and which is acknowledged to
have been the subversion of Christianity." Stubbe made the inflam-
matory accusation that "a Doctor . . . is no Teacher, he is a dumb
Dog, an insignificant piece of Formality in the University. . . ." All
theological degrees were to be abolished, Stubbe advocated, because
they were not instituted by Jesus, because they were the pillars and
upholders of prelacy, presbytery, and tyranny, and because people
had been seduced into error and iniquity by their use.[59]

Degrees were also attacked by William Dell, the Master of Caius
College, Cambridge, who readily acknowledged the apparent anom-
aly between his university position and his criticism of university
practices. His defense reveals him as a stubborn man of dedicated
principles who held his ground (and collegiate position) in the face
of opposition:

> I neither do, nor will relate to the University, as it is polluted with
> any of the Abominations herein mentioned: But as by the Provi-
> dence of God alone, I have been brought to that Relation in which
> I now stand, and continue in it, against the wills and workings of
> many; so through his good pleasure I will remain, till he shall other-
> wise dispose of me; and during my sojurning with them, I will not
> fail to testifie against their evil. . . .

Dell affixed an appendix entitled "A Testimony from the Word
against Divinity-Degrees in the University" to his *Plain and Necessary Confvtation of Divers Gross and Antichristian Errors*. Divinity
degrees were condemned because they made men proud and because
they were a snare to the simple, causing them to believe whatever
they heard. Furthermore, Dell argued, the Gospel made all ministers
equal, but academic degrees changed that simplicity by establishing a

hierarchy of clergy. Reflecting basic sectarian belief in the freedom of
those without higher education to preach, Dell criticized the universities for granting to men "through power received from Antichrist . . . [and] chiefly for money, Divinity-Degrees; and through
those Degrees it gives Authority and priviledge to Batchelors in
Divinity to expound part of the Scriptures, and to Doctors to expound and profess all the Scriptures. . . ." Degrees were sought by
teachers with a pretended knowledge in divinity greater than that of
lay Christians and used in order to "get the uppermost seats in the
Synagogues and greetings in the Markets. . . ." [60]

Titles were attacked with equal vigor and for many of the same
reasons. Burrough rejected them as unapostolic,[61] and Lawson regarded even the title of bachelor of arts as a sign of heathenism. "In
the Primitive Times," he explained, "Gospel Ministers . . . affected
not Titles, nor itched after the same, to gain Reputation of the Children of this World; . . . Batchelors of Arts, Master of Arts were
not heard of among them; Heathen Learning & Arts, . . . they bore
lively Testimony against: But the Divine Call being lost, . . . then
they entertained Heathen Learning and Heathen Arts, to qualifie
them for the Work of the Ministry; then arose an Insatiable itch after
Titles. . . ." [62] According to Dell the teaching of Jesus prohibited
Christians from being called "doctor." Antichrist used titles as well
as divinity degrees to ensnare students.[63] Webster, who regarded the
scholastic theology of the divines as a chaos of "hel-hatc'ht" disputes,
proposed doing away with the use of the title "divine" altogether.
Likewise, although he would not oppose men being called "masters"
and "doctors" because of their attainment of natural and civil knowledge, "to have these titles given them as able, or taking upon them
to teach spiritual things, is vanity and pride, if not blasphemy.
. . ." [64] Even the Puritan John Owen renounced titles, though not
without an ulterior motive. Elected by the University of Oxford as
one of its two representatives in Parliament in 1654, he was barred
from taking his seat by the Clerical Disabilities Act of 1642. He
proceeded thereupon to renounce his episcopal ordination which had
entitled him to be addressed as "reverend" and repudiate his Oxford
D.D. degree bestowed on him without his consent and in his absence in 1653.[65]

The use of titles in medicine received strong criticism from George
Starkey, whose antiprofessionalism in no way dampened his enthusiasm for medical reform. Titles, he contended, were bestowed by the

schools only to allure students and were awarded not on the basis of medical knowledge but for their lectures and disputations on Galen. "By this means the pure fountains of true learning were miserably pudled and poysoned, insomuch that as many as drank of them . . . [were] lulled into a deep sleep, finding honour and riches in that seeming knowledge which they had drank in. . . ." The dubbing of a man a doctor after the conclusion of his academic studies in medicine, "provided he will make a great Feast, and give store of Gloves," was such a costly undertaking for the candidate that it was obviously designed, according to Starkey, to keep all but the rich from becoming medical practitioners, to ensure that the new doctor did not despise the honor of his title in view of the great expense it had entailed, and to serve as an incentive to charge fat fees from the sick and injured.[66] Starkey's condemnation of academic titles revealed class resentment and concern for the poor as well as antiprofessionalism.

Academic dress too was denounced by the sectaries. Henry Stubbe opposed doctoral gowns and hoods because they were used to enhance pride and pomposity. " 'Tis true, that while the Army continued in Action," Stubbe wrote in 1659, " 'twas thought fit by the University Men in part to lay them aside, at least for a while; but since the honest party of the Armies have been scattered and weakened in great measure, they have again brought them into full Credit and Fashion. . . ." [67] Lawson regarded the use of an academic gown and cap as heathenish and an unacceptable symbol of the class distinction of university graduates. He was incensed at the use of academic garb by ministers, which to him was Popish because Pius IV (1559–1565) had commanded that the clergy be clad in the gowns and habit peculiar to them. True ministers, he contended, wore plain clothes, not "Distinct Robes and Colours. . . ." [68] John Saltmarsh averred that it was "not an Vniversity, a Cambridge or Oxford, a Pulpit and Black gowne or Cloak, makes one a true Minister of Iesus Christ. . . ." Such outward distinctions were unknown to the simplicity of the apostles.[69] The scarlet robes of the doctors of divinity reminded Dell of the robes in which Jesus was mocked. The universities, reformed only slightly, he contended, remained the same as they had been when England was Catholic with respect to their "heart, bowels, bones, marrow, sinews and blood," retaining such Antichristian forms as academic hoods, caps, scarlet robes, doctoral rings, kisses, gloves, and "their Doctoral Dinner and Musique.

. . ." [70] Hugh Peter repudiated "those ornaments (or rags rather) the monuments of Idolatrie, viz. gown, caps, Matriculations, with the manie ceremonies about Commencements. . . ." [71] An anonymous writer defended the use of academic and clerical garb, admitting that it was not apostolic, but contending that it was conducive to order and dignity. [72] The Puritan John Owen, however, apparently disapproved of academic dress, even though he was Vice-Chancellor of Oxford. [73]

The zeal of some sectaries carried them beyond the denunciation of abuses in education to vitriolic attacks on the institution of the universities themselves. A Quaker preaching at Aberdeen in the mid-1650s condemned the university in that city as "a cage of unclean birds." [74] The Quaker James Parnell made the same charge, and was particularly irate that colleges were called by such names as Christ, Trinity, and Emmanuel. He suggested instead that the colleges be renamed "Glazier's Hall, or Bull-and-Mouth, or Synagogue. . . ." [75] Burrough thought all universities were of Popish institution, and Winstanley called them "the standing ponds of stinking waters" which spread the curse of ignorance, confusion, and bondage throughout the world. Universities were the "successours of the Scribes and Pharisees houses of learning." [76]

These sectarian criticisms of the degrees, titles, and academic dress of the universities reveal religious motivation. They also indicate social resentment against those who were privileged to attend the universities and earn the right to display the external credentials of intellectual attainment. Those without means had little or no opportunity to attain such status, without which they had little respect. In these criticisms there was a tendency toward social leveling: Those who obtained a university education might not be leveled intellectually, but they could be restrained from visibly and audibly manifesting their social superiority.

Epilogue: The Sectarian Quest for an Educated Lay Society

The sectarian reformers of Puritan England sought a society in which men were motivated by the Spirit in religion (as did the Puritans), educated in subjects with utilitarian value (as did the liberal Puritans), and free from reliance on a professional caste (as the Puritans generally did not). The sectaries attacked religion, academic education, and professionalism, but as men who sought a deeper religious experience, a more relevant education, and universal knowledge in law and medicine. If the sectaries sought to destroy anything, it was only to build better structures where the old had been. The society they envisaged was utopian in its dream that all men might possess basic legal and medical knowledge, but it was not a dream they believed incapable of fulfilment. Their dream was founded on education and the role it could play if the academic institutions were radically reformed. Their critics viewed the sectaries as enemies of education and knowledge,[1] but the real foe of the sectarian reformers was only an educational system steeped in tradition and dedicated to the propagation of esoteric knowledge to the initiated. In attacking this behemoth the sectaries began to pave the way for the development of an educational system more responsive to the needs of society and more inclusive of the people within that society.

What the sectaries wanted was not professionalism but lay intellectualism. They rejected the idea of a society where a select group of specialists monopolistically victimized men through theology, law, and medicine. What they sought was a society where medical knowledge would be so widely dispersed (through formal medical training and self-education via basic medical works such as the translated *Pharmacoepia Londinensis* of Culpeper) that no family lacked proper medical education. They sought a society in which religious knowledge was equally available without charge to all who were enlightened by the Spirit.

In each case the sectarian view of society, reflecting feelings of class antipathy, embodied antiprofessionalism, directed against the clergy, the lawyers, or the medical doctors. Yet the abolition of the lawyers was not intended as a prelude to total ignorance of the law. Simplification and reform of the law was a *sine qua non* of their social program. Part of the motivation for that reform was a desire that all men possess sufficient legal knowledge to do without professional legal specialists. This was antiprofessionalism but not antiintellectualism. The same holds true for medicine: What the sectaries wanted was not abolition of medical knowledge, but the diffusion of that knowledge to as many as possible in order to provide better medical care. Starkey, for example, complained that medicine had "degenerated unto the formality of a Profession . . . ," but he was not an advocate of medical ignorance.[2] Only in the case of their anticlericalism were the sectaries antiintellectual and antiprofessional simultaneously.

Yet the antiprofessionalism of the sectaries was not unqualified. They were not interested in abolishing medical specialists as such, but in smashing their monopoly of medical knowledge. Winstanley probably came the closest to doing away with medical specialists when he made medicine part of the trade of husbandry, which could be selected as one of five possible trades to study. Nor was the antiprofessionalism of the sectaries extended to university professors as a whole. The sectaries did criticize academic dress, titles, and ceremonies, but the brunt of their attack was restricted to professors of divinity. The sectaries criticized university professors because they were part of an educational system which included theological instruction and because of the limitation of higher education to two universities. The former defect was to be remedied by removing theology from the curriculum, and the latter by founding new colleges and universities. In neither case was the remedy the abolition of the professional class of professors *per se*. Calling for such an abolition would clearly have been out of keeping with the whole tenor of the sectaries' programs for educational reform.

Because the sectaries were strongly motivated by religious conviction the bulk of their attack on professionalism was directed against the clergy. Less was said about lawyers, though the attack against them was more pronounced than that against medical doctors. The reason for this hierarchy of concern was more than religious. Any man could regard himself as an expert in religion without particular jeopardy to his physical or material well-being, as long as he was not unduly radical. But when it came to law, however, he took a considerably greater risk in attempting to be self-sufficient. Yet sectaries called for the reform and simplification of English law in order to make such self-sufficiency more attainable.

In the case of medicine there was the greatest risk to physical well-being in actively criticizing the medical establishment. The layman, even if he had read Culpeper's *Pharmacoepia Londinensis*, was not qualified to handle serious medical problems. Unless he was a firm believer in magic or in the immediate and miraculous healing powers of the Spirit he was realistic enough to recognize this. Furthermore the number of sectaries with sufficient medical knowledge to enable them to criticize medical practice was slight. Its four principal critics—Webster, Culpeper, Starkey, and Biggs—did have a reasonable amount of scientific knowledge.

The criticisms of disciplines such as law and theology also reflected antiprofessionalism. One clever manifestation of this—designed to serve as a propaganda medium to the lower classes—was a Digger song with the theme "Gainst lawyers and gainst Priests, stand up now, stand up now. . . ." One of the most sustained and outspoken attacks against the bar came from the Digger Winstanley, who developed the theme (common among the radicals) that lawyers were associated with the hated Norman Conquest. Ever since 1066, Winstanley protested, the lawyers had upheld the Norman interest and subjugated the common people in slavery. William had dictated that the laws be written in Norman French, and had then appointed his own men to expound them to the English in return for a fee, thus inaugurating the trade of lawyers. It was so bad, said Winstanley, that a man could not plead his own case in court but had to hire a lawyer to represent him. "The imaginary Judicature, called the Law of Justice; which indeed is but the declarative will of Conquerors . . ." concerning the manner in which their subjects were to be ruled, was to be condemned along with those lawyers who bound "heavie burdens upon mens shoulders, which you yourselves will not touch with the least of your fingers." Winstanley likened the law upheld by lawyers to a fox and the people to geese whose feathers were continually being pulled. Winstanley proposed a remedy a year after the Commonwealth was founded: "Old Whores and old Laws, picks men[s] pockets, and undoes them: If the fault lie in the Laws, and much does, burn all your old Law-Books in Cheapside, & set up a Government upon your own Foundation. . . ." Winstanley also criticized the professionals who sat as judges, damning them because they oppressed the people rather than delivered them from oppression. Instead of relieving people who had been wronged and preserving the peace, the justices and other officers of the state trod heavily on the poor while permitting the offending rich to go free, "laying aside the letter of their laws, as the Priests doth the Scriptures. . . ." By smooth words they imprisoned and oppressed men and let the poor lie in prison.[3]

The anonymous author of *Tyranipocrit* called for the abolition of lawyers and laws prejudicial to the welfare of the Commonwealth.[4] John Lilburne, whom Thomas Edwards called "a darling of the Sectaries,"[5] accused the lawyers of promoting tyranny in order to foster discord in England "without which they cannot live and grow rich and great. . . ." Consequently Lilburne insisted that the people press for the abbreviation of the legal codes, their composition in English, and the right to plead their cases themselves. The present system of law he, like Winstanley, regarded as a Norman yoke enslaving the Anglo-Saxons; its discard would mean "farewell jangling Lawyers. . . ." If only true religion could be increased as well, he argued, there would be no need for an abundance of lawyers. The judges too were censored by Lilburne for enjoying "their crimes, and the prize and reward of them: . . . but through whose favour is it they have not expiated their Crimes with their blood: . . . but the Lawyers? who wisely consider it may be their own Case another day."[6] Edward Burrough demanded the overthrow of the laws as a prelude to a reign of God on earth, and George Fox called for righteous and equitable laws to be administered by honest men.[7]

These sectarian criticisms did not lack justification. In the mid-seventeenth century one of the quickest and most certain ways of obtaining wealth was the legal profession. In the Interregnum, judges, possessing legal tenure in their offices, received a salary amounting in 1652 to £1,000 per annum.[8] The legal and medical professions both drew men motivated by lucrative rewards as well as those whose first concern was humanitarian service. Sensing this and its inherent injustice, especially to the lower classes, the sectaries criticized the evils of the existing system. The common people, if they wished to be heard in court, had little recourse other than hiring expensive lawyers, for legal documents and laws were sometimes in Latin or Norman French, barristers debated legal points in Norman French, and indictments in courts of law were read in Latin. In 1650 some progress was made when the Rump legislated that all books of law and all court proceedings be in English, though this practice was abandoned at the Restoration.[9] The Rump's action undoubtedly pleased sectaries such as Lilburne, who had urged that Parliament have the same regard for the laws of the land as it did for the Bible when it approved the latter's publication in English.[10] Thomas Collier had voiced similar concern in a sermon preached in September, 1647, at the army's headquarters at Putney: "Oppression or Grievance is in writing our laws in an unknown tongue, that the French should be better read in our English laws than those to whom they pertain." [11] But the language of the law and legal proceedings was only one grievance. Winstanley struck out at another when he complained that "England is a Prison; the variety of subtilties in the Laws preserved by the Sword, are bolts, bars, and doors of the prison; the Lawyers are the Jaylors, and poor men are the prisoners. . . ." [12] In the same vein the Quaker George Bishop called for a simplification of the administration of common law.[13]

In the appeals of the sectaries for legal reform and repression of greedy lawyers there runs a continuous stream of complaint about the abundant expenses entailed in legal action, due not only to high lawyers' fees but also to lengthy legal processes. It has been estimated that in 1653 some 23,000 cases had been awaiting settlement in Chancery for as long as five to thirty years.[14] It is no wonder that Winstanley wrote: "When the Atturney and Lawyers get money they keep a cause depending seven yeares, to the utter undoing of the parties. . . ." Judges and lawyers, Winstanley accused, deliberately went outside the law in order to prolong suits and squeeze the parties involved for as much as they could. In his utopia he would have neither judge nor lawyer, the functions of whom would be assumed by the bare letter of the law alone.[15] William Walwyn verbally thrashed the noted Puritan spokesman and martyr William Prynne for taking, as a typical English lawyer, three times as much money in fees as his fellow lawyers in Popish countries, chiding him for not doing something that heathens themselves would have done *gratis.*[16] Lilburne denounced lawyers who attempted to "get the wealth of the Land into their hands by fishing in troubled waters: incouraging men in unlawful and quarrelous suites, pleading wicked Causes for large Fees, prolonging suites; and making men spend in long suite unto twise the value of their just Right, and debt for which they sue, and by taking treeble fees, and keeping them, though they faile their Clyant, and have been imployed at other Barres, when his Cause was to be pleaded." [17] The antiprofessionalism of the sectaries is clearly apparent in these demands, yet they did not call for an abolition of law but its reform so that each man could serve as his own lawyer. This was not antiintellectualism but educated laicization, enforced by strong feelings of class antipathy.

Much the same might be said of the sectarian position in regard to the ministry. The Puritan martyr John Bastwick's *Letany*, published in 1637, was a preview of what was to come in the anticlerical tracts of the sectaries. Written in English, Bastwick's tract was aimed at the common man in order to rouse him to action against the clerical pomp he resented. Racy and vulgar, it appealed to base emotion, not logic. The episcopalian clergy were condemned for pretending to have the keys of heaven and of hell, shutting out and thrusting in whom they pleased, all the while picking men's pockets. The stately buildings of the prelates, the sumptuousness of their fare, and their pomposity were viewed as superior to that of the nobility and equal to a king's splendor. Things had become so bad, complained Bastwick, that "nobody, without penalty, may pisse within the compasse of their yards and courts." The scurrility of his harangue, an infamous predecessor of the worst that followed in Puritan England, reached its peak in this abusive invective:

> If wee looke upon . . . the priests and prelats of our age, and see their pride, faste [*sic*], impudency, inmanity, prophanesse, unmercifullnes, ungodlinesse, &c., one would thinke that hell were broke loose, and that the devills, in surplices, in hoods, in copes, in rochets, and in foure-square cow-turds upon their heads, were come among us, and had beshit us all. Pho, how they stinke. For they open the very schooles to ungodlinesse and unrighteousnes, impiety, and all manner of licentiousnes; not onely teaching men to be wicked, and rejoycing in it, but constrayning them thereto.[18]

Keeping in mind the lengths to which this Puritan anticlericalism went, nothing that was said by any sectary could be either surprising or out of keeping with the tenor of the times.

The antiprofessionalism of the sectaries directed towards the clergy did not reach the same level of abuse attained by Bastwick but it was equally pointed. Webster accused the clergy of using scholastic theology to enhance their reputations and rob those foolish enough to hear them preach. The clergy were making a trade out of the ministry.[19] Thomas Collier complained that

> we must have idlers, and them only, Drones that never knew what it was to live lawfully in the world, by a particular Calling, that must be put into the Priests office, that they may eat a piece of bread, cloath themselves with the wooll, and feed themselves with the fat; and none must preach but themselves, lest their idleness and baseness should be discovered.

He was confident that there were many in England who lacked a higher education, but who knew more natural philosophy, logic, and rhetoric than the clergy.[20] Lawson spoke disparagingly of their Popish black gowns and coats, and Anna Trapnel accused them of preaching nothing but "their University language, their head-piece language, their own sense. . . ."[21] Dell accused them of desiring to preach only to the rich and powerful, not to the poor. The clergy preached to attain personal glory, Dell believed, else they would not mingle philosophy with divinity, thinking "to credit the Gospel with Termes of Art," and "sprinkle their Sermons with Hebrew, Greek, Latine, as with a perfume acceptable to the Nostrills of the world." The clergy preached for personal gain, making the ministry a trade to live by, hence they ran "from one place to another, from a lesser to a greater Living. . . ." Dell proposed abolishing the clergy altogether as a distinct order, believing with John Huss "that all the clergy must be quite taken away ere the church of Christ can have any true reformation."[22]

Quaker writings abound with manifestations of antiprofessionalism directed against the clergy. Samuel Fisher likened the clergy, the universities, and professors of divinity to mad Tiberian Massorites.[23] Edward Burrough accused the clergy of preaching where they could make the most money, moving from pulpit to pulpit in an everlasting quest to improve their financial status. "They are filthy dreamers, studying for what they speak, and dreaming without the Spirit of

God an houre in a Pulpit, and what they know it is naturally, by naturall learning, and naturall arts, and in that knowledge they are also corrupted, in pride, and vaine glory. . . ." [24] George Fox condemned the clergy for spending a week studying a scriptural text, adding to it their own opinions and quotations from heathen authors, and then preaching to the people on Sunday by the hourglass for money. "Are ye not all a company of idle fellowes, bred up at Schools in the filthiness of the earth, pride, and filth: and when ye come out ye raven after great Benefices. . . ." Because the clergy made merchandize out of the words of Jesus, Fox repudiated them as imposters who maintained themselves in pride and idleness, in hoods, veils, and changeable apparel.[25] James Parnell described Cambridge-educated ministers as "Diviners & Sorcerers, Witches and Magicians. . . ." [26]

An antiprofessional attitude toward the clergy was also a pronounced element in Leveller and Digger literature. James Maclear aptly observed that "Leveller leaders placed such great store by rational autonomy and freedom of the individual that an intellectual anticlericalism was an inevitable result." [27] To John Lilburne the clergy were sworn enemies of Christ,[28] relying, as Richard Overton insisted, on delusions, false glosses on Scripture, sophistications, and godly pretences. In a brilliant caricature of the clergy as Mr. Persecution, Overton ridiculed their attempt to use university training as an impregnable bastion against attacks on their position. Mr. Persecution—at this juncture a Presbyterian minister—was pictured as saying: "I have been of all the Universities of Christendom, have taken all their Degrees, proceeded through all Ecclesiasticall Orders and Functions. . . ." [29] Walwyn unmercifully castigated the clergy for hovering about dying men hoping for a fat fee or legacy. The learned, he said, lived at the expense of those without education, and so became aroused when the unlearned presumed to know as much as they. Walwyn believed there was no need for such learned clergy or for their Gothic churches, for "a plaine discreet man in a privat house, or field, in his ordinary apparell, speaking to plaine people . . . such things as he conceiveth requisit for their knowledge, out of the word of God, doth as much (if not more) resemble the way of Christ and the manner of the Apostles, as a learned man in a carved pulpet, in his neate and black formalities, in a stately, high, and stone-built Church, speaking to an audience, much more glorious and richly clad, then most Christians mentioned in the Scriptures. . . ." [30] The author of *Tyranipocrit* denounced the English for having chosen preachers with good grammar and facility in Latin, Greek, and Hebrew, but devoid of experience in an honest, simple life.[31]

Winstanley's radical opposition to the clergy appears on page after page of his works and embraces most of the accusations of other sectarian writers. To him the clergy were tools of corrupt lawyers used to keep the people in bondage and the Normans in power. The principal work of any reformation had to be the reforming of the clergy, the lawyers, and the law, all of which caused the oppression of the people more than monarchy itself. The persecuting priests and the tithe-taking preachers were the Judases that had betrayed Jesus, and now they sought the blood of those who disagreed with them. Even worse, they had

> ingrossed the earth into their hands. A man must not take a wife, but the Priest must give her him. If he have a child, the Priest must give the name. If any die, the Priest must see it laid in the earth. If any man want knowledge or comfort, they teach him to go to the Priest for it; and what is the end of all this, but to get money: if a man labour in the earth to eat his bread, the Priests must have the tenths of his encrease. . . .

The good men of England, bewailed Winstanley, were being used as horses by the clergy, led around by the noses and ridden upon at their pleasure from one religious form to another. To rebel against such humiliation was to invite being crushed by the power of corrupt magistrates. Still, he encouraged the people to overthrow the clergy, who were the backbone of social and political injustice.[32]

Some sectaries specifically blamed the clergy for being a party to the oppression of the poor, while others, such as Overton, merely accused them of indifference.[33] Edward Burrough was indignant that so many clergy had caused the poor to be imprisoned or to have their goods confiscated because they had insisted that they receive their tithes.[34] The author of *Tyranipocrit* damned those who built churches and cloisters, using money that rightfully belonged to the poor.[35] Winstanley was violent in his denunciation of the clergy for their oppression of the poor. He complained that when those without means resorted to Jesus' saying that the poor would inherit the earth, "presently the tithing Priest stops his mouth with a slam and tels him that is meant of the inward satisfaction of mind which the poor shall have. . . ." The eschatological doctrines of the clergy he decried as a cheat, "for while men are gazing up to Heaven, imagining after a happiness, or fearing a Hell after they are dead, their eyes are put out, that they see not what is their birthrights [their land and freedom]. . . ." Furthermore the theology of the clergy was a cloak to deceive the poor, making them believe that they must accept the *status quo* or be eternally damned. The clergy, Winstanley complained, would not work for 12*d.* a day like normal laborers but insisted on £100 or more a year. "They lay claime to Heaven after they are dead, and yet they require their Heaven in this World too . . . ," though they encouraged the poor to be content with their earthly lot so as to win the riches of heaven in the afterlife. One immediate remedy for the poor, Winstanley advocated, was a repudiation of the whole ecclesiastical structure, for "a man by running to hear Divinity Sermons . . . neglects his labour, and so runs into debt, and then his fellow professors will cast him into prison, and starve him there, and there [*sic*] Divinity will call him a hypocrite and wicked man. . . ."[36]

There is clearly a combination of antiintellectualism and antiprofessionalism in the sectarian criticism of the clergy. Out of that anticlericalism came specific demands for social, religious, and political reform. Among these demands were proposals for religious toleration, freedom of nonordained men to voice publicly their views on religion, and abolition of compulsory, state-supported tithes.[37] Throughout the antiprofessional attack on the clergy frequent recurrence was made to charges of Norman influence and to pleas for a return to a primitive form of religion in which professional clergy had no place. Fittingly, the sectaries advocated a lay ministry as the most suitable means of permitting the unrestricted working of the Spirit. Yet it was not religious ignorance that they advocated in their clerical antiintellectualism, but enlightened laymen infused with spiritual knowledge which they believed could only be obtained through the inner revelatory work of the Spirit divorced from the rational endeavors of man.[38] That there was to be no privileged caste monopolizing spiritual knowledge corresponded to their objection to monopolies of knowledge in the medical and legal realms by equally privileged castes. In the eyes of the sectaries the ultimate goal was not a society dependent on professionals for knowledge of particular subjects, but a society of enlightened, knowledgeable laymen. Their dream of a universally enlightened society is our heritage.

Notes

(Place of publication is London unless otherwise noted.)

CHAPTER ONE

[1] See Richard L. Greaves, *John Bunyan* (Abingdon, England, 1969), Chap. IV.

[2] John F. H. New, *Anglican and Puritan: The Basis of Their Opposition, 1558–1640* (Stanford, 1964), p. 108.

[3] For the sectaries' position on legal reform, see the Epilogue, where this position is treated in the context of their antiprofessionalism.

[4] John Spencer, Καινά καί Παναιά. *Things New and Old* (1658), p. 276. (Hereafter referred to as *Things New and Old*.)

[5] Wilbur Cortey Abbott (ed.), *The Writings and Speeches of Oliver Cromwell* (Cambridge, Mass., 1947), IV, 161.

[6] Spencer, *Things New and Old*, p. 367; and Edward Waterhouse, *An Humble Apologie for Learning and Learned Men* (1653), p. 119.

[7] Joseph Sedgwick, *A Sermon, Preached at St. Maries in the University of Cambridge May 1st, 1653* (1653), p. 11.

[8] *The New England Mind: The Seventeenth Century* (Boston, Beacon Press ed., 1961), p. 79.

[9] Baxter, *Gildas Salvianus, The Reformed Pastor* (2nd ed., 1657), pp. 464–66, quoted in Richard Schlatter, "The Higher Learning in Puritan England," *Historical Magazine of the Protestant Episcopal Church*, XXIII (June, 1954), 187.

[10] Firmin, *Separation Examined* (1652), p. 13.

[11] *The New England Mind*, p. 73.

[12] *An Apologie for the Ministry, and Its Maintenance* (1660), pp. 56–57.

[13] *An Endevovr after the Reconcilement of That Long Debated and Much Lamented Difference between the Godly Presbyterians, and Independents; about Church-Government* (1648), p. 81.

[14] See Mark H. Curtis, *Oxford and Cambridge in Transition, 1558–1642* (Oxford, 1959).

[15] *Ibid.*, pp. 86, 283–84.

[16] M. L. Clarke, *Classical Education in Britain, 1500–1900* (Cambridge, 1959), p. 66.

[17] Haller, *The Rise of Puritanism* (New York, Harper Torchbook ed., 1957), pp. 298–99.

[18] Samuel Eliot Morison, *The Founding of Harvard College* (Cambridge, Mass., 1935), pp. 67–77. On the problem of the reliability of the "Direc-

tions for a Student" usually attributed to Holdsworth, see Christopher Hill, *Intellectual Origins of the English Revolution* (Oxford, 1965), p. 307. The best discussion of the "Directions" is Curtis, *Oxford and Cambridge in Transition*, pp. 108ff., and 131ff. Curtis defends the traditional theory of Holdsworth's authorship in his Appendix. The "Directions" themselves are reprinted in Harris Francis Fletcher, *The Intellectual Development of John Milton*, II (Urbana, Ill., 1961), Appendix II.

[19] See Curtis, *Oxford and Cambridge in Transition*, pp. 113 ff.

[20] Quoted in Charles Edward Mallet, *A History of the University of Oxford* (New York, 1904), II, 387.

[21] Phyllis Allen, "Scientific Studies in the English Universities of the Seventeenth Century," *Journal of the History of Ideas*, X (April, 1949), 223.

[22] Quoted in Hill, *Intellectual Origins of the English Revolution*, p. 64.

[23] *Oxford University Statutes*, trans. G. R. M. Ward (1845), I, 273–74, quoted in Allen, *Journal of the History of Ideas*, X, 226.

[24] See *infra*, p. 73.

[25] Allen, *Journal of the History of Ideas*, X, 227.

[26] *The History of the Rebellion and Civil Wars in England* (Oxford, 1816), Vol. III, Pt. 1, Book x, p. 109.

[27] *The History of the Royal Society of London* (1667), Pt. II, p. 53; quoted in Allen, *Journal of the History of Ideas*, X, 232.

[28] Abraham Wright (ed.), *Parnassus Biceps. Or Several Choice Pieces of Poetry, Composed by the Best Wits That Were in Both the Universities before Their Dissolution* (1927 ed.), "To The Reader."

[29] For his policy toward the Scottish universities, see, e.g., Charles Harding Firth, *The Last Years of the Protectorate, 1656–1658* (1909; reissued New York, 1964), II, 99–100. The University of Dublin was, however, having its difficulties. Humphrey Barrow, a former soldier, proposed to Henry Cromwell "that the Chancellor of this University be moved to a speedy rectification, and rescue of it from disorder." In addition he suggested that the English donate one out of every hundred acres granted to them in Ireland for the purpose of increasing the University's revenue and providing relief for the aged, infirm, and orphans. *The Relief of the Poore, and Advancement of Learning Proposed* (Dublin, 1656), pp. 9, 2.

[30] *The Older Universities of England: Oxford and Cambridge* (Boston, 1923), p. 76.

[31] *Oliver Cromwell and the Puritan Revolution* (1958), pp. 141–42. Ashley's view was earlier expressed by Richard Schlatter, *The Social Ideas of Religious Leaders, 1660–1688* (1940), p. 42.

[32] See James Fulton Maclear, "Popular Anticlericalism in the Puritan Revolution," *Journal of the History of Ideas*, XVII (October, 1956), 450–51.

[33] It should be remembered, however, that there are fundamental differences between the use of the inductive method in religion, where the subject matter is metaphysical and not subject to quantitative measurement, and in science, where the subject matter is physical and subject to such measurement. See Greaves, "Puritanism and Science: The Anatomy of a Controversy," *Journal of the History of Ideas*, section II (to be published in 1969).

[34] For a discussion of that controversy and its broad implications, see Greaves, "The Ordination Controversy and the Spirit of Reform in Puritan England," *Journal of Ecclesiastical History* (to be published in 1969).

[35] *The Compassionate Samaritane* (2nd ed., 1644), pp. 37–38. The tract is reproduced in *Tracts on Liberty in the Puritan Revolution, 1638–1647*, ed. with commentary by William Haller (New York, 1933), Vol. III.

[36] *A Discovrse Opening the Natvre of That Episcopacie, which Is Exercised in England* (2nd ed., 1642), pp. 104ff. The tract is reproduced in *Tracts on Liberty in the Puritan Revolution*, ed. Haller, Vol. II.

[37] *The Coblers End, or His (Last) Sermon* (1641), sigs. A2 *verso*–A4.

[38] *Private-Men No Pulpit-Men: Or, A Modest Examination of Lay-Mens Preaching* (1646), pp. 4, 16, 22, 3.

[39] *A Modest Plea for Private Mens Preaching* (1648), p. 11.

[40] *Gangraena: Or a Catalogue and Discovery of Many of the Errours, Heresies, Blasphemies and Pernicious Practices of the Sectaries* (1646).

[41] In the same year Seaman published another work, opposing Erastians, Brownists, and Enthusiasts. Lay preaching was also condemned, as was the liberal Puritan Sidrach Simpson, one of the Dissenting Brethren in the Westminster Assembly, who had cautiously defended such preaching. See Simpson, *Diatribe, wherein the Iudgement of the Reformed Churches and Protestant Divines, Is Shewed Concerning . . . Preaching by Those Who Are Not Ordained* (1647); and Seaman, *The Diatribe Proved to be Paradiatribe* (1647).

[42] *The Pulpit Guarded with XVII Arguments* (1651).

[43] *The Prerogative Priests Passing-Bell* (1651), fol. A3 and pp. 1, 3, 4, 6.

[44] *The Pulpit-Guard Routed* (1651), pp. 3, 79.

[45] Ferriby, *The Lawfull Preacher* (1652), pp. 6, 17, and Appendix; Saunders, *A Balm to Heal Religions Wounds* (1652), pp. 45, 50–51, 53–55, 120–122, 126–127, 134–136. Collier reasserted his position in *The Pulpit-Guard and Font-Guard Routed* (1652).

[46] *Vindiciae Ministerii Evangelici* (1651), pp. 14–15.

[47] *The Peoples Priviledge and Dvty Gvarded against the Pulpit and Preachers Incroachment* (1652), pp. 1, 4, 15, 22, 57–58.

[48] *Responsoria ad Erratica Pastoris, Sive, Vindiciae Vindiciarum* (1652), pp. 49–50, 74–75, 149–150. Cf. also the same author's *Vindiciae Ministerii Evangelici Revindicatae* (1658).

⁴⁹ *Rump: Or an Exact Collection of the Choycest Poems and Songs Relating to the Late Times* (1662), Pt. I, p. 15.

⁵⁰ Παιδεία-Θρίαμβος. *The Trivmph of Learning over Ignorance, and of Truth over Falsehood* (1653), p. 2.

⁵¹ [Nathaniel Holmes], *Ecclesiastica Methermeneutica, or Church-Cases Cleered* (1652), p. 152 (writing in opposition to the sectary John Jackson's *A Sober Word to a Serious People*). Holmes was a Puritan imbued with millenarian ideas.

⁵² Ἐπισκοπή διδακτικός. *Learning's Necessity to an Able Minister of the Gospel* (1653), p. 34. (Hereafter referred to as *Learning's Necessity*.)

⁵³ *An Apologie*, p. 55.

⁵⁴ See *supra*, note 7.

⁵⁵ *Reliquiae Baxterianae*, ed. Matthew Sylvester (1696), Book I, Pt. 1, sect. 99 (p. 64). The date assigned in the *D.N.B.* for the death of Dell is 1664, but the "Bishop's Transcript" of the Yelden Parish Register gives 1669. See Vera Brittain, *In the Steps of John Bunyan* [1950], p. 425.

⁵⁶ Thomas Goddard Wright, *Literary Culture in Early New England, 1620–1730* (1920, reissued New York, 1966), p. 35.

⁵⁷ *Gods Mercy, Shewed to His People* (Cambridge, Mass., 1655), pp. 38, 47–50, 20. In the same work Chauncy also took note of criticisms similar to Dell's made by John Horne, Διατριβή περι·ποὶοιιχρῷ-ορω[[*Or a Consideration of Infant Baptism* (1654), pp. 154–160; and John Crandon, *Mr. Baxters Aphorisms Exorized and Anthorized* (1654), Pt. I, sigs. C4ff. (Horne's work is hereafter referred to as *A Consideration of Infant Baptism*.)

⁵⁸ *Vindiciae Academiarum* (Oxford, 1654), pp. 58–59. Ward was a Latitudinarian, tractable enough to take the Covenant for the sake of his Oxford position.

⁵⁹ Rufus M. Jones, *Mysticism and Democracy in the English Commonwealth* (New York, Octagon ed., 1965), pp. 85–90; *D.N.B.*, *s.v.* In the same year that Webster published his *Academiarum Examen*, he also published *The Saints Guide, or, Christ the Rule, and Ruler of Saints*. In this work he criticized tithes and the necessity of a university education for the ministry, advocated religious toleration, and revealed his Antinomian sympathies. A reply was forthcoming from the Puritan poet George Wither (1558–1667) in *The Modern Statesman* (1654). Webster vindicated his views the same year in *The Judgement Set, the Bookes Opened, and All Religion Brought to Triall*.

⁶⁰ Epistle to *Vindiciae Academiarum*, pp. 6, 7.

⁶¹ "Histrio-Mastix. A Whip for Webster," *Vindiciae Literarum. The Schools Guarded* (1655 ed.), p. 198.

⁶² *A Treatise of Religion & Learning* (1656), pp. 31–35, 50.

⁶³ *Learning's Necessity*, pp. 32, 35, 38. Sedgwick also took note of

Dell's *The Stumbling-Stone* (1653) by adding an appendix to his published *Sermon, Preached at St. Marie's in the University of Cambridge May 1st, 1653.*

[64] He was also opposed to paedobaptism, yet had his own children baptized.

[65] *Sermon*, p. 18.

[66] *The Quakers Wilde Questions Objected against the Ministers of the Gospel* (1654), pp. 11, 23–24, 41–42.

[67] *The Great Mistery of the Great Whore Unfolded* (1659), pp. 242–243.

[68] N.E., *The Confident Questionist Questioned* (1658); Ives, *Confidence Encountred; Or, a Vindication of the Lawfulness of Preaching without Ordination* (1658).

[69] *A Defence and Justification of Ministers Maintenance by Tythes* (1659), Pt. II, p. 13.

[70] Petto, Martin, Woodall, *The Preacher Sent* (1658); Collinges, *Vindiciae Ministerii Evangelici Revindicatae* (1658); Poole, *Quo Warranto: Or, a Moderate Enquiry into the Warrantableness of the Preaching of Gifted and Unordained Persons* (1658) and *A Model for the Maintaining of Students of Choice Abilities at the University* (1658). Woodall and Petto defended their original position in *A Vindication of the Preacher Sent* (1659).

CHAPTER TWO

[1] Basil Willey, *The Seventeenth Century Background* (New York, Anchor ed., 1953), p. 34. Bacon was one of a number of utopian writers in the sixteenth and seventeenth centuries who helped to popularize the new science. For a study of these writers see Nell Eurich, *Science in Utopia: A Mighty Design* (Cambridge, Mass., 1967).

[2] *The Works of Francis Bacon*, ed. James Spedding, Robert Leslie Ellis, and Douglas Denon Heath, IV (1860), 285–86.

[3] *Ibid.*, IV, 289, 89, 286, 287, 290.

[4] "Three Foreigners and the Philosophy of the English Revolution," *Encounter*, XIV (February, 1960), 7.

[5] Hill, *Intellectual Origins of the English Revolution*, pp. 115–16, 119.

[6] Joseph Frank, *The Beginnings of the English Newspaper, 1620–1660* (Cambridge, Mass., 1961), pp. 158, 272; and Hill, *Intellectual Origins of the English Revolution*, pp. 48–51, 117.

[7] *Works*, III (1859), 219; IV, 88, 341–42; V (1861), 111–12. Cf. Willey, *The Seventeenth Century Background*, pp. 35, 37.

[8] Richard Foster Jones, *Ancients and Moderns: A Study of the Background of the Battle of the Books* (St. Louis, 1936), p. 63.

[9] *The Great Didactic*, trans. and ed. by M. W. Keatinge (New York, 2nd ed., 1910), p. 286.

[10] Trevor-Roper, *Encounter*, XIV, 8.

[11] See Robert Fitzgibbon Young, *Comenius in England* (1932); G. H. Turnbull, *Hartlib, Dury and Comenius: Gleanings from Hartlib's Papers* (1947); and Turnbull, *Samuel Hartlib: A Sketch of His Life and His Relations to J. A. Comenius* (1920).

[12] See A. Wolf, *A History of Science, Technology, and Philosophy in the 16th & 17th Centuries* (2nd ed., 1950), pp. 143–44. Horrocks' works were published posthumously in 1673 by John Wallis, Hartlib's friend.

[13] *Considerations Tending to the Happy Accomplishment of Englands Reformation in Church and State* (1647), pp. 47, 22.

[14] Trevor-Roper, *Encounter*, XIV, 8.

[15] *Considerations*, pp. 36, 47–53.

[16] Haller, *Tracts on Liberty in the Puritan Revolution*, I, 64, n.53.

[17] *A Seasonable Discourse* (1649), pp. 8, 10, 21; *The Reformed School* [1649?], pp. 18–19; *A Motion Tending to the Pvblick Good of This Age, and of Posteritie* (1642), pp. 21, 35, 43.

[18] *The Reformed School*, pp. 38–39, 44, 46; *A Seasonable Discourse*, p. 11.

[19] *A Seasonable Discourse*, pp. 22–26, 17; *A Motion*, pp. 21–22.

[20] *Op. cit.*, reprinted in *The Harleian Miscellany*, VI (1810; reissued 1965), 3–5.

[21] *Ibid.*, VI, 5–6.

[22] *Ibid.*, VI, 12–13.

[23] "Histrio-Mastix. A Whip for Webster," *Vindiciae Literarum*, pp. 214–15.

[24] Maren-Sofie Røstvig, *The Happy Man: Studies in the Metamorphoses of a Classical Ideal, 1600–1700* (Oslo, 1954), I, 55.

[25] *Vindiciae Academiarum*, p. 50.

[26] Allen, *Journal of the History of Ideas*, X, 227; Hill, *Intellectual Origins of the English Revolution*, p. 55.

[27] *Vindiciae Literarum*, p. 27.

[28] *An Humble Apologie*, pp. 145, 193, 7.

[29] *A Sermon*, p. 12.

[30] *A Defence of Humane Learning in the Ministry* (Oxford, 1660), pp. 30, 45, 57.

[31] *Sundry Things from Several Hands Concerning the University of Oxford* (1659), reprinted in *The Harleian Miscellany*, VII (1810), 59–63. J. I. Cope has suggested that the author of this plan was Henry Wilkinson (1610–1673), canon of Christ Church and Lady Margaret Professor of Divinity at Oxford, and a former member of the Westminster Assembly of Divines. "Evelyn, Boyle, and Dr. Wilkinson's 'Mathematico-Chymico-Mechanical School,' " *Isis*, L (1959), 30.

[32] *Puritanism in Old and New England* (Chicago, Phoenix ed., 1955), p. 29.

[33] *An Apologie*, pp. 56–57; and *The Pulpit Guarded*, sig. B1 *verso*.

[34] *Vindiciae Foederis* (1653), p. 129.

[35] *The New England Mind*, p. 66.

[36] Cf. John Collinges, *Responsoria ad Erratica Pastoris*, p. 144.

[37] Waterhouse, *An Humble Apologie*, pp. 225, 94, 124–25.

[38] *A Discovrse Opening the Natvre of That Episcopacie, which Is Exercised in England*, pp. 9–10.

[39] Quoted in Hill, *Intellectual Origins of the English Revolution*, p. 85.

[40] All quotations from Milton are from the copy of his tract *Of Education* [1644] in the William Andrews Clark Memorial Library, University of California at Los Angeles. The tract is conveniently reprinted in the Columbia University edition of *The Works of John Milton*, Vol. IV (New York, 1931).

[41] Cf. his *Seventh Prolusion, Works*, XII (New York, 1936), 246–85, especially p. 277.

[42] Curtis, *Oxford and Cambridge in Transition*, p. 273.

[43] *Paradise Lost* (Mentor ed., 1961), X, 122–25.

[44] *The Prerogative Priests Passing-Bell*, p. 6.

[45] *The New England Mind*, p. 74. Cf. Schlatter: "Not one of the enemies of the learned ministry, so far as I can discover, attacked learning as such." *Historical Magazine of the Protestant Episcopal Church*, XXIII, 172. Cf. Leo F. Solt, "Anti-Intellectualism in the Puritan Revolution," *Church History*, XXIV (December, 1956), 310–11.

[46] *The Saints Guide*, p. 15; and *The Judgement Set*, p. 299 (cf. pp. 286, 289).

[47] *The Works of Gerrard Winstanley*, ed. George H. Sabine (New York, 1941; reissued 1965), p. 271. Cf. James Parnell, *A Collection of the Several Writings* [of] . . . *James Parnel* (1675), pp. 140–141, 349.

[48] *A Word of Reproof to the Priests or Ministers* (3rd ed., 1656), p. 21.

[49] *An Humble Motion to the Parliament of England Concerning the Advancement of Learning* (1649), p. 28.

[50] *Natures Explication and Helmont's Vindication* (1657), pp. 114, 16; *Pyrotechny Asserted and Illustrated* (1658), p. 172.

[51] *Academiarum Examen* (1654), p. 2.

[52] *Works*, p. 576.

[53] *A Whip for the Present House of Lords* [1648], p. 3.

[54] *A Testimony from the Word against Divinity-Degrees in the University*, p. 30; originally published as an appendix to *A Plain and Necessary Confvtation* (1654); and *Works* (1817), II, 217, 222.

[55] Walwyn, *The Compassionate Samaritane*, pp. 36–37; Haller, *Tracts on Liberty in the Puritan Revolution*, I, 39–40.

⁵⁶ *Works*, II, 222.

⁵⁷ *Academiarum Examen*, p. 18.

⁵⁸ *Holy Discoveries and Flames* (1640), p. 104. Saltmarsh, a sectary and a Magdalen College, Cambridge, M.A., was rector of Heslerton, Yorkshire, and subsequently (1647) a chaplain in the New Model Army. For the role of these chaplains, see Solt, *Saints in Arms: Puritanism and Democracy in Cromwell's Army* (Stanford, 1959).

⁵⁹ *Works*, p. 579.

⁶⁰ Frederick B. Tolles, *Meeting House and Counting House; The Quaker Merchants of Colonial Philadelphia, 1682–1763* (New York, 1963 ed.), p. 208; and *The Witness of William Penn*, eds. Tolles and E. Gordon Alderfer (New York, 1957), pp. 42–43.

⁶¹ *A Modest Plea for an Equal Common-Wealth against Monarchy* (1659), pp. 92–93, 50; and *Philosophicall Essayes with Brief Adviso's* (1657), p. 98. For a fuller treatment of Sprigg, see Greaves, "William Sprigg and the Cromwellian Revolution," in a forthcoming issue of the *Huntington Library Quarterly*.

⁶² *Works*, II, 221; and *The Tryal of Spirits both in Teachers & Hearers* (1653), p. 55.

⁶³ *The Power of Love* (1643), pp. 44–45. The tract is reprinted in Haller, *Tracts on Liberty in the Puritan Revolution*, Vol. II.

⁶⁴ Tolles, *Meeting House and Counting House*, p. 207; *Truth Exalted* (1671), pp. 8–9. Penn met Petty before 1669 and Dury in 1677. He was subsequently elected a Fellow of the Royal Society in 1681, and personally knew John Locke, Isaac Newton, John Wallis, John Aubrey, and Robert Hooke.

⁶⁵ *Academiarum Examen*, pp. 91–95, 21–22.

⁶⁶ Epistle to Ward's *Vindiciae Academiarum*, p. 1.

⁶⁷ *Academiarum Examen*, pp. 20–21, 110.

⁶⁸ *Infra*, Chapter IV.

⁶⁹ *A Modest Plea*, p. 53.

CHAPTER THREE

¹ For a careful study of the conditions of the poor in this period, see A. L. Beier, "Poor Relief in Warwickshire 1630–1660," *Past & Present*, No. 35 (December, 1966), 77–100.

² "The History of Trades: Its Relation to Seventeenth-Century Thought as Seen in Bacon, Petty, Evelyn, and Boyle," *Journal of the History of Ideas*, II (January, 1941), 38.

³ The program is described in *The Great Didactic*.

⁴ *The Reformed School*, pp. 52–60.

⁵ *Considerations*, p. 22.

⁶ *The Harleian Miscellany*, VI, 3–6, 12–13.

[7] Webster, *Academiarum Examen*, p. 52; Penn, *No Cross, No Crown* (1669), p. 29; Lawson, *A Mite into the Treasury* (1680), pp. 40–41; Sprigg, *A Modest Plea*, pp. 51–53; and *Philosophicall Essayes*, p. 77. Cf. the latter's *The Royal and Happy Poverty* (1660), p. 42.

[8] See Winthrop S. Hudson, "Economic and Social Thought of Gerrard Winstanley: Was He a Seventeenth-Century Marxist?" *The Journal of Modern History*, XVIII (March, 1946), 19. For Winstanley's activities after the failure of the Digger movement, see Richard T. Vann, "The Later Life of Gerrard Winstanley," *Journal of the History of Ideas*, XXVI (January–March, 1965), 133–36.

[9] *Works*, pp. 576, 579, 577.

[10] *Ibid.*, pp. 526, 577–79. Like Winstanley, Sprigg believed *every* man should have a trade. "Scholars . . . are the greatest murderers of time, unless Masters of some trade or art, wherein to spend their after-meal-houres." *Philosophicall Essayes*, p. 71.

[11] *Works*, pp. 576, 579.

[12] *Ibid.*, pp. 577, 579–80. For a fuller discussion of Winstanley's views, see Greaves, "Gerrard Winstanley and Educational Reform in Puritan England," *British Journal of Educational Studies* (to be published in 1969).

[13] Cf. Foster Watson, *The English Grammar Schools to 1660: Their Curriculum and Practice* (Cambridge, 1908), p. 8.

[14] William Boyd, *The History of Western Education* (6th ed., 1952), pp. 272–73.

[15] William K. Medlin, *The History of Educational Ideas in the West* (New York, 1964), p. 72.

[16] *Considerations*, p. 22.

[17] *A Seasonable Discourse*, p. 8.

[18] *Supra*, 34.

[19] W. K. Jordan, *Men of Substance* (Chicago, 1942), p. 254.

[20] *Vindiciae Academiarum*, p. 62.

[21] Sabine, Introduction to Winstanley's *Works*, pp. 64–65.

[22] *Tyranipocrit, Discovered with His Wiles, wherewith He Vanquisheth* (Rotterdam, 1649), pp. 4, 51–52. On the problem of authorship, see H. N. Brailsford, *The Levellers and the English Revolution*, ed. Christopher Hill (Stanford, 1961), p. 64.

[23] Brailsford, *The Levellers and the English Revolution*, p. 233.

[24] Dell, *A Testimony from the Word*, p. 26.

[25] W. H. G. Armytage, *Four Hundred Years of English Education* (Cambridge, 1964), pp. 22–23; Hill, *Intellectual Origins of the English Revolution*, pp. 108–109, 124; Trevor-Roper, *Encounter*, XIV, 5, 17; Sprigg, *A Modest Plea*, p. 49; Jones, *Ancients and Moderns*, p. 123.

[26] Hill, *Intellectual Origins of the English Revolution*, p. 108; Armytage,

Four Hundred Years of English Education, pp. 22–23; Brailsford, *The Levellers and the English Revolution*, p. 645; Ashley, *Oliver Cromwell and the Puritan Revolution*, p. 142.

[27] Firth, *The Last Years of the Protectorate*, II, 159.

[28] *The Letters and Speeches of Oliver Cromwell*, ed. S. C. Lomas (1904), II, 186–87. Cf. *The Writings and Speeches of Oliver Cromwell*, ed. Abbott, IV, 84, 89–90.

[29] *The Writings and Speeches of Oliver Cromwell*, ed. Abbott, IV, 522–23.

[30] See G. H. Turnbull, "Oliver Cromwell's College at Durham," *Research Review*, No. 3 (September, 1952), 1–7.

[31] *Works*, II, 220–21.

[32] *Vindiciae Academiarum*, pp. 63–64.

[33] *An Humble Motion*, pp. 30, 32, 17.

[34] *A Modest Plea*, pp. 62, 92.

[35] *The Curates Conference; Or a Discovrse betwixt Two Schollers* (1641), p. 2.

[36] *An Humble Motion*, pp. 29–30.

[37] *Op. cit.*, pp. 1–10.

[38] *A Modest Plea*, p. 55.

[39] *Good Work for a Good Magistrate* (1651), pp. 5–7, 11–12; *A Word for the Armie, and Two Words to the Kingdome* (1647), p. 11. For a discussion of Peter's proposals for educational reform see Raymond Phineas Stearns, *The Strenuous Puritan: Hugh Peter, 1598–1660* (Urbana, Illinois, 1954), pp. 311, 371–73, 380–81.

CHAPTER FOUR

[1] *Rump*, Pt. I, p. 18.

[2] Roger Sharrock, Introduction to Bunyan's *Grace Abounding to the Chief of Sinners* (Oxford, 1962), p. xxix.

[3] "Puritanism, Pietism, and Science," in *Science & Ideas: Selected Readings*, eds. Arnold B. Arons and Alfred M. Bork (Englewood Cliffs, New Jersey, 1964), p. 238.

[4] The literature on the problem of a possible relation between Puritanism and science is extensive. Broad treatments of the controversy can be found in Theodore K. Rabb, "Puritanism and the Rise of Experimental Science in England," *Cahiers d'Hist. Mondiale*, VII (1962), 46–67; Leo F. Solt, "Puritanism, Capitalism, Democracy, and the New Science," *The American Historical Review*, LXXIII (October, 1967), 18–29; Douglas S. Kemsley, "Religious Influences in the Rise of Modern Science: A Review and Criticism, Particularly of the 'Protestant-Puritan Ethic' Theory," *Annals of Science*, XXIV (September, 1968), 199–226; and

Greaves, "Puritanism and Science: The Anatomy of a Controversy" (to be published in the *Journal of the History of Ideas* in 1969).

[5] Morison, *The Founding of Harvard College,* p. 77. Contrary to Morison, the new science may have been taught at Cambridge before Barrow's time by individual tutors. See Curtis, *Oxford and Cambridge in Transition,* especially Chap. IX.

[6] Allen, *Journal of the History of Ideas,* X, 233.

[7] *The Diary of John Evelyn,* ed. Austin Dobson (1908), entry for Dec. 10, 1656. A recent study of the religious views of English scientists in the seventeenth century demonstrates that such men were primarily moderate or latitudinarian. "There is not a single unambiguous and fully committed Puritan in the entire scientific leadership," according to B. J. Shapiro. "Latitudinarianism and Science in Seventeenth-Century England," *Past & Present,* No. 40 (July, 1968), 16–41.

[8] *Academiarum Examen,* pp. 34, 105–106, 71.

[9] *Vindiciae Academiarum,* pp. 25, 45–46.

[10] *Astronomical Thought in Renaissance England* (Baltimore, 1937), p. 289.

[11] *Ibid.,* p. 13, n. 11. Recorde left Oxford to practice medicine in London; Dee left Cambridge to study at Louvain, and subsequently refused an offer to lecture on mathematics at Oxford; Hood left Cambridge to lecture on mathematics in London, and later practiced medicine; Wright left Cambridge to lecture on navigation in London; and Gilbert left Cambridge to practice medicine in London.

[12] *Academiarum Examen,* pp. 40–41, 20, 51–52; and Hill, *Intellectual Origins of the English Revolution,* pp. 17–18. Dee's preface was also quoted by the anonymous Puritan author of *A Vindication of Learning from Unjust Aspersions* (1646), sig. C2.

[13] *A Testimony from the Word,* p. 27.

[14] Penn, *No Cross, No Crown,* p. 29; Lawson, *A Mite into the Treasury,* pp. 40–41; and Tolles, *Meeting House and Counting House,* pp. 144–145. Leybourn (1626–1700?) was also the joint author (with Vincent Wing) of the first book on astronomy (*Urania Practica*) in English. *Dictionary of National Biography, s.v.*

[15] *An Humble Motion,* p. 27.

[16] *Vindiciae Academiarum,* pp. 27–28, 41–42, 30.

[17] *Academiarum Examen,* pp. 43 ff., 46.

[18] *Vindiciae Academiarum,* pp. 5, 29–30.

[19] *Astronomical Thought in Renaissance England,* p. 292.

[20] *Academiarum Examen,* p. 103.

[21] Allen, *Journal of the History of Ideas,* X, 227; and Johnson, *Astronomical Thought in Renaissance England,* p. 270.

[22] *An Astronomicall Description of the Late Comet* (1618), quoted in Johnson, *Astronomical Thought in Renaissance England*, p. 271.

[23] Brian Twyne, Fellow of Corpus Christi College, Oxford, was a Copernican, and taught modern astronomical theories to his students between 1605 and 1623. Curtis, *Oxford and Cambridge in Transition*, pp. 120–21.

[24] For Milton's attitude toward astronomy, see George Wesley Whiting, *Milton's Literary Milieu* (Chapel Hill, North Carolina, 1939), pp. 159–64.

[25] Hill, *Intellectual Origins of the English Revolution*, p. 5.

[26] Fletcher, *The Intellectual Development of John Milton*, II, 469.

[27] *Academiarum Examen*, pp. 77–78.

[28] *Vindiciae Academiarum*, p. 36.

[29] *Academiarum Examen*, pp. 41–42.

[30] *Vindiciae Academiarum*, pp. 29, 30.

[31] A. R. Hall, *The Scientific Revolution, 1500–1800* (1954), p. 182.

[32] Hill, *Intellectual Origins of the English Revolution*, p. 306.

[33] *Academiarum Examen*, p. 52.

[34] *Ibid.*, pp. 50–51.

[35] Lawson, *A Mite*, pp. 40–41; and Dell, *A Testimony from the Word*, p. 27.

[36] *Academiarum Examen*, p. 71.

[37] *An Humble Motion*, p. 27.

[38] *A Modest Plea*, p. 53; and *Philosophicall Essayes*, p. 19.

[39] *Academiarum Examen*, pp. 70–71, 76–77. On the authorship of the works attributed to Valentinus and Hollandus, see George Sarton, *Six Wings: Men of Science in the Renaissance* (1957), p. 112.

[40] *Natures Explication*, pp. 34, 109–110. Like Starkey, Penn respected Boyle and recommended that his works be included in libraries of modest size. Tolles, *Meeting House and Counting House*, pp. 144–145. Starkey and Boyle were mutual friends of the New England scientist, Robert Child, who in turn was a friend of Hartlib and was associated with the founders of the Royal Society. See the Epistle Dedicatory to *Pyrotechny Asserted and Illustrated*.

[41] Ronald Sterne Wilkinson, "The Alchemical Library of John Winthrop, Jr. (1606–1676), and His Descendants in Colonial America," *Ambix*, XI (1963), 33–51. One of Winthrop's friends who supplied him with books was Samuel Hartlib.

[42] *Intellectual Origins of the English Revolution*, pp. 122–23.

[43] *Vindiciae Academiarum*, pp. 51, 68–70, 76.

[44] Allen, *Journal of the History of Ideas*, X, 233.

[45] *Academiarum Examen*, pp. 51, 68–70. Cf. Walter Pagel, writing of Robert Fludd—a prime example of the commixture of religion, magic, and

alchemy in the early modern period: "True practical theology is nothing but mystical chemistry which furthers our attempts to uncover the divine light for our own benefit." "Religious Motives in the Medical Biology of the XVIIth Century," *Bulletin of the Institute of the History of Medicine*, III (April, 1935), 269.

⁴⁶ *Academiarum Examen*, pp. 51, 76.

⁴⁷ *Vindiciae Academiarum*, pp. 30, 46, 23, 5. Cf. T. Hall, "Histrio-Mastix," pp. 204–205. The Rosicrucians embraced a combination of mystical religious beliefs, fraternal ideals, and alchemical ideas, the principal inspiration of which came from a series of works published between 1614 and 1616, purportedly written by the order's founder, Christian Rosenkreuz, but actually composed by Johann Valentin Andreae (1586–1654), a friend of Comenius and Leibniz. Margaret Lewis Bailey, *Milton and Jakob Boehme* (New York, 1914), pp. 16–18, 21, 82.

⁴⁸ Lynn Thorndike, *A History of Magic and Experimental Science*, VII (New York, 1958), 435, 439–44.

⁴⁹ Bailey, *Milton and Jakob Boehme*, p. 63, n.1.

⁵⁰ *The Way to Christ Discovered* (1648), Bk. IV, pp. 1–2; *Avrora. That Is, the Day-Spring*, trans. Sparrow (1656), p. 146; *Signatura Rerum*, trans. Ellistone (1651), pp. 77, 1.

⁵¹ Ellistone, Preface to *Signatura Rerum*, sig. A2–A3.

⁵² Bailey, *Milton and Jakob Boehme*, pp. 29–30, 77–78, 81–82, 90. Cf. Thorndike, *A History of Magic and Experimental Science*, VII, 182–83.

⁵³ *Works*, III, 503.

⁵⁴ *Op. cit.*, p. 50.

⁵⁵ *A Mite*, p. 38.

⁵⁶ Fox, *The Vialls of the Wrath of God* (1655), pp. 4, 8; Burrough, *A Trumpet of the Lord Sounded out of Sion* (1656), p. 5; and F[arnworth], *Witchcraft Cast out from the Religious Seed and Israel of God* (1655), p. 2.

⁵⁷ *An Humble Apologie*, pp. 30, 34. Winstanley approved the study of astrology (*Works*, p. 578), as did the anonymous Puritan author of *A Vindication of Learning*. See also Robert Gell, *Stella Nova, a New Starre, Leading Wisemen unto Christ* (1649), a sermon preached before the Society of Astrologers in London, August 1, 1649. Gell (1595–1665) was a former chaplain to the Archbishop of Canterbury and the rector of St. Mary, Aldermanbury, London.

⁵⁸ Schlatter, *Historical Magazine of the Protestant Episcopal Church*, XXIII, 186; Thorndike, *A History of Magic and Experimental Science*, VIII (New York, 1958), 575–80. For Casaubon's belief in witchcraft see also his *Of Credulity and Incredulity* (1670–1672). Glanvill's position is stated in his *Philosophical Endeavour towards the Defence of the Being of Witches and Apparitions* (1666). For an interesting controversy con-

cerning witchcraft involving Bunyan and the Quakers see James Blackley, *A Lying Wonder Discovered* (1659); and W. Y. Tindall, *John Bunyan: Mechanick Preacher* (New York, 1934), Appendix. The Quakers commonly opposed witchcraft. See the references in footnote 56 above, and Samuel Fisher, *Christ's Light Springing* [1660], p. 13.

⁵⁹ Lawson, *A Mite*, pp. 40–41; and Tolles, *Meeting House and Counting House*, pp. 208–209. Penn described Fox as a naturalist as well as a divine, and was surprised at the extent of Fox's knowledge of natural phenomena. *The Witness of William Penn*, p. 42. For a discussion of the botanical interests of Lawson and Fox, see Arthur Raistrick, *Quakers in Science and Industry* (New York, 1950), pp. 244–46.

⁶⁰ *Academiarum Examen*, pp. 73–74.

⁶¹ Cf. Allen, *Journal of the History of Ideas*, X, 233.

⁶² *No Cross, No Crown*, p. 29.

⁶³ *A Mite*, pp. 40–41.

⁶⁴ Nuttall, " 'Unity with the Creation': George Fox and the Hermetic Philosophy," *The Puritan Spirit* (1967), pp. 197–198; and Tolles, *Meeting House and Counting House*, p. 222, n. 51. One of Fox's friends was the Worcester physician, Edward Bourne, also a Quaker.

⁶⁵ *The Sufficiencie of the Spirits Teaching without Humane Learning* (1644), p. 20.

⁶⁶ *A Testimony from the Word*, p. 27.

⁶⁷ *Academiarum Examen*, p. 72.

⁶⁸ *Op. cit.*, quoted in Jones, *Ancients and Moderns*, p. 104.

⁶⁹ *An Humble Motion*, p. 27.

⁷⁰ Jones, *Ancients and Moderns*, pp. 104–105; Hill, *Intellectual Origins of the English Revolution*, p. 123.

⁷¹ Hill, *Intellectual Origins of the English Revolution*, pp. 29, 72, 81–83, 122, 148.

⁷² Thorndike, *A History of Magic and Experimental Science*, VIII, 410.

⁷³ *Academiarum Examen*, pp. 106–107.

⁷⁴ *Six Wings: Men of Science in the Renaissance*, pp. 186–87.

⁷⁵ Thorndike, *A History of Magic and Experimental Science*, VIII, 218–40. See Walter Pagel, "The Religious and Philosophical Aspects of van Helmont's Science and Medicine," *Bulletin of the History of Medicine*, Supplement No. 2 (1944).

⁷⁶ Thorndike, *A History of Magic and Experimental Science*, VII, 232, 233.

⁷⁷ *Academiarum Examen*, pp. 72–74, 106–107.

⁷⁸ *Vindiciae Academiarum*, pp. 35–36.

⁷⁹ Wolf, *A History of Science, Technology, and Philosophy in the 16th & 17th Centuries*, pp. 430–31. For a discussion of the mediocre quality of medical education before 1640 see Curtis, *Oxford and Cam-*

bridge in Transition, pp. 152ff. A broader treatment, reaching similar conclusions, is Phyllis Allen's excellent study, "Medical Education in 17th Century England," *Journal of the History of Medicine & Allied Sciences,* I (January, 1946), 115–143.

⁸⁰ *Pyrotechny Asserted and Illustrated,* pp. 10–11, 78; and *Natures Explication,* Epistle to the Reader and pp. 200, 217, 125. He obliquely criticized university training in divinity on p. 21 of the latter work.

⁸¹ *Natures Explication,* pp. 87, 12, 153–55. Cf. *Pyrotechny Asserted and Illustrated,* pp. 66–67. The acceptance of Hippocrates but not Galen was "one of the hallmarks of Paracelsism. . . ." Allen Debus, "The Paracelsian Compromise in Elizabethan England," *Ambix,* VIII (June, 1960), 88. Debus also demonstrates that as early as the beginning of the seventeenth century the chemical remedies of Paracelsian theory were being accepted even as its occult aspects were generally rejected. Yet in 1659 Meric Casaubon, an Anglican who approved of the study of chemistry and its application to medicine, observed: "Many great Physicians, because of the abuse and danger of it [i.e., chemistry], . . . have done their best (formerly) to cry it down. . . . It is not improbable that divers secrets of it came to the knowledg of man by the Revelation of Spirits." *A True & Faithful Relation of What Passed for Many Yeers between Dr. John Dee . . . and Some Spirits* (1659), Preface.

⁸² *Natures Explication,* Epistle Dedicatory and pp. 115–16, 220, 30, 65, 12, 27; and *Pyrotechny Asserted and Illustrated,* pp. 10–11, 55.

⁸³ *Natures Explication,* Epistle Dedicatory, Epistle to the Reader, and pp. 113, 126–27, 88, 72, 145. (Italics mine.) For an interesting description of contemporary medical practice in action (as Starkey saw it) see pp. 172–73.

⁸⁴ *Advice, Harleian Miscellany,* VI, 7.

CHAPTER FIVE

¹ *Op. cit.,* sig. A3, pp. 47–48.

² *The Reformed School,* p. 47.

³ *The Witness of William Penn,* p. 169.

⁴ Barclay, *Apology for the True Christian Divinity* ([Aberdeen], 1678), p. 218; Lawson, *A Mite,* p. 6.

⁵ *Works,* p. 576.

⁶ *Academiarum Examen,* p. 21. The utilitarian criterion was later adopted by Locke, who contended that there was no reason to require students to study Greek unless they were to become professional scholars. *Some Thoughts Concerning Education* (1693), pp. 233–34.

⁷ *An Humble Motion,* p. 27.

⁸ *A Treatise of Religion & Learning,* p. 58.

[9] *A Discovrse in Derision of the Teaching in Free-Schooles, and Other Common Schooles* [1644], p. 2. This Thomas Grantham is not to be confused with the Baptist preacher of the same name.

[10] *A Mite*, p. 6.

[11] *Academiarum Examen*, pp. 22, 98–100. Cf. *The Witness of William Penn*, p. 170. For Brinsley's educational views, see Joan Simon, *Education and Society in Tudor England* (Cambridge, 1967), pp. 375–381.

[12] *Vindiciae Academiarum*, pp. 43, 17.

[13] *A Modest Plea*, pp. 51–53.

[14] *A Modest Reply* (1659), pp. 20–21.

[15] Richard F. Jones, "Science and Language in England of the Mid-Seventeenth Century," *Journal of English and Germanic Philology*, XXXI (1932), 327, n.35.

[16] Cf. Foster Watson: "The text-books show that the aim of the Grammar School teachers of the 16th and 17th centuries was mainly that the pupil should acquire power of classifying the contents of books read, of analysing the paragraphs, sentences, phrases, words, so as to bring them into comparison with those of other authors. The pupil was expected to show active initiation in gaining control over the material of reading and to register his observations in his note-books and commonplace books so as to use the material from his own independent standpoint of free composition and fluent speech." *The English Grammar Schools to 1660*, p. 8. Cf. Charles Hoole, *A New Discovery of the Old Art of Teaching Schoole* (1660).

[17] See Clarke, *Classical Education*, especially pp. 34–41; Watson, *The English Grammar Schools to 1660*, especially Chaps. XVIII, XIX, XXI, XXX, and XXXII; and Craig R. Thompson, "Schools in Tudor England," in *Life and Letters in Tudor and Stuart England*, eds. Louis B. Wright and Virginia A. LaMar (New York, 1962).

[18] *A Discovrse in Derision*, p. 2.

[19] *A Modest Plea*, p. 54.

[20] See his *Essay toward a Real Character and a Philosophical Language* (1668), pp. 443 ff. Jones wrongly attributed this work to Boyle. *Journal of English and Germanic Philology*, XXXI, 319.

[21] Jones, *Journal of English and Germanic Philology*, XXXI, 324.

[22] *Ibid.*, p. 323, n. 26. The development of mathematical symbols occurred primarily in the sixteenth and seventeenth centuries. The signs for addition ($+$) and subtraction ($-$) appeared first in 1489, but were not generally used until the beginning of the seventeenth century. Recorde first used the sign of equality ($=$) in 1557, and Oughtred the sign of multiplication ($\times$) in 1631. The symbol of division ($\div$) was not printed until 1659, when it appeared in a Swiss work. See Wolf, *A History of Science, Technology, and Philosophy in the 16th & 17th Centuries*, pp. 192–93.

²³ Jones, *Journal of English and Germanic Philology*, XXXI, 323–27.

²⁴ *Ibid.*; J. G. Crowther, *Founders of British Science* (1960), pp. 43–44.

²⁵ *Academiarum Examen*, pp. 24–32.

²⁶ *Vindiciae Academiarum*, pp. 20–22.

²⁷ *A Treatise of Religion*, p. 55.

²⁸ *Beth Hakemoth. The House of Wisdom* (1681), pp. 7–8, 25.

²⁹ James R. Knowlson, "The Idea of Gesture as a Universal Language in the XVIIth and XVIIIth Centuries," *Journal of the History of Ideas*, XXVI (October–December, 1965), 500; cf. p. 501.

³⁰ Armytage, *Four Hundred Years of English Education*, pp. 19–20.

³¹ *Academiarum Examen*, p. 24.

³² Wilkins and Ward, *Vindiciae Academiarum*, pp. 5, 18.

³³ Sedgwick, *A Sermon*, p. 7.

³⁴ *Vindiciae Academiarum*, pp. 45–46, 39.

³⁵ Allen, *Journal of the History of Ideas*, X, 244; Hill, *Intellectual Origins of the English Revolution*, pp. 54, 305.

³⁶ Hall, *Vindiciae Literarum*, p. 49; Dell, *A Plain and Necessary Confvtation*, p. 14.

³⁷ *Academiarum Examen*, pp. 53, 78ff., 59ff., 62, 104, 65. (Cf. Ward, *Vindiciae Academiarum*, pp. 32–33.)

³⁸ *Ibid.*, pp. 52, 5, 88.

³⁹ *Ibid.*, pp. 84–86, 107.

⁴⁰ *Vindiciae Academiarum*, pp. 1–2, 39, 58, 38.

⁴¹ *An Humble Apologie*, p. 151.

⁴² *A Plain and Necessary Confvtation*, pp. 6–7, 21.

⁴³ *Diary*, entry for July 9, 1654.

⁴⁴ *A Consideration of Infant Baptism*, pp. 155, 158–60. Horne was not as radical as sectaries in general about banishing academic learning from the religious realm: "Some lesser usefulness and curiosities some Sciences may afford, as the Mathematicks to find out the bigness of the Ark, the measures of the Temple, &c. Astronomy to tell us what Arcturus, and Orion, and Pleiades are; History and Chronology may seem to help to understand the passages of the Monarchies and Visions of Daniel, &c: and yet there is so great incertainty in them too as to what is Heathen, that they rather trouble then help. . . ." Languages he approved, but not philosophy or physics. Pp. 158, 160. Like Dell, Horne was criticized by Charles Chauncy in New England in 1655. Chauncy, *Gods Mercy*, pp. 46ff.

⁴⁵ *Natures Explication*, pp. 35, 115.

⁴⁶ *Academiarum Examen*, pp. 33–34, 38. Starkey criticized the "rottennesse" of logic as well as philosophy in general, condemning Ramist and Aristotelian logic. *Natures Explication*, Epistle to the Reader and p. 36.

⁴⁷ *Vindiciae Academiarum*, pp. 24–25.

[48] *Philosophicall Essayes*, pp. 3, 13–15; cf. pp. 1–16.

[49] *Works*, II, 219. Cf. Crandon, *Mr. Baxters Aphorisms*, Pt. I, fol. C4.

[50] *Some Thoughts Concerning Education*, p. 220.

[51] "Histrio-Mastix," pp. 220–21, and *The Pulpit Guarded*, p. 9.

[52] Gauden, *Hieraspistes: A Defence of the Ministry and Ministers of the Church of England* (1653), p. 399; and Firmin, *Stablishing against Shaking* (1656), p. 12. Cf. Chauncy, *Gods Mercy*, p. 48.

[53] *Academiarum Examen*, pp. 86–88, 107–108. Cf. Locke, *Some Thoughts Concerning Education*, p. 220.

[54] *Vindiciae Academiarum*, p. 38.

[55] *The Judgment of Non-Conformists* (1676), p. 14.

[56] *A Plain and Necessary Confvtation*, pp. 12, 14, 18, 9, and *The Stumbling-Stone*, p. 30.

[57] *A Light Shining out of Darkness* (3rd ed., 1699) pp. 215, 217–18.

[58] *No Cross, No Crown*, p. 31.

[59] *A Mite*, pp. 40–41.

[60] R.R. and G[eorge] F[ox], *To All Magistrates, Teachers, School-Masters, and People in Christendome* (1660), p. 4. Cf. Fox, *The Vialls of the Wrath of God*, p. 11; and *The Teachers of the World Unvailed* (1656), p. 20.

[61] *The Tryal of Spirits*, p. 55. Dell's criticism of the classics was repudiated by Chauncy. *Gods Mercy*, pp. 35–36.

[62] *Academiarum Examen*, pp. 88–89.

[63] *A Treatise of Religion*, pp. 48, 50.

[64] R.R. and G.F., *To All Magistrates*, p. 5.

[65] *A Testimony from the Word*, p. 27; and *Works*, II, 218–19.

[66] James Westfall Thompson, *A History of Historical Writing*, I (New York, 1942), 626.

[67] See Curtis, *Oxford and Cambridge in Transition*, pp. 120, 132.

[68] *No Cross, No Crown*, p. 29.

[69] *A Mite*, pp. 40–41.

[70] *An Humble Motion*, p. 27.

[71] *Some Thoughts Concerning Education*, p. 217.

[72] *A Treatise of Religion*, p. 43.

[73] *The Reformed School*, p. 60.

[74] Claude V. Palisca, "Scientific Empiricism in Musical Thought," in *Seventeenth Century Science and the Arts*, ed. Hedley Howell Rhys (Princeton, 1961), pp. 91–92, 99; and Crowther, *Founders of British Science*, p. 17.

[75] *Academiarum Examen*, p. 42.

[76] *Vindiciae Academiarum*, p. 29.

[77] *Diary*, entries for July 11 and 12, 1654.

[78] Percy A. Scholes, *The Puritans and Music in England and New England* (1934; reissued, New York, 1962), pp. 162–66, 172–76. Scholes demonstrated that, with the exception of the Quakers, music was commonly regarded as acceptable by Puritans and sectaries. Cf. E. D. Mackerness, *A Social History of English Music* (1964), pp. 80–81, and Greaves, "Music at Puritan Oxford," *The Musical Times*, CX (January, 1969), 26.

[79] Fox, for example, criticized those who delighted in songs and tunes. *The Vialls of the Wrath of God*, p. 11.

CHAPTER SIX

[1] *Historical Magazine of the Protestant Episcopal Church*, XXIII, 170.

[2] Quoted in Geoffrey F. Nuttall, *The Holy Spirit in Puritan Faith and Experience* (Oxford, 1946), p. 47.

[3] *A Survey of the Spirituall Antichrist* (1648), Pt. I, p. 52. Cf. Elizabeth Warren, *The Old and Good Way Vindicated* (1646), p. 17. Warren was an Independent.

[4] *A Sermon*, p. 20.

[5] Cf. Simpson, *Puritanism in Old and New England*, pp. 43–44.

[6] *Works* (Edinburgh, 1861–66), II, 344; IV, 239.

[7] *The Marrow of Modern Divinity*, ed. C. G. McCrie (Glasgow, 1902), pp. 225–26.

[8] Richard Sibbes, *Works*, ed. A. B. Groshart (1862), III, 434, quoted in Nuttall, *The Holy Spirit*, p. 39. Cf. Gauden, *Hieraspistes*, p. 406.

[9] *Vindiciae Literarum*, p. 51.

[10] Sedgwick, *Learning's Necessity*, p. 55.

[11] Nuttall, *The Holy Spirit*, p. 38.

[12] *Grace Abounding to the Chief of Sinners* (1666), sects. 229, 99.

[13] *A Worke of the Beast* (1638), p. 19. The tract is reproduced in Haller, *Tracts on Liberty in the Puritan Revolution*, Vol. II.

[14] *Rump*, Pt. I, p. 46.

[15] *Works*, ed. George Offor (Glasgow, 1861), III, 398.

[16] According to Edward Thompson he also read or was influenced by Sir Walter Ralegh's *Discoverie of the Large and Bewtiful Empire of Guiana* (1596) and *The History of the World* (1614). *Sir Walter Ralegh: Last of the Elizabethans* (New Haven, Conn., 1936), pp. 115, 254.

[17] See Ted LeRoy Underwood, "The Controversy between the Baptists and the Quakers in England 1650–1689: A Theological Elucidation" (unpublished Ph.D. dissertation, University of London, 1965).

[18] *The Spirits Conviction of Sinne*, quoted in Nuttall, *The Holy Spirit*, p. 37. Cf. Sterry, *The Teachings of Christ in the Soule* (1648), pp. 26, 50; and John Everard, *Some Gospel Treasures* (1653; reprinted Germantown, 1757), Pt. I, pp. 37–38, 153.

[19] *Op. cit.* (3rd ed., 1702), p. 93.

[20] *Academiarum Examen*, pp. 17, 16, and the Epistle. Cf. Dell, *A Plain and Necessary Confvtation*, p. 20. Ultimately the logic of the sectarian position drove the Quaker Richard Farnworth to write in 1653: "I am as a white paper book without any line or sentence, but as it is revealed and written by the Spirit, the revealer of secrets, so I administer." Quoted in Nuttall, *Studies in Christian Enthusiasm Illustrated from Early Quakerism* (Wallingford, Pa., 1948), p. 45. The Lockian character of the passage is striking.

[21] Cf. Baxter, *One Sheet for the Ministry, against the Malignants of All Sorts* (1657), pp. 13–14. Fox retorted: "It is lazynesse indeed that hath set up your notes, and reads them by the glasse for money, and who have learned seven years out of books and Colledges, and then gather up out of your authors & books in notes, and thus make a trade of them. . . ." *The Great Mistery of the Great Whore Unfolded*, p. 271.

[22] *Gweithiau*, eds. T. E. Ellis and J. H. Davies (1899–1908), I, 190, quoted in Nuttall, *The Holy Spirit*, p. 155. See Nuttall, *The Welsh Saints, 1640–1660* (Cardiff, 1957), Chap. III.

[23] *The Judgement Set*, pp. 291–92.

[24] See Nuttall, *The Holy Spirit*, p. 36.

[25] *The Saints Guide*, p. 1.

[26] Baxter, *The Vnreasonableness of Infidelity* (1655), Pt. II, p. 166.

[27] *Vindiciae Literarum*, p. 54. See Edward Reynolds, *A Sermon Touching the Use of Humane Learning* (1658), for the development of this principle by a leading Presbyterian.

[28] *A Plain and Necessary Confvtation*, p. 23.

[29] *A Measure of the Times* (1657), p. 30.

[30] *Works*, p. 200.

[31] Johnson, *Wonder-Working Providence* (1654), quoted in Morison, *The Founding of Harvard College*, p. 176.

[32] Dell, *A Plain and Necessary Confvtation*, p. 23. Cf. Crandon, *Mr. Baxters Aphorisms*, Pt. I, sigs. C4, D1 *verso*, E2 *verso*.

[33] *The Judgement Set*, pp. 306, 298.

[34] *Academia Coelestis*, p. 29.

[35] *Works*, pp. 224, 239, 93.

[36] *The Saints Guide*, p. 2.

[37] *Works*, p. 568.

[38] *The Cry of a Stone* (1654), pp. 42–43.

[39] *The Letany of John Bastwick, Doctor of Phisicke* (1637), reprinted in *Somers Tracts*, V (2nd ed., 1965 reissue), 431.

[40] *Responsoria*, p. 150.

[41] Richard Saunders, *A Balm to Heal Religions Wounds*, p. 126. Cf. Chauncy, *Gods Mercy*, p. 50.

[42] *Learning's Necessity*, pp. 40–42.

43 Richard Younge, *The Pastors Advocate* (2nd ed., 1653), p. 15.

44 *An Apologie*, p. 52.

45 Sedgwick, *Learning's Necessity*, p. 51.

46 *Ibid.*, p. 52.

47 *Lay-Preaching Vnmasked* (1644), pp. 23–24.

48 Immanuel Bourne, *A Defence and Justification of Ministers Mainte-nance by Tythes*, Pt. II, p. 14.

49 Quoted in Joseph Ivemey, *The Life of Mr. John Bunyan* (2nd ed., 1825), p. 295, n.*.

50 *The Compassionate Samaritane*, p. 31.

51 *Letters and Speeches*, ed. Lomas, II, 539, 180, 334. "Cromwell was closer to the mystics than he was to any other group of Puritans," according to George Drake. "The Ideology of Oliver Cromwell," *Church History*, XXXV (September, 1966), 262.

52 Winstanley, *Works*, p. 82.

53 Edmund Chillenden, *Preaching withovt Ordjnatjon* (1647), p. 6. Chillenden was an officer in the New Model Army and a General Baptist with Fifth Monarchy sympathies. For a statement of the Quaker position regarding the right of women to prophesy in the church, see Fox, *Women Learning in Silence* (1656), especially p. 6.

54 Stubbe, *A Light*, p. 116.

55 *The Stumbling-Stone*, p. 13.

56 *A Worke of the Beast*, p. 19.

57 *Rump*, Pt. I, p. 263.

58 *A Presentation of Wholesome Informations* (1660), p. 28.

59 *A Light*, pp. 198, 215–16.

60 *A Plain and Necessary Confvtation*, Apology to the Reader; *A Testimony from the Word*, pp. 2–4; *The Tryal of Spirits*, pp. 60, 42–43, 30.

61 *A Presentation*, p. 28.

62 *A Mite*, pp. 42–43.

63 *A Testimony from the Word*, p. 3; and *The Tryal of Spirits*, pp. 30, 60, 42–43.

64 *Academiarum Examen*, pp. 15, 96–97, 11.

65 Nuttall, *The Visible Saints: The Congregational Way, 1640–1660* (Oxford, 1957), pp. 89–90.

66 *Natures Explication*, pp. 10–11, 22–23.

67 *A Light*, pp. 206–207.

68 *A Mite*, pp. 43–46.

69 *The Divine Right of Presbyterie* (1646), p. 12.

70 *The Tryal of Spirits*, pp. 42–43; and *A Plain and Necessary Confvtation*, Apology to the Reader.

71 *Good Work*, p. 4.

72 *A Modest Reply*, p. 4.

[73] Godfrey Noel Vose, "Profile of a Puritan: John Owen (1616–1683)" (unpublished Ph.D. dissertation, School of Religion, State University of Iowa, 1963), pp. 52–53.

[74] Quoted in Firth, *The Last Years of the Protectorate*, II, 103.

[75] *A Collection of . . . Writings*, p. 358.

[76] B[urrough], *A Returne to the Ministers of London* (1660), p. 3; Winstanley, *Works*, p. 238.

EPILOGUE

[1] Modern scholarship has been overly influenced by the harsh and unjust accusations of those who criticized the sectaries. Too often the sectaries have been censored for their purported antiintellectualism. Cf. Miller, *The New England Mind;* and Solt, "Anti-Intellectualism in the Puritan Revolution," *Church History* (December, 1956), 306–316. Schlatter surprisingly described the sectarian reformers as "ignorant radicals." *Historical Magazine of the Protestant Episcopal Church*, XXIII, 187. Mark Curtis called Webster an "ignorant critic," an incredible accusation in the light of the latter's broad range of academic interests and his knowledge of much of the latest scholarly thought, on the Continent as well as in England. If Webster did in fact study at Cambridge, Curtis' accusation damages rather than enhances his argument that both universities, mostly through the work of tutors but also in their lectures, were educating men in the sciences as well as the arts and the professional subjects. *Oxford and Cambridge in Transition*, p. 232; cf. p. 274.

[2] *Natures Explication*, p. 19. Sprigg made a similar charge: A physician "is of that kind of animals [*sic*] that thrive best in the worst aire and like vermine lives on the soars and putrefactions of corrupted nature." *Philosophicall Essayes*, p. 42.

[3] *Works*, pp. 664, 590, 311, 464, 468, 358, 188. For a discussion of the use of the Norman Conquest theme by critics of England's legal system in the 1640s and 1650s, see Stuart E. Prall, *The Agitation for Law Reform during the Puritan Revolution, 1640–1660* (The Hague, 1966), pp. 25, 36–45, 56–57. Sir Edward Coke and his fellow lawyers saw, in opposition to the critics, the feudal law of the Norman period as the basis of England's common law, and therefore viewed its development with respect.

[4] *Tyranipocrit*, p. 16.

[5] *Gangraena* (2nd ed.; 1646), p. 128.

[6] *A Whip*, p. 13; *Regall Tyrannie Discovered* (1647), p. 25; and *Englands Birth-Right Justified* [1645], pp. 36–37. The latter tract is reproduced in Haller, *Tracts on Liberty in the Puritan Revolution*, Vol. III.

[7] Burrough, *A Measure*, p. 27; and Fox, *A Collection of the Several Books and Writings . . . by . . . George Fox* (2nd ed., 1665), p. 91.

⁸ Christopher Hill, *The Century of Revolution, 1603–1714* (Edinburgh, 1961), p. 141.

⁹ Brailsford, *The Levellers and the English Revolution*, p. 121; and Prall, *The Agitation for Law Reform*, pp. 36, 38–39.

¹⁰ *Englands Birth-Right*, p. 8.

¹¹ *Puritanism and Liberty, Being the Army Debates (1647–48) from the Clarke Manuscripts with Supplementary Documents*, ed. A. S. P. Woodhouse (Chicago, 1951), p. 395. Also cf. Burrough, *A Trumpet of the Lord*, p. 4, for a similar complaint.

¹² *Works*, p. 361.

¹³ *A Tender Visitation of Love* (1660), p. 17.

¹⁴ See Brailsford, *The Levellers and the English Revolution*, p. 122; and Prall, *The Agitation for Law Reform*, pp. 57–58.

¹⁵ *Works*, pp. 327, 505, 512.

¹⁶ *A Helpe to the Right Understanding* (1644), p. 2. The tract is reproduced in Haller, *Tracts on Liberty in the Puritan Revolution*, Vol. III.

¹⁷ *Englands Birth-Right*, p. 37. Even Cromwell castigated the lawyers, complaining on one occasion that the law merely served to maintain them. See Prall, *The Agitation for Law Reform*, p. 112.

¹⁸ *Letany, Somers Tracts*, V, 413, 415, 427.

¹⁹ *Academiarum Examen*, p. 16; and *The Saints Guide*, Epistle.

²⁰ *The Pulpit-Guard Routed*, pp. 3, 38.

²¹ Lawson, *A Mite*, p. 47; and Trapnel, *The Cry of a Stone*, p. 50.

²² *The Tryal of Spirits*, pp. 29–31; *Works*, II, 224; and *The Stumbling-Stone*, "To the Reader."

²³ *An Additionall Appendix to the Book Entituled Rusticus ad Academicos* (1660), p. 26.

²⁴ *A Measure*, pp. 16–18.

²⁵ *A Paper Sent Forth* (1654), pp. 4, 1–2; and *The Great Mistery*, p. 115.

²⁶ *A Collection of . . . Writings*, p. 207.

²⁷ *Journal of the History of Ideas*, XVII, 464.

²⁸ *A Copie of a Letter, Written . . . to Mr. William Prinne Esq.* (1645), pp. 4–5. The tract is reproduced in Haller, *Tracts on Liberty in the Puritan Revolution*, Vol. III.

²⁹ *The Araignement of Mr. Persecvtion* (1645), pp. 18, 40. The tract is reproduced in Haller, *Tracts on Liberty in the Puritan Revolution*, Vol. III.

³⁰ *The Compassionate Samaritane*, p. 41; *The Power of Love*, p. 48; and *A Prediction of Mr. Edwards His Conversion, and Recantation* (1646), p. 14. The latter tract is reproduced in Haller, *Tracts on Liberty in the Puritan Revolution*, Vol. III.

[31] *Tyranipocrit*, p. 28.

[32] *Works*, pp. 358, 505, 194, 199, 187, 100, 241. Cf. Maclear, *Journal of the History of Ideas*, XVII, 460. I must agree with Maclear (p. 457) when he says that Winstanley was "probably the most extreme and thorough-going critic of the clergy's role in society that the Interregnum produced."

[33] *A Remonstrance of Many Thousand Citizens* (1646), p. 16. The tract is reproduced in Haller, *Tracts on Liberty in the Puritan Revolution*, Vol. III.

[34] *A Measure*, p. 15.

[35] *Tyranipocrit*, p. 10.

[36] *Works*, pp. 388–89, 568–69, 409, 570.

[37] See Margaret James, "The Political Importance of the Tithes Controversy in the English Revolution," *History* (June, 1941), 1–18.

[38] See Maclear, "The Making of the Lay Tradition," *Journal of Religion*, XXXIII (April, 1953), 113–136.

Select Bibliography

(Place of publication is London unless otherwise noted.)

PRIMARY SOURCES

Bacon, Francis. *The Works of Francis Bacon*, eds. James Spedding, Robert Leslie Ellis, and Douglas Denon Heath, 14 vols., 1857–1874.

Bampfield, Francis. *Beth Hakemoth. The House of Wisdom*, 1681.

Barrow, Humphrey. *The Relief of the Poore, and Advancement of Learning Proposed*, Dublin, 1656.

Bastwick, John. *The Letany of John Bastwick, Doctor of Phisicke*, 1637. Reprinted in *Somers Tracts*, Vol. V, 2nd ed., New York, 1965 reissue.

Baxter, Richard. *One Sheet for the Ministry, against Malignants of All Sorts*, 1657.

———. *Reliquiae Baxteriannae*, ed. Matthew Sylvester, 1696.

———. *The Vnreasonableness of Infidelity*, 1655.

Biggs, Noah. *Mataeotechnia Medicinae Praxeos*, 1651.

Bishop, George. *A Tender Visitation of Love*, 1660.

Boehme, Jacob. *Avrora. That Is, the Day-Spring*, trans. John Sparrow, 1656.

———. *Signatura Rerum*, trans. John Ellistone, 1651.

———. *The Way to Christ Discovered*, 1648.

B[oreman], R[obert]. Παιδία-Θρίαμβος. *The Trivmph of Learning over Ignorance, and of Truth over Falsehood*, 1653.

Bourne, Immanuel. *A Defence and Justification of Ministers Maintenance by Tythes*, 1659.

Burrough, Edward. *A Measure of the Times*, 1657.

———. *A Presentation of Wholesome Informations*, 1660.

———. *A Returne to the Ministers of London*, 1660.

———. *A Trumpet of the Lord Sounded out of Sion*, 1656.

Chauncy, Charles. *Gods Mercy, Shewed to His People*, Cambridge, Mass., 1655.

Chillenden, Edmund. *Preaching withovt Ordjnatjon*, 1647.

Clarendon, Edward, Earl of. *The History of the Rebellion and Civil Wars in England*, 3 vols. in 6, Oxford, 1816.

Collier, Thomas. *The Pulpit-Guard Routed*, 1651.

Collinges, John. *Vindiciae Ministerii Evangelici*, 1651.

———. *Vindiciae Ministerii Evangelici Revindicatae*, 1652.

Comenius, Jan. *The Great Didactic,* trans. and ed. M. W. Keatinge, 2nd ed., New York, 1910.

Crandon, John. *Mr. Baxters Aphorisms Exorized and Anthorized,* 1654.

Cromwell, Oliver. *The Letters and Speeches of Oliver Cromwell,* ed. S. C. Lomas, 3 vols., 1904.

——. *The Writings and Speeches of Oliver Cromwell,* ed. Wilbur Cortey Abbott, 4 vols., Cambridge, Mass., 1947.

Dell, William. *A Plan and Necessary Confvtation,* 1654.

——. *The Stumbling-Stone,* 1653.

——. *A Testimony from the Word against Divinity-Degrees in the University, ad cal. A Plain and Necessary Confvtation,* 1654.

——. *The Tryal of Spirits both in Teachers & Hearers,* 1653.

——. *The Works of William Dell,* 2 vols., 1817.

Dury, John. *A Motion Tending to the Pvblick Good of This Age, and of Posteritie,* 1642.

——. *The Reformed School* [1649?].

——. *A Seasonable Discourse,* 1649.

Evelyn, John. *The Diary of John Evelyn,* ed. Austin Dobson, 1908.

Firmin, Giles. *Stablishing against Shaking,* 1656.

Fisher, Samuel. *Christ's Light Springing,* [1660].

——. *An Additionall Appendix to the Book Entituled Rusticus ad Academicos,* 1660.

Fox, George. *A Collection of the Several Books and Writings . . . by . . . George Fox,* 2nd ed., 1665.

——. *The Great Mistery of the Great Whore Unfolded,* 1659.

——. *A Paper Sent Forth,* 1654.

——. *The Teachers of the World Unvailed,* 1656.

——. *The Vialls of the Wrath of God,* 1655.

Gauden, John. *Hieraspistes: A Defence of the Ministry and Ministers of the Church of England,* 1653.

[Grantham, Thomas]. *A Discovrse in Derision of the Teaching in Free-Schooles, and Other Common Schooles,* [1644].

[Hall, John]. *An Humble Motion to the Parliament of England Concerning the Advancement of Learning,* 1649.

Hall, Thomas. *An Apologie for the Ministry, and Its Maintenance,* 1660.

——. "Histrio-Mastix. A Whip for Webster," published as an appendix to *Vindiciae Literarum,* 1655 ed.

——. *The Pulpit Guarded with XVII Arguments,* 1651.

——. *Vindiciae Literarum. The Schools Guarded,* 1655 ed.

Haller, William (ed.). *Tracts on Liberty in the Puritan Revolution, 1638–1647,* 3 vols., New York, 1933.

Hartley, William. *The Prerogative Priests Passing-Bell,* 1651.

Hartlib, Samuel. *Considerations Tending to the Happy Accomplishment of Englands Reformation in Church and State*, 1647.

———. *The True and Readie Way to Learne the Latine Tongue*, 1654.

Hoole, Charles. *A New Discovery of the Old Art of Teaching Schoole*, 1660.

Horne, John. Διατριβη περι Παιδο-βαπτισμου, *Or a Consideration of Infant Baptism*, 1654.

How, Samuel. *The Sufficiencie of the Spirits Teaching without Humane Learning*, 1644.

Lawson, Thomas. *A Mite into the Treasury*, 1680.

Leigh, Edward. *A Treatise of Religion & Learning*, 1656.

[Milton, John]. *Of Education*, [1644].

A Modest Reply, 1659.

Parnell, James. *A Collection of the Several Writings* [of] . . . *James Parnel*, 1675.

Penn, William. *No Cross, No Crown*, 1669.

———. *Truth Exalted*, 1671.

———. *The Witness of William Penn*, eds. Frederick B. Tolles and E. Gordon Alderfer, New York, 1957.

Peter, Hugh. *Good Work for a Good Magistrate*, 1651.

———. *A Word for the Armie. And Two Words to the Kingdome*, 1647.

P[etty], W[illiam]. *The Advice of W.P. to Mr. Samuel Hartlib, for the Advancement of Some Particular Parts of Learning*, 1648, reprinted in *The Harleian Miscellany*, VI, 1810; reissued New York, 1965.

[Poole, Matthew]. *A Model for the Maintaining of Students of Choice Abilities at the University*, 2nd ed., 1658.

R., R., and F., G. *To All Magistrates, Teachers, School-Masters, and People in Christendome*, 1660.

Reynolds, Edward. *A Sermon Touching the Use of Humane Learning*, 1658.

Rous, Francis. *Academia Coelestis: The Heavenly University*, 3rd ed., 1702.

Rump: Or an Exact Collection of the Choycest Poems and Songs Relating to the Late Times, 1662.

Saltmarsh, John. *Holy Discoveries and Flames*, 1640.

Sedgwick, Joseph. Επισκοπή Διδακτικός. *Learning's Necessity to an Able Minister of the Gospel*, 1653.

———. *A Sermon, Preached at St. Maries in the University of Cambridge May 1st, 1653*, 1653.

Sheppard, William. *The Peoples Priviledge and Dvty Gvarded against the Pulpit and Preachers Incroachment*, 1652.

Sherlock, Richard. *The Quakers Wilde Questions Objected against the Ministers of the Gospel*, 1654.

Spencer, John. Καινὰ καί Παναιά. *Things New and Old*, 1658.

[Sprigg, William.] *A Modest Plea for an Equal Common-Wealth against Monarchy*, 1659.

——. *Philosophicall Essayes with Brief Adviso's*, 1657.

Starkey, George. *Natures Explication and Helmont's Vindication*, 1657.

——. *Pyrotechny Asserted and Illustrated*, 1658.

[Stubbe, Henry.] *A Light Shining out of Darkness*, 3rd ed., 1699.

Thurman, Henry. *A Defence of Humane Learning in the Ministry*, Oxford, 1660.

Tomlinson, William. *A Word of Reproof to the Priests or Ministers*, 3rd ed., 1656.

Trapnel, Anna. *The Cry of a Stone*, 1654.

Tyranipocrit, Discovered with His Wiles, wherewith He Vanquisheth, Rotterdam, 1649.

A Vindication of Learning from Unjust Aspersions, 1646.

Ward, Seth. *Vindiciae Academiarum*, Oxford, 1654.

Waterhouse, Edward. *An Humble Apologie for Learning and Learned Men*, 1653.

Webster, John. *Academiarum Examen*, 1654.

——. *The Judgement Set, the Bookes Opened, and All Religion Brought to Triall*, 1654.

——. *The Saints Guide, or, Christ the Rule, and Ruler of Saints*, 1654.

Winstanley, Gerrard. *The Works of Gerrard Winstanley*, ed. George H. Sabine, New York, 1941, reissued 1965.

Wood, Anthony, *Athenae Oxonienses*, ed. Philip Bliss, 5 vols., 1813–1820.

Workman, Giles. *Private-Men No Pulpit-Men: Or, A Modest Examination of Lay-Mens Preaching*, 1646.

SECONDARY SOURCES

Allen, Phyllis. "Medical Education in 17th Century England," *Journal of the History of Medicine & Allied Sciences*, I (January, 1946), 115–143.

——. "Scientific Studies in the English Universities of the Seventeenth Century," *Journal of the History of Ideas*, X (April, 1949), 219–253.

Brailsford, H. N. *The Levellers and the English Revolution*, ed. Christopher Hill, Stanford, Calif., 1961.

Braithwaite, William C. *The Beginnings of Quakerism*, 2nd ed., Cambridge, 1955.

Clarke, M. L. *Classical Education in Britain, 1500–1900*, Cambridge, 1959.

Conant, James. "The Advancement of Learning during the Puritan Commonwealth," *Proceedings of the Massachusetts Historical Society*, LXVI (1936–1941), 3–31.

Crowther, J. G. *Founders of British Science*, 1960.

Curtis, Mark H. *Oxford and Cambridge in Transition, 1558–1642*, Oxford, 1959.

Eurich, Nell. *Science in Utopia: A Mighty Design*, Cambridge, Mass., 1967.

Fletcher, Harris Francis. *The Intellectual Development of John Milton*, 2 vols., Urbana, Ill., 1956, 1961.

Hall, A. R. *The Scientific Revolution, 1500–1800*, 1954.

Haller, William. *The Rise of Puritanism*, New York, Harper Torchbook ed., 1957.

Hill, Christopher. *The Century of Revolution, 1603–1714*, Edinburgh, 1961.

————. *Intellectual Origins of the English Revolution*, Oxford, 1965.

Houghton, Walter E. "The History of Trades: Its Relation to Seventeenth-Century Thought as Seen in Bacon, Petty, Evelyn, and Boyle," *Journal of the History of Ideas*, II (January, 1941), 33–60.

James, Margaret. *Social Problems and Policy during the Puritan Revolution*, 1930.

Johnson, Francis R. *Astronomical Thought in Renaissance England*, Baltimore, 1937.

————. "Gresham College: Precursor of the Royal Society," *Journal of the History of Ideas*, I (October, 1940), 413–438.

Jones, Richard Foster. *Ancients and Moderns: A Study of the Background of the Battle of the Books*, St. Louis, 1936.

————. "The Humanistic Defense of Learning in the Mid-Seventeenth Century," *Reason and the Imagination: Studies in the History of Ideas, 1600–1800*, ed. J. A. Mazzeo, New York, 1962.

————. "Science and Language in England of the Mid-Seventeenth Century," *Journal of English and Germanic Philology*, XXXI (1932), 315–331.

Kemsley, Douglas S. "Religious Influences in the Rise of Modern Science: A Review and Criticism, Particularly of the 'Protestant-Puritan Ethic' Theory," *Annals of Science*, XXIV (September, 1968), 199–226.

Maclear, James Fulton. "The Making of the Lay Tradition," *Journal of Religion*, XXXIII (April, 1953), 113–136.

————. "Popular Anticlericalism in the Puritan Revolution," *Journal of the History of Ideas*, XVII (October, 1956), 443–470.

Mallet, Charles Edward. *A History of the University of Oxford*, 2 vols., New York, 1904.

Merton, Robert K. "Puritanism, Pietism, and Science," reprinted in *Science & Ideas: Selected Readings*, eds. Arnold B. Arons and Alfred M. Bork, Englewood Cliffs, New Jersey, 1964.

Miller, Perry. *The New England Mind: The Seventeenth Century*, Boston, Beacon Press ed., 1961.

Morison, Samuel Eliot. *The Founding of Harvard College*, Cambridge, Mass., 1935.

Mullinger, J. B. *The University of Cambridge*, 3 vols., 1873–1911.

Nuttall, Geoffrey F. *The Holy Spirit in Puritan Faith and Experience*, Oxford, 1946.

———. *The Puritan Spirit*, 1967.

———. *Studies in Christian Enthusiasm Illustrated from Early Quakerism*, Wallingford, Pa., 1948.

Prall, Stuart E. *The Agitation for Law Reform during the Puritan Revolution, 1640–1660*, The Hague, 1966.

Rabb, Theodore K. "Puritanism and the Rise of Experimental Science in England," *Cahiers d'Hist. Mondiale*, VII (1962), 46–67.

Sarton, George. *Six Wings: Men of Science in the Renaissance*, 1957.

Schenk, W. *Concern for Social Justice in the Puritan Revolution*, 1948.

Schlatter, Richard. "The Higher Learning in Puritan England," *Historical Magazine of the Protestant Episcopal Church*, XXIII (June, 1954), 167–187.

Scholes, Percy A. *The Puritans and Music in England and New England*, 1934; reissued New York, 1962.

Shapiro, B. J. "Latitudinarianism and Science in Seventeenth-Century England," *Past & Present*, No. 40 (July, 1968), 16–41.

Solt, Leo F. "Anti-Intellectualism in the Puritan Revolution," *Church History*, XXIV (December, 1956), 306–316.

———. "Puritanism, Capitalism, Democracy, and the New Science," *The American Historical Review*, LXXIII (October, 1967), 18–29.

———. *Saints in Arms: Puritanism and Democracy in Cromwell's Army*, Stanford, 1959.

Stearns, Raymond Phineas. *The Strenuous Puritan: Hugh Peter, 1598–1660*, Urbana, Ill., 1954.

Thorndike, Lynn. *A History of Magic and Experimental Science*, Vols. VII and VIII, New York, 1958.

Tolles, Frederick B. *Meeting House and Counting House: The Quaker Merchants of Colonial Philadelphia, 1682–1763*, New York, 1963 ed.

Trevor-Roper, H. R. "Three Foreigners and the Philosophy of the English Revolution," *Encounter*, XIV (February, 1960), 3–20.

Turnbull, G. H. *Hartlib, Dury and Comenius: Gleanings from Hartlib's Papers*, 1947.

———. "Oliver Cromwell's College at Durham," *Research Review*, No. 3 (September, 1952), 1–7.

———. *Samuel Hartlib: A Sketch of His Life and His Relations to J. A. Comenius*, 1920.

Vincent, W. A. L. *The State and School Education 1640–1660 in England and Wales*, 1950.

Watson, Foster. *The English Grammar Schools to 1660: Their Curriculum and Practice*, Cambridge, 1908.

———. "The State and Education during the Commonwealth," *English Historical Review*, XV (January, 1900), 58–72.

Willey, Basil. *The Seventeenth Century Background*, New York, Anchor ed., 1953.

Wolf, A. *A History of Science, Technology, and Philosophy in the 16th & 17th Centuries*, 2nd ed., 1950.

Young, Robert Fitzgibbon. *Comenius in England*, 1932.

Index

This book was set in Janson Linotype. Printed by letterpress on Warren's #66 Antique manufactured by S. D. Warren Company, Boston, Mass. Composed, printed and bound by Quinn & Boden Company, Inc., Rahway, N. J.